Black Issues in the Therapeutic

Black Issues in the Therapeutic Process

Dr Isha McKenzie-Mavinga
London Metropolitan University

Cover image: Iponri (c) Fowokan George Kelly

First published 2009 by
PALGRAVE MACMILLAN

Palgrave Macmillan in the UK is an imprint of Macmillan Publishers Limited, registered in England, company number 785998, of Houndmills, Basingstoke, Hampshire RG21 6XS.

Palgrave Macmillan in the US is a division of St Martin's Press LLC, 175 Fifth Avenue, New York, NY 10010.

Palgrave Macmillan is the global academic imprint of the above companies and has companies and representatives throughout the world.

Palgrave® and Macmillan® are registered trademarks in the United States, the United Kingdom, Europe and other countries.

ISBN 978-1-4039-9572-8   ISBN 978-1-137-19979-9 (eBook)
DOI 10.1007/978-1-137-19979-9

This book is printed on paper suitable for recycling and made from fully managed and sustained forest sources. Logging, pulping and manufacturing processes are expected to conform to the environmental regulations of the country of origin.

A catalogue record for this book is available from the British Library.

Library of Congress Cataloging-in-Publication Data

McKenzie-Mavinga, Isha, 1948–
    Black issues in the therapeutic process / Isha McKenzie-Mavinga.
        p. cm.
    Includes bibliographical references and index.
    ISBN 978-1-4039-9572-8
    1. Psychiatry, Transcultural. 2. Cross-cultural counseling.
    3. Blacks – Mental health. I. Title. [DNLM: 1. African Continental
    Ancestry Group – psychology. 2. Psychotherapy – methods. 3. Cultural
    Competency. WM 420 M4775b 2009]

RC455.4.E8.M43 2009
616.890089'96073—dc22   2008043236

10 9 8 7 6 5 4 3 2 1
18 17 16 15 14 13 12 11 10 09

Contents

Foreword

Isha opens this book by quoting from a poem by LeRoy Clarke, a Trinidadian artist and poet. She explains that the poem depicts the pace, patience and humility that are needed to understand black issues in the therapeutic process. I have always appreciated Isha as a fellow traveller on the very long and painful road towards equality, absence of discrimination and removal of abuses of power between individuals and groups, particularly between those deemed 'black' and 'white'. There is no doubt that she has been subject to the pace of the journey, has had to be patient and has demonstrated extraordinary humility in her ongoing development as a colleague deeply devoted to the optimum delivery of sensitive, informed and humane psychotherapeutic practice.

In her doctoral thesis Isha noted how her own sense of fear and concerns for survival had been frequently raised during the research process and, in reflection, noted:

- the importance (from survival to compassion) of her ongoing commitment to development and therapeutic growth (this process facilitating her own capacity to work openly and with acceptance of a wide range of trainees)
- the considerable challenges of facilitating groups of black and white counselling/psychotherapy trainees to explore these issues, particularly when strong emotions and difficulties (such as pain, defensiveness, aggression, projection, silence, and allegations and fears of racism) are released in the group
- the value of having located 'compassion' for the many points of view and people expressing them within this subject.

This book, then, represents the author's accumulated experience of many years of counselling, counsellor training and research. Indeed, this text is based upon Isha's doctoral research and it constitutes a material outcome of and for concerns that have been deeply personal to her own experience in the world, and which, through teaching and the research process, have found wider resonance and validation in the experiences of others, both black and white.

The author's own valuing of creativity is wonderfully demonstrated in her choice of chapter titles, selected extracts of poetry, images and therapeutic examples. This creativity is exemplified in her approach to the original research, which I had the privilege to read, and in her work on 'black issues' with students and staff on the counselling courses she is involved with. It is further evidenced in the suggestions of methods for counselling and psychotherapy trainers to employ in conducting similar 'awareness' raising work.

The term 'black issues' is usefully defined early in the text and conceptualised within the more frequent attention that has been given, historically, to issues of 'race', racism, culture and so on. It is a term that has long been used by Isha, and I believe it has now entered the lexicon of trainers and trainees, practitioners and theorists alike as a most useful encapsulating concept within which to explore these complex dynamic phenomena.

This work truly complements other recent research work conducted in this field by colleagues such as:

- Duncan Lawrence, who in 2003 published the results of his survey into race and cultural issues on counselling courses
- Val Watson, who surveyed the experiences of black students on counselling and psychotherapy courses (2004)
- Aileen Alleyne, who researched the complexities of introjection and black identity wounding (2005)
- Harbrinder Dhillon-Stevens, who explored anti-oppressive practice in psychotherapy (2004)
- Sara Razzaq Bains, who studied the multiple impacts of racism within family and collegial settings (2008)

Isha's work has already impacted significantly upon the professional training and research fields. A national straw poll of counselling/psychotherapy courses conducted in 2007 by one of the major professional bodies revealed that the majority of courses found tackling the issues that are explored in this book extremely challenging, with many recognising that inclusion was, at best, minimal. This text is thus a timely and valuable contribution to the emerging literature on this theme in counselling and psychotherapy and the learning here could also be usefully employed in much other professional training (e.g. social work, teaching, probation, nursing).

This book constitutes a most valuable resource for the counselling and psychotherapy field. I trust it will find a wide and appreciative readership.

COLIN LAGO
Sheffield
August 2008

Acknowledgements

Thanks to the Almighty Creator and the benevolent ancestors who have kept me safe and guided me when I have struggled to articulate what has been said but not heard and what has been written but not done. For the challenges and learning that help me continue to grow and understand my own black issues and my role as a black woman, writer, therapist, teacher and parent.

Special thanks to: my students, clients, supervisees, colleagues and counsellors for contributing and our journeying; my children Andrea, Phillippa, Joshua and Aaron and their children, who inspire me; my family in Britain and T&T; Thelma Perkins; my sista writers Wendy Francis and Hyacinth Frazer; Rev. Anita Mckenzie, Dr Margaret Andrews, George Kelly, Ebun Culwin, Patricia Gonsalves, Jenny Harrison, Luke Daniels, Rosmarie Kossov, Dr Kathy Raffles, Dr Aileen Alleyne, Dr Kate Maguire, Dr Harbrinder Dhillon-Stevens, Dr Val Watson, Professor Derek Portwood, Colin Lago, Arike, Shahed Shah, Christine Smith, Paula Collens, Sue Holden, Val Blomfield, Ramesh Talwar, Joyce Thompson, Beryl Coley, Leroy Clarke, Makemba kunle, Byron, Jacinta, Angela, WJ, Dr Pat Adin-Tetty, Ozcar and Vicky, Caroline Ravelo, Eugene Ellis, Anthony Dowling, Eddie Osei-Frimpong, Jacqueline Hughes, Doreen Robinson, Kay Lacka, Francie Van-Hout, Paula Collens, Jane Stavert, Barbara Moiraq, Goldsmiths College, Metanoia Institute and the Psychology Department of London Metropolitan University, all of whom acknowledged my work and encouraged me to stick with it and remain visible in the face of isolation, rage and fear.

A Space to Contemplate

Just so . . .
In the quiet way that time plays on tiles
Its archaic lace imprisons space
Takes us in
Lets us no further than its eyelids
To wait a little more
To wait, I say,
        For horizons at our feet
But wait if you want!

        Habit has a history of nursing wounds
        Their spears dulled
        Displayed
        Slaves adapt privilege granted
        To caress it long enough
        Their own
        A freedom
        Independence.

But wait if you want

        Only light like time
        A resolute
        Burning with the will of dawn
        Must rent the bush

Turn each wing
        With aching pace
Softening each boulder
With the patience of snails.

Excerpt from 'In a Quiet Way',
LeRoy Clarke (1981, p. 25)

LeRoy Clarke, a Trinidadian artist and poet, represents in his poem 'In a Quiet Way' an image of the impact of slavery and colonisation. His paintings of gigantic images combining past and present multicoloured landscapes of mind, body and soul invite spectators to observe, to listen to their responses and to engage in a 'space to contemplate'. I have included this poem to show respect for the integration of creativity that influences and is influenced by personal development. *Douens* depicts the same pace, patience and humility that are needed to understand black issues in the therapeutic process. These qualities were required for the study that supports this book (McKenzie-Mavinga, 2005).

Introduction

This book is the product of a study I undertook in 2005. In this study, counsellors who had trained over the previous two decades on a variety of courses reported that they had not experienced a space to contemplate, or received sufficient input to support, the experiences of black people, in either training or counselling settings. To address these issues, the study placed counsellor training in higher education under the spotlight.

Discussions with trainees showed that concerns about racism featured highly in their interactions and needed to be worked through. Trainees were clearly asking how one makes the therapeutic space safe enough for a dialogue about racism.

As chapter 1 shows, my research demonstrated that themes such as fear and safety were features of the trainees' process of exploring and understanding black issues. Four concepts that evolved from the study – shared concerns, finding a voice, recognition trauma and a bridge from fear to transformation – are therefore used as useful partitions in this book. These partitions represent different phases of the self-development process of understanding black issues. The study showed that sharing concerns assisted trainees to find a voice where previously they felt silenced. Their narrative demonstrated that they were keen to open up a dialogue about black issues but needed safety to unravel the sticky and often emotional impact of racism. Concern was displayed in different ways by black and white trainees. White trainees expressed a fear of losing their assumed power in the unconscious schema of institutional racism. Black trainees experienced fears associated with their emancipation from the role of the oppressed. I have named the processing of these fears and feelings for both black and white trainees 'recognition trauma', because this term gives meaning to the emotional process of exploring black issues. In her study of racial oppression in workplace contexts, Alleyne (2005) mentions a process akin to recognition trauma:

> Deep scrutiny and analysis of my findings, coupled with observable evidence from private practice, suggested there was an influential internal force that co-existed alongside external and interpersonal

experiences of oppression. I see this significant outcome as having particular relevance to black people as a whole and for all therapists who work with black identity wounding and other issues of cultural trauma. (p. 293)

Trainees' feelings about racism, guilt, history and trust needed to be processed to form a bridge that would enable their progress from fear to transformation.

A previous study by Lawrence (2003) surveyed counselling students about race and cultural issues during their training. The survey highlighted that white students felt more comfortable on their training than their black counterparts. All students felt that the race and culture of their tutor would affect their training experience. Respondents were consistently saying that 'there was a gap in what could be an opportunity to work through the diversity of race and culture within their counselling training' (p. 123).

This book contributes to ways of filling gaps identified in Eurocentric approaches to counselling and therapy training. It supports the dynamics of change, widening participation and diversity, rather than assuming that Eurocentric theory, more relevant to white middle-class individuals, can be applied systematically. The main concepts in the study are presented along with proposals to support the training and continuing professional development of counsellors in their work with individuals and groups in the caring professions. This book offers a response to some of the questions and concerns raised by trainee counsellors. It is written in an integrative, transcultural style that reflects my approach to counsellor training.

What Are Black Issues?

The first challenge that reflected the nature of this question was raised by trainees' demand to define the term 'black'. 'Black' is a political and sociological term, identifying a group of people who have been most vulnerable to the oppression of white racism owing to difference in skin colour. As the most visible minority, this group has been least represented in the field of psychotherapy and counselling. However, it must be noted that individuals from African and Asian backgrounds who have experienced racism may not all subscribe to the label 'black'.

Black people of African and Caribbean heritage are six times more likely to be sectioned under the United Kingdom's Mental Health Act than white people. Asian people are four times more likely to commit suicide than white people (Foundation News, 2003). These facts demand greater emphasis on psychotherapy and counselling provision that not only takes account of, but also works with, black issues to increase resources for those at risk of entering the mental health system or committing suicide. To support this effort, this book focuses primarily on people of African and Caribbean heritage. However, the themes and discussions can be used as a model for work with other minority group experiences.

As opposed to a focus on black people per se, the word 'issues' has been linked to the concept of 'black'. The term 'black issues' was placed at the centre of the study and included in workshops so that responses to it could be examined. The approach was intended to be emancipatory so as to broaden understanding of the experiences of both black and white trainees in relation to black issues. 'Issues' in this context therefore refers to any concern, problem, dynamic, feeling or experience raised about black people, by themselves or by white people. Using a broad definition of the term allows for the relationships, personal development and theoretical context of experiences to be taken into account. Conclusions drawn from my experience as a counsellor trainer suggest that unless black issues are raised in the context of racism, general experiences pertaining to culture or everyday life are likely to be raised mainly by black people themselves. This often causes the training group to become overwhelmed with powerful feelings related to racism. I have known this scenario to occur when training approaches do not facilitate listening skills that appropriately reflect black issues or explore the impact of racism.

The Need for Change

As diversity in the student population increases, the demand to provide services for the wider, multicultural population grows. This requires training to address the dynamics of racism and the experiences of black people.

The Race Relations Act 1976 (Amended 2000) now gives public authorities, including higher education authorities, a 'statutory general duty to promote race equality' (CRE, 2002). Developments in social policy are necessary for creating frameworks to address power structures that maintain marginalised voices. The Race Relations Act does not use the term 'black issues', but it does apply regulations to race issues (equal rights and access, regardless of colour or creed) that my study indicated were a significant area of black issues. The Act suggests that as a community of practitioners 'we' are responsible for change in the educational process. In view of this responsibility, counsellors/therapists can be empowered to discover the voice of change within their training experience. This book proposes ways of understanding black issues and ways to develop practice that challenges an over-reliance on Eurocentric approaches, as defined in the following quotation:

> Psychology as an organised discipline, as taught and practised, ascribes little value to the experiences of black people. They are important only in so much as they reinforce white people's sense of superiority. Out and out eurocentricism permeates assumptions, outlook and instruments of psychology. But it is this psychology that has stormed through the world to be adopted even by black nations, uncritically and wholesale. (Howitt and Owusu-Bempah, 1994, p. 127)

In keeping with this statement, this book encourages readers to extend their therapeutic repertoire and address biases that encroach on black self-pride and cultural identity.

A Model of Integrating Black Issues into Counsellor Training

During the study, I was compelled to check my own 'colour blindness' as a black woman. Working within a white middle-class counsellor training framework, I questioned how engaged I was in a dialogue about black issues with colleagues and trainees. Some trainees questioned my right as a black tutor to challenge Eurocentric paradigms within education, and others viewed the inclusion of black issues as an additional problem for them to solve. As a tutor I needed to develop my compassion towards individuals who expressed negative responses. This approach provided a supportive model for counselling trainees.

In this book, I present aspects of the study that may help readers understand the process of trainers and trainees developing a race sensitive or Afrocentric discourse. I also address some of the black issues that the study did not have room for because the issue of racism became overwhelming. The study highlighted the importance of understanding how an individual's feelings about racism run the risk of taking over the listening process for black clients in a therapeutic setting. I found that when racism overwhelms discussions, emphasis gets placed on white people's feelings of fear about being members of the oppressor group. This presents a challenge of supporting both black and white trainees to develop their listening skills and their understanding of black issues in the therapeutic process. The classroom is an ideal setting for trainers to support the process of understanding this dynamic, by facilitating the expression by both black and white trainees of feelings and experiences that include the impact of racism.

Questions, concerns and experiences related to black issues that require understanding and reflection often remain unresolved owing to lack of space in training programmes. We must not underestimate the impact that racism can have on training programmes. I have heard white trainees suggest that living in an area where they rarely see black people or not having black clients excludes them from the dynamics of race and black people's experiences. On the other hand, some trainees believe that a friendship with black people or being black British absolves them from the conflicts of stereotyping and prejudice that sometimes impact intercultural relationships. If they are not addressed, these forms of denial can be transferred into therapeutic relationships. Trainees must be encouraged to dialogue about black issues and the impact of racism during their training. Lack of space for these issues constitutes silence, a silence that may also be viewed as colour blindness. Tuckwell (2002) asserts her understanding of silence in relation to racism:

> There is a silence generally within our profession concerning racism, but I believe also that a silence can too easily develop in the consulting room. It is a dangerous silence for the therapy because it contains too much background noise for it not to infect all other work we try to do. A frequent response by the black patient is to stop and leave therapy, often silently. Another response is not to enter in the first place, which is the loudest silence of all. (p. 138)

In my attempts to break the silence I found that the notion of 'understanding' featured prominently. Trainee counsellors have frequently expressed an urgency to gain clarity and guidance on how to work more effectively with black issues. Questions about how to understand, explore, address and overcome powerful feelings linked to black issues have been raised like a mantra over and over again. This showed an important need to examine their concerns and questions. I have therefore interspersed the questions throughout the chapters to encourage readers to share in further exploration of them. Kareem and Littlewood (1992) exemplify the impact of Eurocentric training on processing silence:

> Such intensive training can sometimes be compared to a kind of colonisation of the mind and I constantly had to battle within myself to keep my head above water, to remind myself at every point who I was and what I was. It was a painful difficult battle not to think what I was told to think, not to be what I had been told to be and not to challenge what I had been told could not be challenged and at the same time not to become alienated from my basic roots. (p. 31)

Multicultural, intercultural and transcultural therapeutic approaches have presented various viewpoints on how equality, diversity and oppression in counselling can be approached. These viewpoints provide a useful framework for developing methods to assist the exploration of black issues.

Multiculturalism

Multiculturalists Vanoy Adams (1996) and Feltham and Horton (2000) suggest attention should be paid to the many cultural reference points that affect relationships. Ponterotto et al. (2001) argue:

> Essential elements of multicultural therapy competence are the therapist's awareness of his or her own cultural heritage, world view and the related values, biases and assumptions about human behaviour, and an understanding of the worldview of the culturally different client. (p. 25)

Multicultural authors tend to dissolve the dominance of white Eurocentric approaches to therapy using a cultural paradigm. A general cultural paradigm can limit attention to the experiences of black therapists/counsellors and clients, because black issues can be neither confined to cultural specifics nor generalised to a focus solely on racism. A process of dilution can take the focus off particular concerns about black issues and place it on the parallel experiences of other minority groups, missing vital opportunities to explore this concern. Scheurich and Young (1997) referred to the power dynamics that uphold this institutional process as 'epistemological racism'.

It is clear that attention has been paid to addressing gaps in multicultural theory; however, exploration of the experiences of black counsellors and black clients has been limited. This lacuna plays a role in perpetuating the colour blindness of Eurocentric paradigms in the training of therapists.

Although the issues of all minority groups are an important concern, there is a demand for a specific emphasis on models that address and work with black issues. We cannot therefore take for granted that a multicultural theory offers enough for trainees to understand the specific nature of black issues and ways to address them.

Intercultural and Transcultural Approaches

Interculturalists Kareem and Littlewood (1992) and Lago and Thompson (1996) attempt to deal with the specific problem of colour blindness by suggesting that therapists should pay attention to relationships between cultures and within cultural groups. Kareem and Littlewood (1992) suggest, 'Intercultural therapy should never be allowed to become some specialised therapy targeted at black people, but simply therapy that takes into account these issues' (p. 12).

Eleftheriadou (1994) and d'Ardenne and Mahtani (1989) get closer to the relationship aspect of diversity in their use of transculturalism by suggesting that we must transcend our own cultural reference points, whether they are similar or different, and thus experience ourselves empathically within the culture of another person or group. d'Ardenne and Mahtani (1989) distinguish the transcultural approach: 'We have chosen the term "trans" as opposed to "cross" or "inter" cultural counselling because we want to emphasise the active and reciprocal process that is involved' (p. 5).

In keeping with the need for an active and reciprocal process, Kareem and Littlewood (1992) suggest:

Psychotherapists who are analytically trained learn to work with and understand the patient's inner world only, and therefore for some there is resistance in dealing with psychological problems that originate in the real (outer) world. However most black people would admit that the most traumatic feature in their personal lives is to be black in a white society. (p. 25)

It follows that if training promotes an active and reciprocal approach to black issues, then the provision of therapy will become culturally active and reciprocal. This process can afford therapists and clients of African and Asian heritage a more equal share of the pie.

My study resulted in the following main proposals:

- Being active in providing a space for sharing and exploration in training can model greater confidence and dialogue about black issues in client work.
- The different experiences of black and white trainees must be valued.
- Understanding can be supported by modelling the process and dialogue on black issues in training workshops.
- To support the emancipatory and transformative process of the training group, the trainer's personal development process must include an understanding of racism and knowledge of black issues.

All this amounts to an evolving process of understanding ways to find meaning for the emotional wisdom that produces awareness and transformation linked to black issues. The specific process underpinning black issues unfolds in the four parts of the book outlined below. Each part has its own brief introduction. These parts can be likened to stages of the therapeutic process: catharsis, elucidation, exploration and transformation. The chapters in each part represent the emotions of this process. The book ends with suggestions for workshop exercises to assist the exploration of black issues in training.

Questions about black issues raised by trainee counsellors who participated in the study have been integrated throughout the book. I encourage readers to pay attention to these questions and use the content of the book to open dialogue about black issues with colleagues and clients.

The Book's Structure

Part I, 'Shared Concerns', presents an outline of the study (McKenzie-Mavinga, 2005) based on trainees' shared concerns. Encouraging trainees to share their concerns and open a dialogue about black issues was an important feature of the study. Feelings attached to black issues and building connecting responses are considered in Chapters 2 and 3.

Chapter 1, 'A Can of Worms', outlines the study that informs and supports the book. The outpouring of questions and emotions related to black issues can be described as 'a can of worms' because the volatile theme of racism was the biggest concern expressed by trainees.

Chapter 2, 'Feeling It in Our Bones', explores the challenges of journeying through some of the feelings that trainee counsellors associated with black issues and the impact of racism on their client work. Ways to develop a broader understanding that challenges Eurocentric approaches and promotes greater connection to black issues are considered.

Chapter 3, 'A Black Empathic Approach', underscores the importance of a way to understand and connect to the experience of being 'black' in Britain. Drawing on the humanistic concept of empathy, 'a black empathic approach' is used to develop a connection to feelings about difference and sameness and a shared understanding of racism.

In Part II, the concept of 'Recognition Trauma' has been used to assist readers to understand the emotional context of working through the impact of racism on individuals. Therapists are encouraged to engage with ways of understanding responses to black issues and the internal process of racism by developing traditional ideas such as Jung's archetypes.

Chapter 4, 'Healing Ancestral Baggage', engages with transpersonal aspects of black issues by exploring the dynamics of relationships, customs and inherited distress that get passed on by previous generations and expressed in the present. Discussions with trainee counsellors give a flavour of their experiences of working through their concerns about racism. Aspects of psychoanalytic theory are drawn on to support an understanding of the concept of ancestral baggage and the process of recognition trauma.

In Chapter 5, the symptoms and affects of internalised racism are explored using the concept of 'The Black Western Archetype'. To help explain this concept I present a review of therapy with Jacinta, a black lesbian who experienced beatings and used counselling to build her esteem.

Chapter 6, 'Cultural Schizophrenia', addresses issues that affect the mental health treatment of African and Caribbean people. Cultural schizophrenia is a concept used to describe symptoms of mental distress that can be exacerbated by living within or having been influenced by dual or multiple cultures. I present an interview with Angela, a middle-aged African Caribbean woman caught up in the revolving door of the mental health system.

The title of Part III speaks for itself: 'Finding a Voice' expresses the challenging yet liberating experience of becoming un-gagged. The study assisted trainees to open a dialogue where there had been silence. Here I have provided a space for the voices of black men and women to be presented.

Chapter 7, 'Breaking the Bonds', presents a model of group work and black women sharing experiences through therapeutic writing. The effects of patriarchy, slavery and colonialism have meant that black women inheriting the trauma of these experiences may be subject to oppression of self over long periods.

Chapter 8, 'The Wounded Warrior', centres on some important aspects of working with black men. A dialogue with a black male psychotherapist, Arike, is supported by the experiences of two Caribbean men: Leroy, an artist, and Byron, a drummer. Byron expresses the importance of feeling the rhythm from within the African experience and of African male role models. He also shares his views on gay issues in the black community.

Counselling and psychotherapy theory is a tool that provides a framework for understanding a personal context of black issues and the impact of racism. Part IV, 'A Bridge from Fear to Transformation', shows how theory can be developed to include cultural constructs that may support black issues. A shift from fear generated by the impact of racism to an active engagement with black issues is supported by experiences of and ideas for working with black issues in the therapeutic process.

Chapter 9, 'Therapeutic Styles and Approach to Client Work', presents the experiences of Beryl and Joyce, African Caribbean counsellors trained in Britain, and the work of Dr Pat, a Ghanaian therapist. Joyce has returned to Jamaica to practise her counselling skills; Beryl uses her African-centred counsellor training to contextualise relationships within the black family. In response to questions about an African-centred approach, Dr Pat talks about how the principles of African tradition can be applied as a healing instrument.

Chapter 10, 'Going All the Way', concludes by drawing together some key learning points from the narratives of trainers and trainees. Some constructive suggestions are made for preparing trainees to explore and understand black issues. These training suggestions have been offered in response to trainees' questions about practice, theory and process.

Part I

Shared Concerns

Part I outlines the study and the trainees' shared concerns identified in my findings. The strength and volume of trainees' concerns opened a can of worms. Attention is focused on the need to create a dialogue about these concerns. The study was intended to make a difference to counsellor training. This meant responding to trainees' need to open a dialogue about black issues with their clients. To assist trainees with this process, I have developed the concept of a black empathic approach. For me the act of sharing concerns draws together the voices of many into one. The saying 'I feel it in my bones' came to mind when I reflected on the powerful yet virtually unseen, unexplored nature of black issues, which seemed to come alive when trainees were considering the impact of racism.

1

A Can of Worms

This chapter describes and explains the study that provided the framework for this book and supported the inclusion of a space to explore black issues in counsellor training. I first describe the process and key findings of the study. This discussion is followed by excerpts from a dialogue with trainee counsellors and colleagues reporting their experiences of diversity and the emotions evoked by the study. The metaphor in the title of this chapter, 'a can of worms', denotes the cathartic outpouring of concerns and emotions expressed by trainees when they explored black issues. In an attempt to discover the nuances of trainees' understanding, this chapter reflects on their narrative journey from silence to finding a voice, which came about during discussions while they were engaged in black issues workshops.

I quote a poem that I wrote, titled 'Invisible', to give readers a flavour of the personal experience that motivated this study. Phrases used in the poem describe the impact of racism, isolation and the historical backdrop on the processes of my own understanding.

Invisible

They talk over my head
They lean across my desk
They stand beside me
They ask someone else

They ignore my request
They take it off the agenda
They try to convince me
They say it's my problem

They arrive after me
They stand in front
They queue behind me
They get served first

They turn their backs
They want to shake hands
They gave children guns
They stole my lands

They wounded my heart
They tortured my body
They blinded my heritage
They made the trail bloody

They show their tears
They want compassion
They carve their smiles
They follow fashion

They misinterpret my words
They don't want my opinion
They wear their guilt
They can't see I am broken

They fail to hear me
They want me silenced
They shrink away
They call my power violence

They invite challenge
They leave me on the frontline
They include me when
They want a token

They say show me how
They have their problems
They want it written
They don't want it spoken

They come for my soul
They have already taken
They want me the same
They make me different

They want to be conscious
They want to do it right

They want me visible
They want me out of sight
Isha McKenzie-Mavinga
(October 2002)

Describing my experiences in a poem was a way of acknowledging my personal relationship with the theme of black issues and some of the difficulties in engaging my colleagues in the study. Collection of data was influenced by the impact of racism on individuals and by the silencing nature of institutional racism. Scheurich and Young (1997) use the term 'epistemological racism' to describe the power dynamics that stem from these elements of institutional racism. Although they were aware of my minority position in higher education, trainees reminded me of the impact of my own epistemological role in the hierarchy of training. The majority of trainees were women, and I was aware of my role as black woman, and the duality of being both researcher and tutor. In addition, I was reminded of the impact of my own Eurocentric training and upbringing.

The best way to limit these influences was to present trainees' original narratives and not try to interpret their experiences. This was achieved using a process of listening and reflection, similar to that of a counselling relationship. On reflection, the heuristic nature of this process comes to mind.

Moustakas (1990) used the term 'initial engagement' (connection to and ownership of a burning issue) to describe the heuristic nature of the researcher's relationship with the theme of the study: 'The task of the initial engagement is to discover an intense interest, a passionate concern that calls out to the researcher. One that holds an important social meaning and personal compelling implications' (p. 27). The initial engagement of the study and its outcome grew out of trainee counsellors' expressed concerns about exploring black issues in their training and client work. I was curious about these concerns as I had not had an opportunity to explore black issues in my own training. I interviewed a number of experienced practitioners to find out whether they had been offered opportunities to explore black issues in their training.

These interviews corroborated my own concern about not having black issues addressed in our training. The practitioners involved in the interviews had all been colleagues at various stages of my journey as a counsellor trainer. None of them had previously discussed their training with me. Excerpts from these interviews are presented here, followed by a summary of key responses and interviewees' strategies for coping. Names have been changed to provide anonymity.

The interviewees and their comments

- Paulette is a white, Jewish woman who trained as a person-centred counsellor in 1978. She runs a private practice and works as an external moderator for counsellor training courses.

> **Paulette**
> People were not aware of black issues or areas like disability at the time I trained. There was not much inclusion in those days.

- Ragina is an Indian, Hindu woman who trained as a person-centred counsellor in 1992. She runs a private practice and coordinates an integrative counselling course.

> **Ragina**
> I don't feel that I learnt a lot of theory regarding black issues when I was training.

- Anton is an African Caribbean man who trained in person-centred counselling in 1989. He runs a private practice, has worked as a group therapist with black men in high-security mental health care, and teaches person-centred counselling.

> **Anton**
> If we had not brought those issues up as black people, they would not have come up.

- Phillip is a white, gay, Irish man who trained in integrative and Adlerian counselling in 1990. He teaches integrative counselling.

> **Phillip**
> The issues of race did not get addressed in any formal sense. It only came up in the context of our client work. In my Adlerian training course we had one session on race and racism. So across the whole of that there has not really been a focus on black issues.

- Bibi is a British Asian, Pakistani and Muslim woman who trained in psychodynamic and person-centred counselling in 2001. She is studying for an MA in counselling.

> **Bibi**
> I experienced the tutors as not being able to handle it; they seemed to change energetically, in their facial language. It seemed they were less confident and maybe even cautious. I think they were frightened at the prospects of having to hold many different levels of student expression. Expressions of anger and anguish, annoyance that they could become mis-represented.

Summary of key themes emerging from interviews

Key themes were summarised and considered as pointers for data collected later:

- My intense interest allayed isolation and became a shared concern.
- The interviews broke silences that inhibit dialogue about black issues.
- There was no experience of explicit discussion of black issues in the interviewees' training.
- Individuals used other forums to develop their knowledge of black issues.
- Black issues have been considered external to the training curriculum.
- Black issues have been regarded as belonging to black trainees.
- The need to bring black issues into the training curriculum was confirmed.

Strategies for coping with the missing element of black issues

- Paulette confirms she gained her initial understanding of racism from a black colleague and her awareness of herself as a white person outside of training.
- Ragina goes outside of training to black student peers.
- Phillip wonders whether a black therapist may bring elements missing with his white therapist and supervisor.
- Bibi and Anton had to challenge the racism of their training to have their experience valued.

Role of the Black Expert

These accounts suggest that learning about black issues was influenced mainly by the input of black trainees and black staff, who are few and far between. This role of educator was one that I had found myself filling as a trainee counsellor. A trainee in Watson's (2004) research shares this sentiment:

It's harder work getting the issues taken seriously because it's down to ... it feels as though pressure is on you as the one Black person to represent all sorts of things or to raise all sorts of things whether you want to or not. Or if you don't then your silence is taken as agreement or collusion with the things that might happen. (p. 47)

The black student bearing the role of educator on training courses (the black expert role) may be forced to experience what Straker et al. (2002) view as the 'continuous trauma' of their often-disempowered position in a white-dominated society. Straker et al. see this trauma as an interruption in the ongoing process of self-development. In performing the role of the black expert, the black trainee becomes distracted from his or her self-development process and burdened with white trainees' self-development and the need to explain racism. For therapists this should happen only in the context of listening to clients.

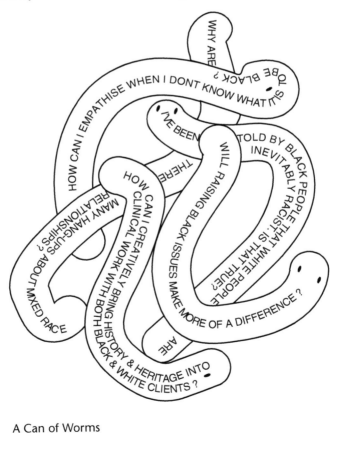

A Can of Worms

My colleagues' voices echoed some problems of discussing black issues in training settings. Bibi said, 'We have opened the door, but we have not been able to enter'; Paulette, 'It felt dangerous and difficult.' During discussions with trainees I tried to introduce black issues in a wider context, but these discussions became focused on black people and racism. Issues about white practitioners and their relationships with black people and with each other were contentious. Wading through a great mire of transferred feelings of guilt, fear, anger and denial, trainees were asking questions such as 'How do we open a dialogue about black issues when the discussion seems difficult and dangerous?' They wanted more than the information provided in the literature. They needed to gain confidence through a deeper process of exploration and understanding during their training. Reports seemed to indicate that the volatile nature of black issues created tensions that inhibited discussions. The key themes listed below came out like opening a can of worms.

Key themes considered during the second phase of study

- a need for opportunities to voice experiences and concerns about working with black issues
- the different experiences of black and white trainees
- the different experiences of African and Asian trainees
- powerful feelings and blocks attached to the exploration of black issues
- valuing the input of black trainees and trainers
- fixed Eurocentric models and the need for new perspectives
- lack of professional input on black issues
- expectations of white trainees to learn from black trainees and trainers (role of the black expert, trainee facilitator role)
- impact of racism
- lack of input on black issues from white trainers
- concerns about not having black issues supported in supervision and further personal development

Reflections on key themes

- Opportunities to explore black issues provided by visiting tutors may not be integrated into the main system of training and may not be followed up by core tutors.
- It is clear that the number of black students on counsellor training courses is growing, and their training needs must be considered in

the light of their cultural experiences and experiences of racism and minority oppression in Britain.

• Concerns about black issues may not be fully addressed; they may be dispersed into issues of humanity, multiculturalism and diversity.

Just as the context of understanding is important for the role of a counsellor, it became clear that the context of understanding was an important feature in the process of dialogue about black issues in training.

The second phase of the study was rather like the early stages of the therapeutic relationship, where the therapist finds out the concerns of a client and attempts to create a focused dialogue where exploration can take place. Similarly, some of the themes that emerged during this process helped to inform the ethical considerations of the study. In the therapeutic relationship, it is usually the contents of the client's presenting problem and his or her history that shape the relationship. Likewise, the concerns that trainees expressed helped to shape the context of the study:

White trainee counsellors' concerns

• 'How can I empathise when I don't know what it is to be black?'
• 'How do I explore early childhood experiences of racism?'
• 'Is it patronising to change the nature of counselling when working transculturally?'

Black trainee counsellors' concerns

• 'What is expected of me as a woman of colour?'
• 'Do I verbally raise the difference if I feel it isn't a difference?'
• 'Children seem to focus less on skin colour, so why does colour become more noticeable when children become adults?'

Trainees' primary concerns appeared to be existential and very much based on their feelings about the theme of black issues. It was clear that they needed to voice and explore some of the emotions attached to the concerns that they had shared about understanding black issues. The main thrust of the study then turned into an attempt to understand the concept of black issues as a phenomenon and how this concept may or may not be addressed in the therapeutic process. Moustakas (1990) called this attention to feelings and reflective process during research 'explication' (p. 30).

I found that listening to trainees' shared concerns evoked a strong sense of familiarity and helped me to recognise the emotional patterns of oppression in myself. Loss of faith that dominant oppressor groups would change their attitudes towards black women was illuminated, and I needed to use my own therapy to discharge my deep feelings of rejection and humiliation.

I had not been working on this loss of faith in my own co-counselling sessions with white counsellors. I had abandoned them as my white mother had abandoned me. This awareness and the fact that in co-counselling both counsellor and client have a mutual agreement to lead helped me decide to take the lead on this important part of our therapeutic relationship. The theory and training that support co-counselling promote a high expectation that counsellors will contradict oppression and internalised oppression in the counsellor, in the client, and in their relationship. Internalised oppression is viewed as negative and unconscious acting out or acting towards self in negative ways that can be emotionally harmful and distort identity. Skin bleaching and skin scraping caused by a wish to be white are extreme cases of internalised racism. Being open to my own process of internalised racism with my white counsellors, not just with my black counsellors, transformed me into a more empathic listener. It was a two-way process that I believe assisted my white co-counsellors to overcome their fixation with black issues and get on with the business of working through their white guilt and shame about racism. Through this process I began to experience a new place inside of me that would reach out rather than dismiss individuals who had difficulty accepting the personal as opposed to the political context of black issues.

Listening to trainees' responses and reflecting on my own therapeutic process has helped me to understand that racism has an impact on white people as well as black people. Awareness of my own responses and blocks contributed to the reflective process of transcribing interviews and discussions with trainees and colleagues. It is often at the point of responding to black issues that therapists get blocked if their training or practice has not sufficiently exposed them to these concerns and supported their difficulties. My poem 'Transcription' represents my engagement with this transformative process:

Transcription

I face the blank page/yawn, feel hysterical
Laughter and tears beneath the surface

With a prod my chest may exude this mass
Afraid, my pen will cease to flow

I stop to itch my nose/aware of stopping
Stopping may distract attention
My thinking once curbed, I wonder
Can this narrative transform knowledge?

Holding this pause/this moment in history
A space to unravel, to mind and observe
A cathartic matrix of writhing worms
Each ventricular journey a precious growth

Illumination of newborn concepts/routes
Past to future unfolding wisdom and notion
Tapestries of experiences embrace tentatively
Ignite the passion of learning new other ways
                    Isha McKenzie-Mavinga (2005)

Through the transformation process of the study I became clear that racism needs to be explored by anyone involved in the process of understanding black issues. Below I reflect on some of the ethical concerns that emerged from trainees' responses to this theme.

My tutor–researcher role

As a tutor in the role of researcher there were times when I became consumed with fear – a silencing fear that cautioned me not to want to share or disclose the experiences and data that emerged. It felt very much as though the data were red hot and would burn me. On one hand, I was responsible for trainees' learning; on the other, I was engaging them with a theme close to my heart, which could be viewed as imposing my own agenda on them. I withdrew into periods of incubation when I revisited my fears of attack, rejection and humiliation relived from past experiences. In the face of this I was encouraged by my black peers to remain visible, because there have been many great inventors, people of colour, who have disappeared. Feminist researcher Field Belenky and colleagues (1986) refer to the process of emerging visibility through language in terms of George Elliot's phrase 'the other side of silence':

If we had a keen vision and feeling of all ordinary human life, it would be like hearing the grass grow and the squirrel's heartbeat,

and we should die of that roar which lies on the other side of silence.
(*Middlemarch*, quoted in Field Belenky et al., 1986, p. 13)

Understanding my own process as a tutor helped build an emotional
space for trainees to share their concerns about black issues. This created new awareness and a release from their associated negative feelings.
Denzin (1989) considers the relevance of these processes to a kind of
catharsis: 'Emotionality and shared experience provide the conditions
for deep, authentic understanding' (p. 33). In Freudian therapy, Freud
(1909) and Breuer related the term 'cathartic' to the act of speaking out
whatever events were happening at the time a symptom occurred. The
symptom then disappeared. Freud encouraged his trauma patients to
use this method and linked it with the discharge of repressed emotion.

For myself as tutor–researcher and also for trainees, a cathartic
process appears as a sharing, going public and expression of pent-up
response and emotion about black issues not previously attended to in
our training. This process provided a means of relieving silence and
tension, an opportunity to begin a dialogue and a way of understanding the concept of black issues in relation to the action and process
of counselling – in Freud's and Breuer's terms, an expression that can
lead to change.

In the study, change was initiated by finding meaning to bridge the
gap between trainees' shared concerns and what could be viewed as
their process of understanding black issues.

The role of the black expert

The role of the black expert becomes evident when white trainees look
towards black peers for their learning about black issues, as opposed to
learning from white peers, trainers and other sources. This was evident
in the black interviewees' experiences. This dynamic was significant in
the study because references to black people's developmental process
and their relationships with each other were rarely made by white trainees. White trainees did not voice concerns about rejection from white
clients or white peers, whereas black trainees showed concerns about
working with both their black and their white peers. Feelings such as
guilt were expressed by white trainees. Black trainees offered information to white peers about their experiences. They addressed their concerns in terms of the impact of racism on themselves. They also showed
concern about being accepted and dealing with white people's feelings
about racism. The situation of black trainees' learning space being used
to cope with or respond to white trainees' feelings about racism is an

important issue in training. Mutual support is needed so that black trainees' self-discovery is not compromised.

The following concern is illustrative: 'I'm curious how some people react in a defensive way when black issues are mentioned. Are whites feeling attacked by the guilt of our history?' The question clearly raises issues about the responses of white trainees and about the training of black counsellors working with black clients. To avoid burdening black trainees, both black trainees' and white trainees' concerns must be supported by course trainers.

Issues of fear, safety and finding a voice

Powerful feelings, defences and blocks attached to the exploration of black issues and concerns about racism were evident in some interviewees' and trainees' statements. These responses reflected trainees' fears about the safety of sharing their experiences.

- 'Why do I find this difficult?'
- 'Why do I feel more comfortable as a black counsellor when presented with a black client?'
- 'Would I ever be seen as good enough, as a white counsellor, to deal with black issues by a black client?'
- 'How can I hold on to my sense of being black in a white counselling world?'

Trainees knowing and 'not knowing' about racism

The concerns referred to above speak volumes about trainees' attempts to make sense of black issues and, most important, about where shifts in the transcultural elements of counsellor training may be needed. Some trainees expressed knowledge about the dynamics of racism, whereas others seemed to be in a place of not knowing. Trainees' responses were both self-reflective and about their concern for clients. This indicated the importance of an ethical context for approaching discussions about black issues in training. Trainees therefore need to experience safety to explore black issues, find their voice and develop ways of integrating theoretical models to support their work. Trainers can facilitate these challenges and support feelings that arise out of this process. This may include a need to understand their different levels of awareness about black issues.

Differing levels of awareness meant that trainees and colleagues took at least a year to develop a shared understanding and acceptance of the concept of black issues. On reflection, over a twenty-year period in the field of counselling and psychotherapy I have found that varying levels of awareness and understanding about black issues are displayed. These variations create a tension within training groups. The tension needs to be explored on a personal and professional level. This process of acknowledgement and working through can act as a model for under-standing and facilitating therapeutic relationships.

The following three key areas are examples of the varying levels that affect trainees' and tutors' capacity to understand black issues:

- a hierarchy of oppressions that can dominate discussions about black issues
- the need for a shared knowledge of the sociological contexts of black issues
- experience located in the impact of racism and colonialism

Further Analysis of Trainees' Concerns

As a means of coding the information collected in the study I revisited the collection of trainees' shared concerns, paying particular attention to my discovery that within trainees' questions, racism was referred to many times. I decided to look for other terms that were repeated. These were identified as 'guilt', 'history' and 'trust'. I divided the questions into four categories based on trainees' level of training: 'Certificate and skills', 'Year one', 'Year two' and 'Others' (for example, collaborators and conference delegates). (See Figure 1.) The terms used to identify these themes are shown in Figure 2. Table 1 is divided according to the three universities that were involved in the study. Concerns were divided into six categories (rows), and examples from these categories are presented here:

- Black trainees: 'How can the historical view of a black person not being suitable to support a white person be addressed?'
- White trainees: 'What if I am racist to a black client?'
- Political: 'Why do I feel really resentful towards being politically correct?'
- Self-reflective: 'Why do I feel nervous when I hear the term "black issues"?'
- Theoretical: 'Are black people always victims? If men hold the power, how can black men be victims and perpetrators?'
- Clients: 'How do I raise issues of race and culture and difference with a client who doesn't raise it, but as a counsellor I feel it is an issue?'

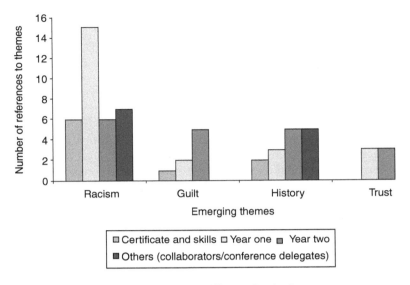

Figure 1 Key Emerging Themes in Different Study Groups

When I had completed this coding, it became clear that the issue of 'racism' was referred to most often. The category of 'history' was referred to considerably less frequently, yet it was the second-commonest theme. This seemed to indicate that the historical context of black issues is an important element in trainees' attempts to understand black issues in the therapeutic process. Concerns about the process of racism are layered on top of history, guilt and trust issues, and these emotions demanded more immediate attention. In therapeutic relationships, repetitive themes are usually seen as indicators of significance in the client's emotional process. Using the study as a parallel process, I paid particular attention to the relevance of these themes in the counsellor training group. It was important to recognise that although concerns about racism seemed to become a priority, responses to these issues differed between black and white trainees.

For trainees, sharing their different responses and concerns about black issues became a way of finding their voice on transcultural issues. Sharing evokes profound realisation as part of the emancipation process. In transcultural counselling, the counsellor is required to examine his or her own prejudices, assumptions and personal responses to the client's cultural experiences and belief systems (Eleftheriadou, 1994).

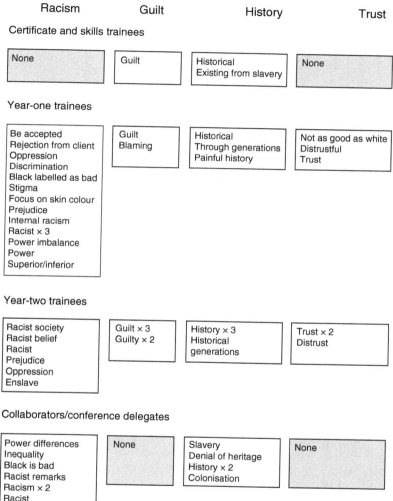

Figure 2 Repeated Themes

Themes that evolved from the trainees' process of self-examination during the study evoked a range of emotions from fear to transformation, with racism, guilt, history and trust issues being expressed as part of this experience.

Since racism emerged as the dominant theme and trainees had different ideas about what racism is, let's take a look at some contemporary

Table 1 Synopsis of Shared Concerns

	University 1	University 2	University 3	Others	Common concerns
Black trainees	Not being as good as white counterparts Client rejection Eurocentric models	Internalised oppression Defensiveness and guilt of white counterparts Anger of black and white trainees	Black on black comfort Black on black concerns Maintaining identity and acceptance		Focus on black on black-and-white history Acceptance, defensiveness, anger, Eurocentric theory Internalised oppression Acknowledgement of history
White trainees	The effect of whiteness and effectiveness with black clients How do I empathise with the other?	What if I am racist? Effect of my guilt My prejudice	Black clients' distrust of me Am I good enough? How to respond to black issues	(Year 2) Competency with black clients Limitations, trust, a healthy alliance My prejudice Racism, power	Being effective with black clients Levels of empathy Competency, guilt Racism to black clients Isolation, trust, power
Political	Why black issues, what about other oppressions? Why focus on black people? What is 'black'? Why are other groups excluded?	Does it matter? What about other differences? Political correctness	Anti-racism Too much focus to the exclusion of others Learn black issues without politics White liberal guilt	(Year 2) Political correctness Bad feelings Historical impact on black and white people Is the colour of the therapist relevant?	Why black issues? Negative feelings Other groups Oppression Political correctness Guilt

Self-reflective	White racism Will I understand? Negative stereotypes Intellect v. emotions Where do I start? Different identities Black on black, white on white	Inadequacies, difficulties How to address black issues or not Power issues	Nervous about the term 'black'	(Year 2) Empathy Covert racism. Historical view of inadequate black person Power Pressure of getting it wrong Blame, guilt, isolation Feeling intimidated	Impact of my white racism, stereotypes How will I understand? Empathy levels Black on black, white on white Inadequacies How do I address black issues? Overt and covert racism Power Pressure of getting it wrong Blame guilt, isolation, intimidation
Theoretical	Will black remain a central issue, is it always present, is it possible to go beyond this? Do black men have power or not?			(Year 2) Breaking down hate defences	Is black a central issue or not? Going beyond Gender issues (black men) Hate defences
Clients	Overt racism My own prejudice	What if I am racist or prejudiced?	Difficulty discussing black issues Responding to victims of racism Identity issues	(Year 2) Differences in black people's experiences Oppression in the transference The link between black issues and trust	Differences between black people Racism and prejudice in practice Oppression in the transference Historical impact on black and white Learning from the black client

definitions. Tuckwell (2002) describes individual racism as 'consisting of personal attitudes of racial superiority, leading to behaviour that is discriminatory in nature' (p. 17). Howitt and Owusu-Bempah (1994) discuss 'old racism' and 'new racism' in the context of evolving discourse. For example, they define myths that black people are inferior as old racism, and new racism as including the concept of cultural racism: 'Because racism's clothes have changed, because it is now expressed in terms of culture rather than biology, many believe that it is now little more than an embarrassing appendage to psychology' (p. 9).

This stage of acknowledging the greater concerns about racism was most painful and challenging for the trainees, much as when deeper feelings begin to surface in the second phase of a therapeutic relationship. I became concerned about the strength of feelings that trainees expressed when engaged with the theme of black issues. There appeared to be a block; discussions became focused on black trainees' experiences of racism, and some white trainees felt silenced. This process of powerful response to racism I have named 'recognition trauma'. It is a process whereby the powerful emotions of individuals relating to black issues either come to the fore or create a block. Trainees were facilitated to work through these emotions and to voice their experiences. Responses indicated that there had been shifts in communication and a greater understanding. However, the implications of 'recognition trauma' for client work needed to be considered. Discussions with trainees highlighted a transformative process which included their willingness to acknowledge the issue of fear and develop a safe space to address racism and the powerful feelings associated with it.

The following transcripts show how trainees used discussion to process the impact of recognition trauma on their development as counsellors and their client work. The discussions highlighted a transformative process that included their willingness to acknowledge the issue of fear and develop a safe space to address racism and the powerful feelings associated with it.

A black trainee articulates her experiences of racism, her pride and, on the other hand, the impact of internalised racism. She applies her understanding to the skill of empathy with black and white clients and to herself in the role of black client with a white counsellor. White trainees discuss their ethnicity and their experiences of learning from a black tutor, black peers and black clients in the black expert role. There was a real sense of transformation. The narrative also validates the impact of the workshops, and it can be seen that for the most part, trainees' understanding of black issues in the therapeutic process was linked to the impact of racism.

Black female trainee

It is that black issues is not just about racism, it is to do with the way black people relate to other black people as well as how they relate to white people. For me in counselling situations as a black woman what is going through my head, is my client thinking I am not good enough? I am wondering what she is thinking about me and how I can be there with her. In relation to how it affects my relationship with other black people. At times it is helpful. When a young black man comes to me and he is telling me about his respect, having young black people that look up to him, I find it easier to understand where he is coming from, because within my culture as the older child we have to set examples that young people follow. So it makes it easier for me to enter into their frame of reference. But there are times, because of history, because of racism and because of the way I have the experience of being black, I am wondering you know when I am with another black person, because I don't see black people in key posts very much, one of the questions is how did they come to be where they are?

Black trainees felt empowered to talk explicitly about racism and question white tutors about their ability to empathise with them. White trainees took ownership of their own cultural links with each other and the impact this has on their understanding of black issues. Power and fear in relation to racism were repeatedly expressed and I see this as a feature of recognition trauma. A white participant shared her experiences of not feeling understood 'as a white woman' and feeling 'intimidated' by me, the black tutor. Concerns about clinical work and placement support for discussing black issues were shared, and issues of power and history surfaced.

Turkish Asian female trainee

It applies to me as well. What we are learning here is enormous, it is major learning. Before this course I thought I had learned enough reading, studying about history and black people. But when I started the course I realised that I really did not know anything. Just knowing the history and having black friends or being in a black community, it doesn't mean that we know the culture of black people. Because black people have their own culture, women have their own culture. How we develop this culture and how this culture can intervene between us as a counsellor and our clients and in this society. So I learned a lot about myself and my own issues and my inner world. I try with this learning to bring my inner world to its reality. Sometimes I feel the same as you. So this culture of learning, of oppression is so concrete, it makes it very difficult to forget or lose it. It can easily come to the counselling setting or whatever setting. So in my workplace, I can easily be destroyed in a minute by somebody who I have experienced a history of being oppressed by. I don't really know, this is what I really need to learn more of. How to build confidence and how to acknowledge and recognise my own self in an appropriate way. How to present myself as I am and not to be oppressed when it comes from my history. I said that I learned a lot, but how does the learning support me? There is more to learn.

The narrative showed trainees challenging each other and getting to grips with their learning about and understanding of black issues in their lives, in their training and in their clinical work. Understanding was derived from trainees' own cultural reference points. Safety and fear as a feature of recognition trauma are concerns referred to in relation to racism by both black and white trainees. Both groups have different experiences of racism and different needs. The most interesting revelation was the expression by a white man of the power of black people sharing their experiences. This was likened to a burning-bush experience, a personal epiphany about recognising the power of the impact of racism and, also, the power of black women's expressed feelings about their experiences. This brought to light a differentiation between the fear of the white man and the fear of the black woman. The white man expresses fear of being called a racist. The black woman expresses fear of being rejected.

White male trainee

When I started on the training my knowledge of black issues and any other cultural issues was quite poor. Coming down to London from Bury St Edmunds, a white middle-class area, was a learning curve for me. Being on the course has helped me to increase my learning and my understanding of black issues. The real difficultly is that it has made me look at my own prejudices. I don't believe when people say they don't have prejudices, we all have prejudices. It's coming to terms with that and trying to understand what these prejudices are and where they come from that is important. The black issues workshops have created a lot of uncomfortable feelings for me. At times I have felt quite unsafe, much challenged and quite criticised being a white male. I have had to work through that. At times I have come away from the workshops feeling angry and quite defensive. Over the two years I have tried to work through that and really asked myself why am I getting angry? Are there some prejudices I have got to face? I still don't really know the answers. It has really made me look at it in a very honest way. The black issues workshops make you look at it in the face. To me as well it is about safety and being safe to feel able to say what you really think and work through what you really think. Sometimes I have not felt particularly safe to be really free and say how I really felt.

Black issues workshops became part of the curriculum during the study, and evaluative discussions outside the teaching sessions enabled something to happen outside the training that did not happen during the black issues workshops. A mutually safe, non-judgemental, empathic environment that facilitated discussion about racism was provided. Trainees were offered a place for a cathartic process where feelings of guilt and the impact of history were explored.

Black female trainee

My interest in coming to this evaluation is the motivation of getting feedback through a transcript. I have learnt a lot about black issues that I did not know in the beginning and I have gained insight of black issues that happen every day, everywhere, every time. I have also gained insight and learning from other colleagues and tutors concerning black issues. In the beginning I was so afraid to talk about black issues. I felt that I would hurt other people's feelings, those who are not black. But seeing the example set by the tutors in one of the workshops, as they talked openly and transparently about black issues, I felt well I can express myself and learn from others as they learn from me as well. I thought that if black issues were brought into the course it has widened my understanding.

The summary in Figure 3 shows that in later discussions second-year trainees focused less on theoretical and political concerns and more on concerns about client work. The role of the black expert also featured to a lesser degree, but remained implicit within trainees' narrative. However, towards the latter part of the study black trainees found

Shared concerns at beginning of year 1

Black trainee counsellors
What if a client rejects me when I am a counsellor, because of my African/ Caribbean heritage?
Why is it that I don't feel as good as white contemporaries?
Most of the theory and models are from non-black backgrounds; this has an impact on black culture, it does not fit into the way we think, how can we work with this?

White trainee counsellors
Do I have to have had personal experience of oppression to be an effective counsellor to a black person?
How can I imaginatively extend my own experience?
As a white woman how can I be effective in counselling black clients?
How will being white affect my relationship when counselling black clients, and how able will I be?

Political
Why does there have to be a separate area of 'black issues', where has it come from?
Shouldn't black issues be about celebrating diversity?
Why do I feel discriminated against when we discuss black issues?
Why are blacks labelled bad most of the time?
Why is there stigma around trans-racial relationships?
Do we focus too much on the colour of each other's skin and consequently generate unnecessary barriers?
How are black gay/lesbian/bisexual/transgender people treated in their own community?
As an African/Asian gay person, how do you perceive you are accepted or not within the gay community?

Reflective
Will I be fully open to and understand black issues?
Do I compensate in my behaviour when I deal with black issues, to hide my prejudice?
Why do I feel more comfortable with non-white people or people from non-Western cultures?
When there are two people with the same first name in a group and one is white and one black, and we don't know each other very well, is it okay to refer to them as white Kathy and black Kathy?

Theoretical: None

About clients:
Does my client identify me as his/her counsellor, do I know his/her culture?

Shared concerns at beginning of year 2

Black trainee counsellors
I am wondering why, as a black woman, up to now, I have not thought of bringing black issues into my relationships with white clients.

White trainee counsellors
How do we avoid stepping into a socially conditioned posture of white racism, overtly or covertly, in the therapeutic dyad, and avoid the sociopolitical implications of race by focusing solely on psychological processes. (Useful framework: Tuckwell, 2002)

My beliefs in the past year have changed drastically. I feel that to be empathic with a client who has had bereavement, my own experience of loss plays a major part. Without personal experience of loss I feel quite inept. How can I therefore be a substitute for a black counsellor, who may understand and have experienced oppression personally? I ask these questions from the viewpoint of a black client who is looking for a counsellor who truly empathises with the issue of oppression.
Sometimes I, as a white person, want to hear a black person's perspective, but I often feel that this is perceived as not okay, why is that? And how come wanting to listen and understand can make me feel uncomfortable and confused? As a white counsellor, am I over-identifying with black issues?

Political: None

Theoretical
I have learnt a lot about black issues, but still I find it difficult to convert this into theories.

Reflective
Learning about black issues gave me knowledge and understanding of dynamics and feelings of black people – the history and psychological impact on individuals, but I am concerned about how this learning would be positive in relationships between black and other ethnic minorities.
Will I patronise my black friends because of their history and see them as weak and as needing my protection and not identify with white supremacy and try to unconditionally validate blacks and dismiss the reality?
As a counsellor, how can I remain empathic when I am being attacked by the other?

About clients
What if this is an issue with racism in the counselling process, and every time I reflect on it the client changes the subject, then I address that and the client says that is not what I am trying to say but you still feel something is not right? Resistance on the client's behalf. ... Should I address my fear, uncertainty of dealing with black issues with my client?
Is my fear of black issues a transference?

Figure 3   University 1: Shared concerns at beginning and end of workshops

their voices and challenged this dynamic. This change appears to have enabled white trainees to take more ownership of their whiteness – a painful yet empowering experience for both groups.

Trainees were invited to comment on their experiences of the black issues workshops during their training. They were asked how useful the workshops were in supporting all areas of their training, including their counselling placements. Their feedback was gathered during recorded discussions and by using questionnaires as evaluation forms. I then asked my colleagues to comment on the evaluation. I have listed the main themes of this evaluation below.

Summary of pertinent and repeated themes presented by trainees

- An emphasis was placed on the importance of sharing concerns, including the tutors' concerns, and their commitment to addressing black issues.
- Trainees gained awareness and exploration of their own and others' cultures.
- All trainees reported that the workshops had contributed to their understanding of the impact of racism, oppression and power issues.
- An interest in whiteness and blackness and the impact of one on the other was shown.
- The facilitation style was considered helpful by nine out of eleven trainees.
- Ten trainees thought that both black and white tutors were helpful.
- Points made about what was unhelpful related to friction between black and white trainees.
- Comments were made about divisions in the group and needing more time on black issues and other cultural issues.
- Some important points were made about support to explore black issues in clinical supervision: all trainees experienced support in their course supervision; only five of eleven trainees reported support in their placement supervision.
- Some white trainees' responses showed that they continue to rely on the 'black expert' for knowledge and personal development on black issues.
- Responses from colleagues reflecting on this summary validate the positive impact of the workshops and point to issues of safety, finding a voice and the need for further exploration of oppression and other cultural issues.

Conclusion

The study began by using the concept of shared concerns, which allowed trainees to express their levels of understanding of the concept of black issues that had been introduced into their training. Out of this experience came the identification of certain categories within which trainees appeared to express their concerns (for example, 'black trainees', 'white trainees').

Out of the silence came the need for trainees to find their voices. The concept of recognition trauma gave meaning to the fear experienced by both black and white trainees when they realised the impact and context of racism on their lives. In addition, the theme of power was recognised in the context of white trainees witnessing the feelings of black trainees sharing their experiences of racism.

Self-challenge, equality issues and the needs of both black and white trainees and clients played a key role in the study. A reconciliation of social history and transferring knowledge into deliverable techniques was considered. The study played a role in creating new social forms and opening up theory. Eurocentrism was challenged in the process and approach of the study – in particular, by not leaving the responsibility of raising black issues to black trainees or expecting trainees to find out about black issues in counselling outside of the training, as had happened to most of the trainers. The question of how black issues are addressed was explored through the process of understanding trainees' relationship with the phenomenon of black issues.

Trainees' narratives showed that an understanding of black issues comes about through sharing concerns about their peer relationships, their practice and their experiences of the impact and dynamics of racism. Allowing a cathartic process and discussion about racism to take place in a safe, confidential space seemed to be an important parallel to the counselling relationship. The ability to recognise feelings such as fear, hurt, rejection and anger that connect with the process of recognition trauma appears key to the process of understanding black issues. Links between the workshop experience of black issues and other aspects of training, such as clinical supervision and training placements, need to be developed.

By this point, I was feeling that we had reached a critical impasse. Although there were no limits to the themes open for discussion within the paradigm of black issues, responses to the concept were showing that black issues had been superseded by concerns about racism. An important outcome of the study, therefore, is the knowledge that in counsellor training, experiences of racism need to be addressed to create a deeper understanding of black issues in the therapeutic process. This was reconfirmed in the process of data collection, in trainees' responses and in the outcome of the study. Enabling trainees to express their concerns and work through them during training can contribute to the emancipation process of finding a voice on black issues.

The main themes to emerge from the study have provided pointers for counsellor training. These will be identified at the end of each chapter.

Pointers for therapists (including trainers and trainees)

- Create discussions that explore and value the separate experiences of black and white trainees.
- Facilitate trainees to find their voice and share their own experiences of diversity.
- Explore and model supportive listening to experiences of racism and the impact of racism on trainees.
- Create group exercises that explore and raise awareness of feelings such as fear, guilt and mistrust associated with black issues.
- Engage in discussions about black history, white history, mental health and oppression in relation to black issues.
- Acknowledge that some trainees' language, culture and social disposition may limit their initial response to black issues.
- Revise traditional approaches to therapy and develop a multidimensional training approach that allows the flexibility to work with black issues in the therapeutic process.

2
Feeling It in Our Bones

The phrase 'feeling it in our bones', used as the title for this chapter, intuitively suggests the need to attend to the deeper feelings that come up in response to black issues. Chapter 1 explained how my study (McKenzie-Mavinga, 2005) culminated in the identification of concerns about racism. Discussions about general life experiences of black people were overtaken by questions that go far beyond skin colour to the structure of our feelings. We touched on the bones of emotional conflicts associated with an understanding of black issues. Concerns that arose – such as the following, voiced by a trainee – have endorsed the need to reframe the context of counsellor training:

> Why is it that in nine years of training, in inner city London, I have only had one black and one Asian trainer and why is it that I am still struggling, not to intellectually understand the concept of 'black issues', but to feel it in my bones?

This chapter explores the struggle for a space that allows therapists and clients to feel it in our bones. Trainees raised concerns about their dialogue with black clients and the impact of racism on black–white counselling relationships. Readers are challenged to examine the Eurocentric impact on counselling theory and to develop the basic core conditions of therapeutic relationships to help understand the process of black issues.

The Eurocentric impact on counselling theory incorporates traditional approaches such as those proposed by early schools of psychoanalysis. In these approaches behaviour and the internal psychological processes were observed, interpreted and measured against stereotypes of human personality traits and the lifestyles of white middle-class therapists. For example, Freud (1909), whose medical career started in 1837, introduced the concept of the 'Oedipus complex' based on the development of children and their relationship to the ideal white middle-class heterosexual parent couple. Interpretations of internal responses to the dichotomy of these typological parents may not necessarily apply to families with same-sex parents or a child raised within an extended family, as is quite often the case in working-class families and families originating from non-Western parts of the world. The concept of 'individuation', a therapeutic aim proposed by Jung (1970), can also be viewed as a Eurocentric imposition on individuals raised within these families whose cultural reference points may be defined in more collective ways: 'This progression from the unconscious to the conscious and from the ego to the self Jung named as *individuation*' (p. 672).

Many contemporary therapeutic approaches have been developed from these original concepts and therapists of today recognise the importance of adapting their approaches to a more diverse multicultural society. Therapists who remain aware of the extent to which Eurocentric approaches have dominated counselling theory will be advantaged in their understanding of black issues in the therapeutic process.

The study highlighted the different needs of black and white counsellors, at the same time valuing trainees' need to develop a philosophical and theoretical base for their practice. It became apparent that white trainees needed to discuss their feelings of guilt and fear about addressing black issues. Black trainees needed to develop their specific learning needs, such as understanding the impact of racism in their own lives and the lives of their clients.

The discourses of counselling and psychotherapy have been programmed in ways that provoke a response to the distressing elements of black–white relationships rather than the personal development issues attached to racism. Dalal (2002) addresses this problem as though it were a defence mechanism:

> Racism and prejudice are group phenomena; they grip large numbers of people at the same time. … Whilst racism is a group phenomenon it does not operate on all individuals homogeneously, thus there are always variations with instances going against the general trend. It is my contention that certain facets of racism and prejudice only make their presence known when the field of view is a broad and general one, and that the device of focusing on the particular is a means of negating its presence. (p. 63)

In my study white trainees associated with the gripping sensation mentioned by Dalal that occurred when racism was brought into the discussion. They explained this as a fear that they might be singled out as the racist (tutors would attempt to hunt the racist among them). This kind of fear may be seen as a defence against the impact of racism, since racism is cultivated as a group phenomenon. If it is not addressed, this sensation can permeate training and perpetuate institutional racism by creating blocks in communication about black issues.

An institution consists of a collection of people, who in Dalal's group phenomenon may not always be aware of the blocks that racism can cause. By trying to understand and engage with powerful feelings of fear and guilt evoked by racism, institutions and individuals are taking an opportunity to develop a new discourse – a discourse that explores the impact of racism and its related emotional blocks, one that engages in a confident dialogue about black issues, less dominated by fears about racism.

I believe that the underlying hurt in our own personal lives attaches itself to our conflicts about the nature of racism. When this aspect of conflict was echoed within counsellor training groups, defensiveness was apparent rather than deepening empathy. According to Rogers (1990), empathy requires both attitude and expression for it to become an accurate therapeutic skill that enables the client's further expression. Conveying warmth and empathy is a means of supporting the emotional context of defences; however, when a hostile theme such as racism is being discussed, empathic responses may be challenged and impose barriers on further expression. O'Brien and Houston (2007), who discuss integrative counselling, acknowledge empathy as a core therapeutic skill:

> It is Rogers again that points out that the therapist's attitude of involvement and empathy needs not only to be there, but to be communicated so that the client knows it is honestly there. If the therapist manages to listen well, and shows that she has accurately picked up the client's story, and his inner, even out-of-awareness feelings and thoughts, this empathic responding is again likely to help the client stay with even painful experience, as well as to feel confidence in the therapist. (p. 73)

Empathy can be summarised as a way of 'feeling it in our bones', but this feeling needs to be a mutually engaging experience. Empathy in the context of black issues requires the support of knowledge and the historical context of racism. An understanding of the different psychological processes of racism for both black and white counsellors may also be helpful. In addition, the development of compassion and objectivity to differentiate between the personal, sociological and political elements of racist dynamics is needed. This may seem like a tall order, as therapists may need to be aware of defences associated with racism and find ways that empathy can help them understand these. Experienced therapists may be able to draw on empathic approaches that meet the emotional context of hostile oppressions such as racism. Defences against racism may be seen as particular unconscious processes associated with humiliation and rejection based on skin colour. If we are aware that discussions about racism in the training situation can be painful and sometimes hostile, we can expect discussions in a therapeutic setting may also be painful. Davey and Cross (2004, p. 42) define defences as a mediator between a threat and something vulnerable. Defences such as denial and distancing can manifest to avoid the painful consequences of naming the oppression of racism and making it conscious.

Hurt associated with racism can dissolve into long-term defensive attitudes and a false self, resulting in behaviours that suggest a process of internalised racism. Davey and Cross expand on Jacobs' evaluation of the false self: 'The false self is a natural part of development, built up on a basis of compliance ... a defensive function, which is the protection of the true self' (Davey and Cross, 2004, p. 51; see Jacobs, 1995, p. 58). Therapists may need to develop their empathic skills to allow clients to work through defences related to black issues. Empathic responses to defences against racism need to consider the internalisation processes of racism as part of an individual's experience. In this context empathy needs to reflect the particular nature of the defence, which may act as a protection against the lowering of self-esteem and the devaluation of identity.

Attention to the different responses that black and white people have to racism means offering a kind of race-specific empathic response that considers the concept of 'black issues' in all its guises. Silence, a nod or a brief reference to the client's description of his or her experience of racism may not be enough. A dialogue lacking in empathic responses that connect with black issues runs the risk of not providing enough safety for the client to discuss experiences of racism. To develop specific and accurate empathy towards black issues, therapists need to develop awareness of their own attitude to racism. They will then be less likely to respond from their own defences against racism and better able to provide attention to the theme of black issues. This is what I mean by 'feeling it in our bones'.

Fernando (2006) addresses the issue of safety and the development of appropriate attention to specific cultural and ethnic concerns:

> In a modern Western country where psychotherapy is a service that is available for people with mental health problems, people from all cultural and ethnic backgrounds have a right to access such therapies in a form that is appropriate for them. (p. xvii)

Access to appropriate services is dependent on training that incorporates an expectation that trainees will engage with the cultural aspects of black issues and oppressions in the therapeutic relationship. The questions below, which were raised by both experienced and trainee counsellors, show their concern about appropriate services and how they might develop their therapeutic practice to address black issues:

- 'How do I address, or when is it appropriate to address, the difference between black and white in the therapy session?'
- 'What might there be embedded in the wisdom of black and white cultures around healing and justice that could reinforce the process of individual enlightenment and change?'
- 'As a white counsellor working with a black client, is it true to say that another dimension in terms of power and status comes into play, which may affect the relationship, or is this proposition racist in itself?'
- 'Is black as an issue always present in the therapeutic relationship between black and white therapist and client? If so, is it possible, desirable, to fully go beyond this? Will it always remain the central issue?'
- 'Is it necessary for me to look closely at my own prejudices and examine them in the light of my counselling someone from a black African/Asian heritage? Will the non-white person think the counselling situation once again enslaves them?'

These sensitive questions focus a great deal of concern on the process of black and white individuals working together. Therapists need to develop an understanding of cross-racial dynamics. It may also be helpful to explore the intra-group dynamics among black people and among white people. Trans-theoretical frameworks that span therapeutic approaches may be helpful in exploring these dynamics. For example, how do we develop empathic responses within a black-on-black therapeutic relationship or a white-on-white therapeutic relationship? How do we apply other core concepts such as being non-judgemental and unconditional? Although empathy may be developed to employ an understanding of and a connection to the experience of racism, there is a contradiction. Racism is an experience born out of judgemental, cultural conditions; therefore the skill of being unconditional in the face of racism may be challenged.

Educational Disposition and Accountability

International delegates at a conference organised by the British Association of Counselling and Psychotherapy on 22 May 2004 emphasised being active and accountable for the social and cultural aspects of therapy. Delegates from New Zealand expressed the importance of placing counselling in the cultural context of the country's Maori communities. South African delegates considered the impact of the Apartheid system and the colour bar on counsellors and clients. US counsellors stated that accreditation of professional counsellors requires evidence of their ability to understand and work with diversity, cultural context and racial oppression. These global examples have implications for the accountability of counsellor training in Britain. Whether in Britain racism and oppression are addressed in ways that develop theory and support therapeutic dialogue on black issues in training is questionable. The multicultural theories that Feurtes and Gretchen (2001) reviewed indicated 'a need to translate useful concepts into deliverable techniques for ethnic minority clients' (p. 530). Although there is sufficient evidence of this need, the authors were unable to offer concrete suggestions as to how we turn this transfer into practice. This seems to be the missing link that trainees in my study highlighted.

It is important to find ways to fulfil trainees' need to work through their understanding of race and culture. Counsellor training can be expanded to support the dynamics of change rather than assume that Eurocentric theory, which often dominates these needs, can be applied systematically.

Authors Morrow et al. (2001) support the challenge to Eurocentrism in counselling theory by reflecting on multicultural writing:

Although traditional research methods have assembled a wealth of knowledge within the field of counselling, the 'compass' used to guide such knowledge has been a Eurocentric paradigm that reflects the perspectives of white middle class males. ... Intuitively, the multicultural researcher questions the effectiveness of such paradigms when applied to marginalized populations. ... How can the worldviews of people of colour be understood when the researcher's 'compass' is directed by the polarities of a Eurocentric worldview? (p. 576)

These authors speak of the compass being directed by white males. Although traditional Eurocentric theories, which dominate the teaching of psychotherapy and counselling, may have been directed by white males, this is not entirely true of the counselling population, which appears to be dominated by white females. This racial and gender makeup creates a discourse more likely to be challenged by the minority voices of black people and men.

Dalal (2002) views racialisation as a process of discovery through identifying with the terms 'black' and 'white'. This definition matters because participants in the study used these terms to describe themselves. Before carrying out the study, I had felt shut down and confined to discussing black issues and the work of black writers such as Fanon (1986) and hooks (1991) in my own black circles. Now contemporary writers such as Dalal (2002) have opened doors for my own voice to be heard. Reflecting on the dilemma of being shut down, I am aware that previously I had conformed to my pre-assigned role as a tutor. I had been representing ideas and concepts that get trainees through the curriculum but not furthering their personal understanding of black issues to help develop the theoretical backdrop to their practice.

Given the constraints of established theories that have not fully addressed black issues or racial oppression in their methods, we need to draw insights from transcultural approaches. Transcultural theory places an emphasis on the therapist's own personal development and suggests that therapists should examine their own cultural frameworks and prejudices to transcend the client's world. This approach encourages them to seek ways of entering the client's frame of reference and cultural experience from within. For therapists who have similar cultural backgrounds to their clients, Eleftheriadou (1994, p. 34) suggests an 'emic' approach. This means focusing on the particular; therefore the needs of black trainees should be accommodated within training. It is important to consider that any theoretical framework that stems from traditional Eurocentric psychoanalytical therapies must be questioned as to its cultural applicability by both trainers and trainees.

Theory is the demonstration of an ability to present ideas and concepts. It can play the role of challenging and nurturing understanding and developing a framework for learning, creativity and practice. The learning individual can also challenge and contribute to theory and its potential use with diverse client groups. The training of counsellors and psychotherapists involves self-exploration and the use of ideas and concepts as a framework for understanding real-life connections and relationships with clients. This is particularly important when working therapeutically with black issues. As mentioned above, multicultural writers have recognised an imbalance in the theoretical representation of frameworks for understanding diversity and cultural perspectives. This representation has been recognised as being dominated by Eurocentric theories. Left unchallenged, this situation can perpetuate institutional racism and other oppressions. In my study, counselling trainees expressed their need to understand anti-oppressive practice and ways of working with black issues. In addition, trainers expressed a need to develop as role models in transcultural relationships to address the complexities of diversity and oppression, particularly racism, within their teaching. Their voices, expressing this loss in their own training, are presented below.

Ragina

I don't feel that I learned a lot of theory regarding black issues when I was training. It was a self-directed course. I felt that there was no didactic teaching of any theories to address the issue of diversity and difference in counselling. We did not actually look at whether any of the prevailing theoretical approaches lend themselves to working with people from a non-European culture. I was aware that our training was not readily applicable to people from my culture and therefore, my work with Asian people would have to be carefully considered keeping the appropriate values in focus. We did some workshops and I was part of a group that decided to work on equal opportunities. Then we had a black support group, which was very helpful. We took our insights back to the main group. ... My training is different from my culture; I wanted to know how to adapt it. I found myself mainly working cross-culturally. I was researching mental health needs of Asian women in Greenwich. I realised that there were not many counsellors of Asian heritage. This meant that Asian women who went to get help from mental health services were given drug treatment. The interviews were heavily biased because if they did not speak English, they were not offered professional interpreters; they were using members of the family like the husband or the children. I met Jafar Kareem at NAFSIYAT and I met Phillip Rack and Maurice Lipsedge. I had to do a lot of work on myself outside of the course, as it wasn't really available. My tutors were trying to create an awareness of the Person Centred Approach; they were willing, but not aware of culture.

Ragina shared that it was the black participants on her training programme who mainly supported her experiences of working with black issues. Kareem draws an important parallel to this dilemma. In his discussion of racism in therapy and societal transference, he suggests:

> Most psychotherapists who are analytically trained learn to work with and understand the patient's inner world, and therefore for some there is resistance in dealing with psychological problems that originate in the real (outer) world. However, most black people would admit that the most traumatic feature in their personal lives is to be black in a white society. (Kareem and Littlewood, 1992, p. 12)

He goes on to say:

> From the point of view of the intercultural therapist, I believe that it is the responsibility of the therapist, from the very outset, to facilitate the expression of any negative transference which is based on historical context, and not leave the onus on the patient.

Here, Kareem addresses the fact that inadequate training can place the patient in the role of the black expert, as in Ragina's experience. The black student bearing the role of educator on training courses may experience what Straker (in a concept proposed during her presentation at a specialist seminar at the Metanoia Institute in 2004) identifies as the 'continuous trauma' of his or her often-disempowered position in a white-dominated society. For Straker the 'self-structure' of individuals is intruded upon by traumatic situations. Straker describes two main types of trauma: 'developmental' and 'environmental'. She explains the concept of 'continuous trauma' as the experience of environmental situations that continue to affect the individual and stir feelings related to the original frightening or hurtful experience. These painful feelings or symptoms interrupt the normal self-building process that Straker refers to as the 'going on being of self'. She saw this process as being resolvable by soothing: 'It is important to have another who will perceive affect accurately and sooth it.'

Ragina attempted to complement her 'going on being of self' with attendance at the black support group. She used projects external to the training as a way of 'soothing' the experience of environmental trauma produced by the dominant Eurocentric nature of the training and her past experience.

If trainers are sufficiently aware of and confident about black issues, they can act as the 'another' that Straker talks about. Acting in this reflective role can counter the impact of institutional racism. Straker uses the term 'empathic attunement' to describe the important role of the therapist entering the world of the traumatised individual. Ragina's experience demonstrates the importance, if not necessity, of entering the cultural and historical framework of individuals and assisting them to work through this type of traumatic phase during the therapeutic process. The impact of racism can be regarded as a traumatic phase whether it is acknowledged by clients or not; therefore trainees must be encouraged to draw on theory that assists understanding of this impact on their therapeutic work.

Kareem believes that few training organisations are prepared to take up the intercultural challenge and that individuals feel inhibited about raising issues of racism in their training. In an experience that I can identify with, he suggests that individuals may experience a great pressure to keep quiet so as to complete their training:

> My own internal ego and superego had become replaced with the external institutional superegos of my training models. ... I constantly had to battle with myself to keep my head above water, to remind myself at every point who I was and what I was. It was a painful and difficult battle not to think what I had been told to think, not to be what I had been told to be and not to challenge what I had been told could not be challenged and at the same time not become alienated from my basic roots and my basic self. (Kareem and Littlewood, 1992, p. 31)

The silencing of trainees is an important ethical concern. Trainees of today, both black and white, share this experience of silencing, yet (as we see in the following transcript) the silencing is experienced very differently by black individuals:

Anton

My training was a kind of a self-directed training; you never knew what was going on from one week to the next. There were three black students out of twelve on the course. If we had not brought those issues up as black people, they would not have come up. They came up inasmuch as it was relevant for us to deal with what was going on between us as students on the course, about what goes on generally on training between white people and black people. There is a lack of awareness of what was important for the black people. There was a very loose structure. I remember I had to write an essay. I was writing about issues to do with race; it was pretty raw. The external examiner was saying, 'It is very subjective, but who can blame him.' I was angry because I was making a particular point about how racism affects me and he seemed to be saying that I was on a rant, but who could blame me sort of thing. I initiated time together as black students and we processed for ourselves and taught each other. Then we went back into the main body of students. There was no relevant reading material. I had already trained as a co-counsellor and that developed my understanding of racism and internalised oppression.

As a trainer, in the early nineties, it was good because I was not on my own. There was another black trainer. We started together. The reason I left after five years is that I did not feel that I could be myself. There is something about being black and being in a leading position; people have a lot of expectation of you and they get disappointed if you don't match their expectations. What is tough is that I would like to be there for me, but as you know, as a black person, rarely can you be there as yourself; you have to represent. As a black man there was an inner struggle about being there as a facilitator of people and being there as a black person among a majority of white people. Both the black and the white people would have expectations of me and where is my space to be. So I would find that I was very measured in how I engaged in a formal setting. I don't think that people really got to see me. I don't think the course was set up to deal with the distress that was happening.

If one person is sick the whole community is sick. As practitioner if you haven't pulled yourself outside of Western training, you are faced with a massive shift to be sensitive and open to different ways. For example, in indigenous communities hearing voices is accepted and we would have to change our concepts. They would be irrational. White people define the parameters and they define black people as having an identity crisis. They don't know that they have an identity crisis. There is a crisis and it has to do with who I am. What is my place in the scheme of things? Where do I come from and what is my purpose? If we have not been born into a community that helps us with those questions life is very hard to manage. So what you see manifesting is people who are wrestling with those issues.

To show that we are in pain often meant that we were exterminated by the dominant ones. So we had to ensure that generations who came after did not show this either. We have become a group of people who had to over time suppress something that needs to be healed. We had to push our feelings down. In the present day we are seeing the signs of this coming out. The signs have been there but people could not recognise it. A lot more black people are conscious of this now and there is an enormous piece of grieving to do. So yes there is a crisis, but not 'our' identity crisis. The meaning is put into the word 'black' and it is hard for us to resist. So it becomes hard for us to value ourselves. So it is about the value that is put on whiteness. It's not in the books; it's unchartered territory. It has not been put down in a form that we can share, which is the way that we have learned. So even in our black supervision group, what are our reference points?

Anton expressed concern about how we reinvent ourselves and find an authentic voice within the context of training. Some black trainees shared Anton's experience of shut-down-ness and exclusion as black people in training. Like Ragina, Anton had to rely on personal development sources external to the training for his cultural development, rather than receiving appropriate support from the training. hooks (1996) uses feminism to critique Eurocentric theory and its impact. In a section on 'Reuniting that which has been broken', she says that as a woman she too went outside of her group and she learned to think critically about colonialism from men: 'In rooms, which it seemed no women were allowed to enter, they gave me ways to invent and make myself' (p. 81). She refers to a psychotherapy session where she spoke about what stands in the way of love, concluding that 'to face love you have to face fear'. According to Read (1996), hooks recreates her feminist self through her rediscovery of Fanon's much-neglected writing advocating the pursuit of love. 'Today, I believe in the possibility of love, that is why I endeavour to trace its imperfections, its perversions' (p. 80).

The possibility of using dialogue to develop love rather than fear was the biggest motivator for my study. Anton's concern about the loss and misunderstanding of black cultural identities has been echoed by other black men who have encountered dissonance in the institutions of counselling and psychotherapy. In the following quotation, hooks

(1996) offers insights from her way of transcending the gender divide that support my own understanding of personal development during the study:

> I knew how to move through the body of the father to discover myself. In my girlhood, it had not been possible to imagine one-self as a thinker/writer/interrogator without projecting oneself into the phallic imaginary, into the body of the father. Only by jour-neying through the body of the father could I connect with the mind. ... Fascinated by my journey through the body of the father, I forgot about mothers. The feminist movement returned me to the body of the mother. (p. 80)

hooks shares an experience of being born again in the body of the mother, being liberated beyond patriarchy, 'An act of finding, listen-ing to the female voice' (p. 81). Her experience offers a way of under-standing that going outside a group experience can help one transcend a discourse of oppression – in other words, to use the different other to reflect who you are. It is this act of finding and listening to my black self that I am being born into through attempting to discover how we under-stand black issues within the Eurocentric body of psychotherapy and counselling – by exploring with the oppressor group and building on self-knowledge gained from this experience. The following excerpt high-lights considerations of the particular oppressions that Asian trainees can experience. Attention must be paid to these different experiences so as not to homogenise black peoples:

Bibi

Fifty percent of trainees were of African Caribbean descent. I was the only Asian student and the rest were white. There were twenty-two students in all. A very isolating experience, but there was plenty of opportunity for exploration of black issues presented by visiting tutors. It felt as though there was some resistance when the topic of race came up. I did not know precisely why but wanted to pinpoint it exactly, if possible. Could it be partly due to there being even num-bers racially that tension was equally distributed?

We would always get to the door and not be able to open it. I expe-rienced the tutors as not being able to handle it; they seemed to change energetically, in their facial language; it seemed they were less confident and maybe even cautious. I think they were frightened at the prospect of having to hold many different levels of student expression. Expressions of anger and anguish, annoyance that they could become misrepresented. The issue of difference and diversity as it was named became such a no-go area that it may as well have been called 'dilemma and disruption' as practically all including myself felt uneasy, almost confronted about something, some hidden thing to do with difference. It is clearly very potent.

Race and culture was one of the syllabuses. There was lack of trust and it was mostly about British history. Most of the students aged twenty-five to fifty were raised in Britain and have lived through the seventies period of uprisings when the National Front were around. I was very aware of this at the time. I was quietly aware. That is one of the things I resented, because stereotypes of Asian women are quiet, shy, submissive, whereas if a black woman is quiet she is just a gentle black lady. I want to challenge this distortion. It is not because I am an Asian woman that I am quiet; that is a feature of my individual personality. Interestingly I felt there was more hostility from black students, maybe about why I am so quiet, why I don't speak up? From white people it was somewhat more of a feeling sympathy, like we understand. It was more patronising and even humiliating. All the staff were white, a male Kleinian tutor and a female Rogerian.

I am the only Asian person in a group of twenty-two and race is not stressed here. I feel there is a space for exploration at this level, which feels like a relief. It seems to be addressed in local colleges where there are people who don't have funding for private tuition and who need grants. Whereas perhaps it is my responsibility as it is an MA. The theories we are discussing are very European, Freudian and Jungian, but I believe they can be applied universally too and should be tested against black and Asian studies and given its own differentiated place. I feel there is a space for exploration at this level, which feels like a relief. There is such a gap with people getting together and seeing where we fit, that is why I am continuing with it, but it is a struggle. I'm very lonely in it. Even my family do not know what I am doing.

As a child I witnessed my parents' experience of racism and, thinking back, they would have been the same age that I am now. These were bleak and nasty experiences. Having eggs thrown at your front door and dogs set on you because it is known that you do not have dogs inside the home, being verbally abused, called Pakis and stuff like that. There is going to be residues of that happening now in different forms and at varying levels, whether conscious or subconscious. If I feel safe to bring up something like that I will. I did once bring up something about my own experience in supervision. Ok, it was a caring response, but it was dismissive. I was told, 'You are being too hard on yourself.' My response was, 'That sounds very dismissive because I am saying something about my experience here.' My supervisor said to me, 'Actually I take that back, if I am saying you are being too hard on yourself, I am judging you for your experience.' I really felt as though I had more self-worth after that. It really changed our relationship after that.

There is always that something hidden looking down on. I often need to ask myself, Is it just me projecting an inferiority complex relating to race issues here with this person or is there actually something to be worked on? As an associate, doing volunteer counselling here, I have felt on my own with black issues and I have had to work on my own with black clients here. It would have been lovely to have some support with this in supervision. As an associate I felt I taught in supervision and this is a very interesting concept to me. It is not just about me breaking new ground; let's all break new ground.

Isolation is one of many disempowering experiences for the black practitioner. It appears that even at MA level there is great difficulty understanding these issues. An inner and outer struggle expressed by Bibi was going on as a result of inadequate training in how to address black issues actively. Trainers and supervisors may not always get it right, but finding ways to keep the dialogue open helps to break the black therapist's isolation. A dialogue influenced by psychoanalytical training may try to fit theory to the client's inner conflicts and racial context, devoid of the historical context behind the experience. This may not always be appropriate. Person-centred approaches may focus on the present even when the client's data are based on his or her past. Lago and Thompson (1996), in their discussions on race, culture and counselling, support Pederson's comment on 'neglect of history':

Counsellors, Pederson (1987, p. 21) suggests, are much less likely to attend to clients who talk about the history of their own people. (Examples of this would include clients' stories of forebears, ancestors, religious, ethnic and tribal history and so on.) In many cultures the connection between past and present history makes it necessary for counsellors to understand clearly the client's historical context as a way of understanding their present behaviour. (p. 81)

This suggestion by Pederson may challenge ways in which therapists are trained. The person-centred approach, for example, advocates the use of core conditions that should be enough for therapeutic change. How, then, can the therapist invite clients to explore their cultural background? Trainees have questioned when, or how, to address black issues if they have not been raised by the client. Models such as those presented by Carl Rogers did not adequately demonstrate how this could be done with black clients.

Bibi's epistemology identifies what I would call the 'black-on-black issues' that counsellors and psychotherapists need to have a dialogue about if they are to understand and actively engage with black issues in the therapeutic process. Her narrative shows us that understanding and having a voice on black issues means more than understanding the dynamics of racism.

Conclusion

In this chapter I have addressed the context of the study and presented the insights and training concerns of experienced therapists. I have drawn attention to transcultural writing that supports an exploration of the lack of discussion of black issues in training. The study highlighted that a particular focus on black issues raised overwhelming concern about the impact of racism and therapeutic relationships between black and white people. I have therefore addressed the impact of racism on trainees, experienced counsellors and myself as researcher, writer and listener. Defences raised through the recognition of racism as a component of black issues have been explored. It is clear that the challenging of individual racism can help undermine institutional racism. I have proposed that the gap in mainstream theoretical approaches to the training of counsellors and psychotherapists be closed by developing the core skills used to build therapeutic relationships. This development should consider the process of racialisation in black–white relationships and the impact of racism in the use of therapeutic skill with black issues. In the next chapter I build on the concept of empathy in the context of black issues.

Training is a process that influences learning and should assist trainees to find a common understanding of theory and practice that supports the diverse needs of communities in Britain. Trainees and clients from different cultural groups offer experiences that contribute to this understanding. The theme of 'understanding' features highly in the training curriculum, personal development process and therapeutic process. It is therefore reasonable to try to discover how understanding that relates to diversity comes about. It is important for both trainers and trainees to give voice to their concerns and ways of understanding black issues, as their wish to understand the process of working with black issues can be transformed into action. The comments of a white tutor reflect the emotional conflict, pain and institutional challenge of addressing black issues in counsellor training:

White tutor

I was thinking about the discussion about black and I was reading some of Farhad's stuff on black as a colour and white and the history of the term 'black' and its historical relationship as a word that has been a signifier of all that is negative. Something about putting it in the curriculum and me prioritising it and with that process all the negative stuff has come as well, all the pain and history of the term. I have also felt great joy in the learning that I have shared listening to black and white students and some of the positives that have come out. I think I can get lost in the pain of it, the censorship of it and the whole process of silencing, opposed to staying with the positive. I can lose sight of it more quickly. Something about having this on the course means something about it is about fighting the institutionalised silence on the subject and the social silence on the subject and my personal silence on the subject. Then having to move through all of that to have a relationship with the students and each other and the subject and the issues around it is like trying to have a revolution inside myself. The inner battle is massive, which is obviously part of the external world battle as well. But that external world battle that exists inside myself is as problematic as the discussions I have with other people. The interpersonal experience in the groups with others and the students are challenging, but the challenge begins even before I open my mouth and come into contact with anyone else. In terms of trying to think about it all. Those things start to swirl and I think about the power of oppression. The power of silence is so massive. There is a value in calling it black issues because it is re-prioritising something. Highlighting the fact that everything taught are white issues, we don't actually say that we just call it theory or practice. We don't actually say everything we are talking about is white, because it is invisible.

Pointers for therapists (including trainees and trainers)

- Take a holistic view of the client's personal development and include cultural aspects.
- Decide to address and explore the place of racism and other oppressions in the client's therapeutic process if you sense they may be present in the therapeutic alliance.
- Explore your own prejudices and experiences of oppression so as to be more fully aware of and present with clients' experiences and feelings about black issues.
- Draw on traditional theories and multicultural and transcultural theories of therapy to support the process of working with cultural dynamics, identity and black issues.
- Develop an anti-oppressive stance so as not to perpetuate oppression by exclusion, denial or lack of response to the sociological, historical and cultural impact of Eurocentrism.
- Ask for your learning needs to be met either in training, personal development forums or your own therapy, so that you can explore and understand black issues in therapeutic work.

3

A Black Empathic Approach

Chapter 2 opened up the idea of working with aspects of racism and starting a dialogue about black issues by challenging the dominance of Eurocentric approaches to counselling. This chapter engages with the social, cultural and psychological context of identifying as 'black', or as a 'person of colour'. Using a trans-theoretical backdrop, I make use of the 'feeling in our bones' by exploring the empathic context of black issues in the therapeutic process at a deeper level.

In my own approach as an integrative, transcultural psychotherapist, I pay particular attention to the cultural influences and oppressions in a client's background. This is just as important as paying attention to key past relationships and developmental points in a client's history. A black empathic approach pays particular attention to the cultural influence of racism. As a focus on racism became an important feature of trainees' concerns (as mentioned in Chapter 1), I draw on their questions to help expand this concept.

It became clear that trainee counsellors found sharing through dialogue supportive when they were attempting to understand the contradictions raised by Eurocentric influences on their learning experience. In a study based on conversations with women, Field Belenky et al. (1986) used a method that they called 'connected knowing' for contextualising elements of their dialogue: 'Connected knowing builds on the subjectivists' conviction that the most trustworthy knowledge comes from personal experience rather than the pronouncements of authorities' (p. 113).

In Field Belenky et al.'s study, the 'connected knower' develops procedures built on his or her capacity to empathise to gain access to other people's knowledge. The authors propose that since knowledge comes from experience, avenues for understanding another person's ideas are opened up by sharing the experience that has led the person to form the idea. The approach that I use challenges Eurocentric theory as the authority that Field Belenky et al. speak of. I would like to share with you the experience that has led me to propose the idea of a black empathic approach. This concept is drawn from the idea of 'connected knowing', the therapeutic skill of emotional connection and the shared experience of racism. The humanistic concept of empathy is utilised in virtually all therapeutic approaches. Mearns and Thorne (1988) explain this concept as:

> a process, whereby the counsellor lays aside her own way of experiencing and perceiving reality, preferring to sense and respond to the experiences of the client. This sensing may be intense and enduring with the counsellor actually experiencing her client's thoughts as if they had originated in herself. (p. 39)

Empathy as a multidisciplinary skill provides a useful starting point for a trans-theoretical approach. A trans-theoretical approach considers the use of concepts that can be integrated into a variety of therapeutic models. I shall follow this thread by considering the concept of empathy in the context of a transcultural focus on black issues.

According to Mearns (1994) empathy can be conscious or unconscious. In the process of understanding black issues, I want to encourage conscious empathy built around an awareness of self in relation to black issues. Fears and prejudices that relate to black issues need to be processed then placed aside for empathy to occur in the therapeutic process. While unconscious empathy may cause therapists to avoid being active in the process of acknowledging black issues, explicit connection can encourage therapeutic process on black issues and related power dynamics.

To address the power issues in multiracial therapeutic relationships requires a willingness to place attention on the diverse experiences of black individuals. This attention should include an understanding of the individual developmental processes of black people and how the dynamics of racism may affect them as individuals. This approach relies on the therapist's concern to understand the differences that influence relationships among black people as well as those between black and white people. Although trainees in my study were mainly concerned with the latter, it is important to remain aware of the Eurocentric influence on their responses. Training that lacks a transcultural emphasis on therapeutic relationships may nurture a mono-cultural approach to relationship dynamics built on racist attitudes and the exclusion of black trainees' and clients' experiences. It became clear in the study that this situation can result in the suppression of black trainees' learning needs and allow them to fall into the role of the black expert when racism is being discussed. This is when black trainees begin to facilitate the learning of white peers and their own learning needs take a back seat.

As discussed in Chapter 1, the study demonstrated that when white counselling trainees were paying attention only to their feelings of guilt and fears about racism, space for black trainees' emotions and developmental process diminished. These power dynamics can have a negative influence on the therapeutic process and perpetuate isolation and distress caused by racism. Concerns about engaging empathically with black clients were expressed by several white trainees. Black trainees did not raise concerns about working with black clients; they wanted to share the racism they had experienced from white clients, from their therapists and in their lives.

Trainees must be facilitated to address empathy in the context of black issues. Exploration of the internal experience of self as black or white and the external complexities of healing relationships between black and white people is essential. This approach creates a space for the evaluation of self-esteem, personal development and an appreciation of 'black' identity in a cultural sense. Although the concept of a black empathic approach points to a more dynamic recognition of the emotions of black people, white therapists are invited to locate their ability to engage with this experience. Some of their training needs come to light as I present questions about their capacity to empathise.

Does the therapist have to be black to demonstrate empathy towards a black client?

The training of both black therapists and white therapists is predominantly influenced by a Eurocentric approach that has not fully considered the particular dynamics between black client and white therapist and vice versa. We cannot assume that because these challenges exist, black clients' needs will automatically be met by black therapists. Lorde (1984) challenges the racial dynamic of this question: 'I can't tell you how many good white psychwomen have said to me, "Why should it matter if I am black or white?" Who would ever think of saying, "Why does it matter if I am female or male?"' (p. 161).

It may help if the therapist is black, but whatever the complexion of the therapist, he or she needs to be conscious of and confident about working with black issues. A black therapist will need to be positive about his or her black identity and be willing to use his or her experience positively for the benefit of the client. In an ideal world therapists would be trained to listen to, connect with and celebrate the experiences of black people and other minority groups. Clients aware of the impact of racism on their self-esteem may select their therapist on the basis of the therapist's experience, knowledge of black issues and awareness of their cultural background. On the other hand, they may be searching for the like reflection of a black face, just as women often want a female therapist. The white therapist's response to difference and a non-defensive understanding of racism are key to his or her level of relationship with black clients. For black therapists, empathy can be based on mutual understanding of experiences about being black in Britain or the diaspora, but they must be conscious of identifying and not take these shared elements of heritage for granted.

The awareness of black therapists working with black clients of what it is like to be black will be based on their own experiences and levels of black consciousness. They need to be aware of blind spots influenced by their Eurocentric education. These blind spots can alter the mirroring process. Lack of awareness of this influence can create emotional distance in their therapeutic relationships and inhibit a black empathic approach. On the other hand, being black with black clients can heighten possibilities, but the black therapist must recognise elements of collusion and pseudo-connection based on assumptions of sameness. Support may be needed to separate out their own experiences and allow space for empathic connection and understanding based on both the differences and similarities among black people. Black therapists may not necessarily be concerned about connecting through blackness with their clients. Although this aspect of identity may be an avenue for empathy, their capacity to use a black empathic approach may have been diminished by the Eurocentric influence in their training. Black therapists need to be aware of their intrinsic differences from black clients and separate their own process from the client's experience. These considerations are the nuts and bolts of a black empathic approach. As with any approach, it is important to be aware of collusion and internalised racism. The term 'internalised racism' is used to describe the impact of racism on the black psyche and self-development process. Viewed as unconscious process, internalised racism can be influenced by inadequate or negative reflection of the black identity.

How can I empathise when I don't know what it is to be black?

This question proposes a contradiction to the connecting therapeutic process of empathy. It presupposes that empathy towards black people may be dependent on skin colour. It could be said that empathy is neither colourless nor an opaque internal process that can be coloured in by emotions, devoid of black people's experiences.

The white therapist's capacity to do more than just listen to and respond to a black client's experience may be placed under the spotlight. White therapists asking this question are demonstrating their genuine concern about racially defined difference. Although they may have the capacity to connect to the black client's other life experiences, it may be difficult to connect with a black client's experience of being black without racism getting in the way. The question suggests a concern about connecting to black clients through their blackness and being with them in their blackness, whether this is made explicit or not. The therapist's lack of understanding about the impact of racism and their fears about harming the client if they refer to black issues can influence levels of empathic attunement. Therapists may perceive that gathering knowledge of black people's histories, lifestyles and developmental processes is an onerous task; therefore, white therapists may fear a failure to connect with these experiences and respond using a colour-blind approach. The colour-blind approach dismisses the context of blackness in a client's identity process and approaches the situation using the mythology that 'we are all the same' or 'feelings do not come in colours'. This mythology can evoke a numbing affect in both the therapist and the client, producing further mythology that black people can suppress their pain or do not have feelings about their experiences. A numbing affect influences the capacity to empathise and militates against a black empathic approach. This collective mythology can reproduce a self-fulfilling prophecy along the following lines: I am not black; therefore, I cannot connect to black people's emotions. This situation can be resolved if training, supervision and personal development forums promote self-knowledge and engage with trainees' capacity to empathise with black issues. It is a learning process that requires research into history and culture. The following question reflects a need for further research.

Is empathy going to be enough when someone's history is so very different from mine?

As the client's history is always different from the therapist's history, it is the 'so very' aspect of this question that examines the counsellor's limitations. In the therapeutic process there is always an element of the unknown. Although histories may differ we must bear in mind that history also connects people. The impact of slavery and colonialism means that we have a shared but differently influenced history, as both black and white people have been hurt by the oppression of Western racism. This predisposition adds another dimension to the capacity for a black empathic approach. The prospect of acknowledging the historical context of black issues can make empathy seem out of reach. Therapists raising this question are therefore challenged to develop their knowledge of the client and the relevant histories of black people while setting aside their biases. This requires an exploration of the elements that forge disconnection and a greater effort to share information, as suggested in the following quotation:

> If the African educated on European lines is unable or unwilling to teach the outside world something of the institutions and inner feelings of his people; if for some reason or other, he can show nothing of his real self to those anxious to learn, and to assist him; if he cannot make his friends feel the force of his racial character and sympathise with his racial aspiration, then it is evident that his education has been sadly defective. (Blyden, 1994, p. 16)

Feeling Connected through Shared Experience

'Empathy' is a term used to describe the way individuals transcend the experience of another person. It is a multifaceted process influenced by belief systems, cultural experiences, heritage and the passions, prejudice and pain that we collect throughout our lives. These components make empathy a transcultural experience. In therapeutic relationships an empathic response demonstrates connection to the client's experience. This also breaks isolation by raising the client's awareness of the connection between his or her personal feelings and the experiences of others.

Therapists may easily connect with pleasant experiences shared by clients, but conflicts often arise when painful issues are shared. If we can agree that all living individuals experience the pain and hurt of oppression at some level, we can assume that we have the capacity to be empathic towards someone hurting from the effects of racism. Neither black nor white therapists, however, can take for granted that an ability to empathise takes care of empathic responses when exploring black issues and the historical context of racism.

If the pain and hurt of racism have been buried and become unconscious, the therapist's awareness first needs to be raised Therapists already informed about black issues and the impact of racism may be better placed to offer a black empathic approach. The development of a black empathic approach involves the dissemination of power and recognition of how inequalities may influence the therapeutic relationship. An example of modelling a black empathic approach in a situation that throws up inequality concerns is presented below.

A young woman aged twenty-seven who had recently arrived from the Caribbean, where she had been raised by her grandmother, was referred for mental health treatment by her mother. On her first visit she sat on the centre table facing me. I wondered about her need to face me and show her power of decision not to conform to the two chairs in the room (a very Western form of therapy). I felt that she might also be displaying her difference and making a point about comfortable distance between us as black women. She complained to me that she felt estranged from her mother, from whom she had been separated for twenty-three years. She was sharing accommodation with her mother and aunt. The mother was behaving in an abusive fashion to her because she saw her as exhibiting what is known as 'country behaviour' and because she planned to visit her estranged father in London for help while she was settling in in her new homeland. Although relatives in African/Caribbean families usually play a significant role in childrearing, it became clear that she was hurting from previous abandonment by her parents. She also seemed to be a victim of class oppression and intergenerational conflicts within her Jamaican family. Her depression had undoubtedly been generated from the experience of immigration and loss associated with the fragmentation of her family around the world. I accepted her seating arrangements, and she felt supported by my capacity to draw on cultural and historical knowledge that reflected her disposition. Drawing on knowledge gained from my own marital connection to a Jamaican family and schooling with Jamaican peers, I was aware of the cultural impact on individuals who migrate from the country areas of Jamaica to the heart of London and how this can affect family relationships.

This process of summoning up a black empathic approach challenged my own personal development and prejudices. I am aware that these prejudices have also been triggered on various trips to the Caribbean and Africa when I am prone to looking down on other customs through my Western eyes and judging the living styles of my own black people.

A black empathic approach requires therapists to address these effects of racism and oppressive elements in the therapeutic process. In the therapeutic relationship black and white therapists share the responsibility of psychological healing and development of the black self, which can ultimately lead to healing negative elements in the collective psyche. Fanon (1986) discloses his own experience of being battered by elements of the negative collective psyche in the process of finding his black self:

> I was responsible at the time for my body, for my race, for my ancestors. I subjected myself to an objective examination, I discovered my blackness, my ethnic characteristics; and I was battered down by tom toms, cannibalism, slave ships, and above all else, above all; 'Sho good eatin'. (p. 112)

Using his own journey of self-discovery, Fanon affirms the importance of understanding the developmental aspects of the self and healing the impact of racism on the black identity. The process of discovering negative elements of the black self brings black individuals face to face with the archetypal nature of racism. This idea is explored in more depth in Part II.

It can be difficult for therapists to empathise unless they accept that they may also, in different ways, have been affected by racism. Understanding the dynamic process of racism means understanding that we are also treating a discourse contaminated by the residue of slavery and colonialism. This residue can affect black self-development.

A black empathic approach draws on an awareness of the developmental phases of a black identity (Helms, 1990) and how they can be negatively impacted. I explain some areas of negative impact below.

Negative reflection about physical identity

Common aspects of early negative reflection are focused on skin colour and physical features such as hair texture and nose shape. Historically, these projections featured in the brutality of slavery, which played a role in categorisation based on physical appearance. They were interjected into the black neocolonial family and I have heard black people represent them in comments such as 'di picknee nose too flat, too broad; di picknee skin too dark, too light; di picknee hair too nappy, not good enough'. These kinds of negative reflection formed the basis of rejection. They have served as a measure of esteem within the black family and demonstrate how early oppression can affect upbringing. The black child in her or his early stages of development may have received contradictory messages about parts of the black physical self measured in relation to the white person. Under these conditions, the child learns early to disassociate from parts of his or her physical self. According to Wilson (1987), 'The crux of the matter is that given any combination of orientations black life regardless of class is "white centred". The orbital path of the black psyche is defined by its revolution around the central "white star"' (p. 75). This incongruent mirroring can damage the black psyche and weaken family relationships, like a 'black Cinderella syndrome'. These inner conflicts based on self-hatred and low self-esteem, known as internalised racism, can manifest as denial and defence against the pain of experiencing racism. A black empathic approach can support clients through these defences rather than perpetuate them.

Lack of black cultural representation in education and training

Education in Britain has only recently begun to consider equality issues. In a survey (McKenzie-Mavinga, 1991), I found that black clients played the black expert role with their white therapists. They felt that they had to explain to white therapists about their experiences of racism and describe what racism is. Some believed that they were educating the therapist to make their relationship a little safer to open up about their pain as black people. The white therapists involved had little scope for empathic responses that related to their black clients' cultural needs. This situation highlighted problems on both sides. The white therapists either lacked awareness of their inherent experience of racism or were not trained to be confident in managing their responses to the experience of racism. Clients said that given the choice they would have chosen black therapists, and many of them did. They also stated that they had made these choices because they felt listened to and understood by a black therapist without having to explain. These clients were starting their therapy with an awareness of how racism had affected them and what they needed to feel safe to explore their experiences of being black in Britain. A black empathic approach equips both black and white therapists to process how racism has affected clients.

Lack of positive black role models

Positive role models are those individuals whom we seek to emulate or approach for guidance. They can be parental role models, teachers and leaders. Gandhi and Martin Luther King were viewed as positive role models because of their leadership and non-violent approach to resolving conflicts within their communities. It has always been the case that black communities have positive role models; however, where positive role models are lacking, the brutality of racism and oppression gets reinforced. As black on black violence increases, role modelling for future generations is marred. The experience shared below places my own life in the context of positive and negative role modelling in Britain and the diaspora.

> I sit pondering in the gallery of my sister's home in Trinidad. The house has bars all around. My sister and her husband are in their twilight years. They are recognised as positive role models in their local community. They are frail and live in fear, trapped in a cage like many other elders living on their island. They are afraid of being attacked and robbed in their own home. I too am afraid, because their fears are justified. Every day the newspapers report robbery and murder. The people who kill are black. The people who die are black. I feel helpless because elders in Britain are afraid too, and every week the newspapers report black-on-black killings. Psychological support is not an easy option. These issues are rarely addressed. How do we remain balanced when such terror invades our lives? I try to recall the positive role modelling of my sister and her husband, yet I feel the urge to make judgements and accuse my people of inordinate violence. Trinidad is no more violent than Britain. Every day in England people die on the streets from murder, police brutality and the abuse of racism. I return to England my other home. In the town where I live one in four people is black. Most of the shopkeepers are from minority groups. An African man recently set up shop in the neighbourhood a few yards from my home. He was mown down with a machine gun.

My empathic responses as a psychotherapist are challenged by this confusion caused by negative role modelling. I have firsthand experience of what it is like to have family scattered across the world. I can see that the brutality of slavery and colonialism is rife. The link between home and the difficulties of immigration becomes clearer. Increased knowledge of the global context of relationships among black people assists my development of a black empathic approach, and I must try to remain impartial.

Lack of opportunities to process experiences of racial abuse as a young person

Nathan was eleven years old when he became a victim of the SUS law (a stop-and-search law that permits police officers to act on suspicion alone, based on section 4 of the Vagrancy Act 1824). One day on his way home from school four policemen backed him up against a wall.

They searched his gym bag, then they mocked him, called him names and told him to go home as they had made a mistake. While walking through a petrol station with his school friends on another occasion, he became separated from them and was beaten up by an unknown white man because his friend had looked at the man's wife. At the age of fifteen he was standing on the street with his white friends and a white man rode his motorbike onto the pavement and into the group of young people, shouting, 'Nigger lovers'. The garage owner wiped his CCTV coverage of the beating, and the police failed to take action against the motorcyclist, who was known to live locally.

At the age of eighteen Nathan was encouraged by his cousin to start weight lifting at a local gym. He enjoyed being with older black men, as his father was absent and he wanted to make his body bigger so that 'no one would mess about with him ever again'. This led to further police harassment and a habit of drug-taking to numb the pain of his tearing muscles. The emotional pain of his father's absence and his experiences of racism had not been dealt with. At twenty-two he became confused, depressed and homeless.

Many young black people are acutely aware of the dynamics of racism and become deeply affected by it. Attending to the cycle of abuse connected to the experience of black youths means that the therapist must build a relationship based on understanding the combined experience of adolescence and racism. The therapist's capacity to believe experiences of racism without the client having to explain will assist the development of a black empathic approach. This creates an opportunity to explore the abuse of racism.

Racism in the workplace causing overwork, burnout and mental ill health

The chances of being fully confident in our working lives are affected by our life experience and by opportunities to overcome conditions such as unfair recruitment procedures, low pay, low-status work, bigotry and unfair dismissal. Historically these elements have undermined the confidence and employment chances of black people.

Althea was the only black staff member in a long-established team of residential workers. She had been engaged as a trainee under section 5.2d of the 1976 Race Relations Act (Commission for Racial Equality), which sanctions the recruitment of black staff members to redress low numbers of black and minority group professionals in organisations. Althea's boss was accusing her of incompetence after several complaints that she had been verbally abusive to the staff and residents. She was reprimanded for not fulfilling her job description properly. They were trying to get her to do tasks that she was not yet trained for and that if not carried out properly would create danger to the residents. She refused to comply and became subject to silences and bullying from members of her team.

After her probation period was over, she went off sick every time she experienced conflict with her colleagues. Each time she returned from sick leave her colleagues behaved in a hostile way that she challenged as racism. Althea protested at the hostility of the other staff members and was accused of being racist herself. Clearly the manager and other staff members had very little awareness of the dynamics of racism. Althea said that there was one member of staff who agreed with her that she was the victim of racism from her colleagues. Her manager let the cycle of abuse go on far too long before he admitted that he did not know how to handle the situation. It became clear that he had colluded with his white colleagues and had been afraid to challenge their racism. When Althea's manager attempted to discuss the situation with her, she would clam up because she felt that she had lost her trust in him. By the time head office were called in to investigate Althea's situation, she had 'burnout' and was absent on long-term sick leave. Alleyne (2005) points out the particular nature of this 'workplace oppression' that wears down black employees:

> A general finding in this study has indicated that although workplace oppression for black workers was not overtly about race and cultural differences, interpersonal conflict in black/white relations was frequently set off by subtle, yet silent and 'not so easy to pin down' incidents. Such incidents targeted a racial or cultural signifier of the black person's identity. ... The unrelenting nature of these silent conflicts and subsequent protective stances adopted by black workers to defend against further hurt eventually wore them down. (p. 288)

Alleyne pinpoints the kind of racism that Althea suffered as a kind of affront to her identity. To counteract this invasion of the black psyche, therapists need to develop a black empathic approach and be congruent when assisting black clients to unravel experiences of racism and rebuild their sense of self-worth. The realness of the therapist is key to avoiding the perpetuation of oppression. Supporting clients through their recognition trauma is a step towards a black empathic approach.

Lack of opportunities to work through recognition trauma by processing the pain of racism

Althea was not offered an early opportunity to work through her recognition trauma, because her experience of racism was not acknowledged. The process of recognition trauma can be influenced by the various negative factors discussed above. Racism must therefore be acknowledged and related emotions supported.

Black people need opportunities to feel the feelings about being 'black' people and being viewed as different in Britain. A black empathic approach may offer clients an opportunity to explore the developmental aspects of racism as well as their current experiences of racism. We therefore need to be aware of our responses to racism in our daily lives and how these experiences impact our intimate relationships with peer groups and with clients, whether they are black or white.

Richards (1992) identifies 'ethos' as the special characteristics that link the way we feel about each other and our identity as a group. This way of connecting refers to our expression of emotional responses and reactions, not our conscious or self-conscious responses and reactions. Ethos consists of our passions, excitements, laughter, tears, fears, pain. It is similar to the concept of culture in that it exists and grows in relation to group responses and it cannot thrive in isolation. Richards proposes that ethos and the wide world are closely related and that there exists an African diasporic ethos that consists of our specific spiritual experience inherited from the cultural history of Africa. She goes on to suggest that to understand ethos it is necessary to have a global perspective on African diasporic responses to European culture. This is an essential component of developing a black empathic approach.

A black empathic approach means recognising defences related to the hurt of racism both in the counsellor and in the client. A common defence is the projection of anger and hostility towards the therapist. Fears associated with these projections can manifest in the client's need to cross-examine the therapist about his or her cultural background. As a trainee I asked my white therapist about her awareness of racism. She tried to reassure me by disclosing that she had black friends. In the process of my own recognition trauma, I had brought my hurt from racism along with me, and her reply did nothing to reassure me. It was an echo of something I had heard many times before. I felt that she was not aware of my pain. From a therapeutic point of view, I experienced her incongruence as she tried to hide her naivety about racism. This negated my fears and was a lost opportunity to work through my recognition trauma.

I stayed with her for a while longer but was not convinced of her ability to continue any in-depth discussion about my experiences as a black woman and my hurt from racism. She would address the theme only if I raised it, so I became the black expert in my own counselling sessions. As I became clearer about her lack of connection with my experience and her denial of her limitations, I went into denial myself. There seemed to be nowhere safe to take my feelings about racism. She was a psychoanalytical therapist, yet she was unwilling to include any interpretations about my experiences of racism. Clearly her training had not prepared her for working with black issues. This created a tension between us that was not worked through. When things came to a head, I challenged her about not understanding me because she did not have a black experience. She replied that she did not have a white experience. I then realised that she had not processed her own experience as a white women enough to work with me at the level of my experience and identity as a black woman. She was at this point ready to acknowledge her own racism. I became aware that her dilemma was akin to the process of recognition trauma that I was working through. On reflection, both my therapist and I were hurting. I was becoming the therapist or educator, and effectively at this point the therapy was over.

From this early experience of my own therapy, I have gained a greater understanding of how hurt people may not be fully aware of themselves. The process of working through can provide valuable information about working with black issues. In developing a black empathic approach, therapists are expected to face their cultural limitations and not deny them. An exploration of these limitations can provide clarity and separate out defences and elements of recognition trauma.

Being disconnected from blackness or whiteness suggests a way of functioning below the individual's full potential. Individuals remain slightly invisible to themselves, defending against the fear of adverse attention. Therefore a black client's developmental process can become overwhelmed by defence construction. Defences against blackness are an important means of protection against the fear of another attack. Recognising the defences of racism and communicating this recognition in a caring and connected manner can support a black empathic approach.

A black empathic approach means recognising and understanding invisibility. This invisibility is sometimes apparent in the way black trainees in a large study group stay silent. They engage in discussions about racism and fail to converse with the group about their everyday relationships. This hiding behaviour is usually unconscious, but sometimes it becomes a strategy for defending against their role as a minority in the learning group. A black empathic approach can bring these defences to black trainees' awareness and work with them in the training process.

Conclusion

Racism based on skin tone affects the balance of power in therapeutic relationships. Differences in the experiences of a white person and a black person cannot be used to understand the differences between a light-skinned black person and a dark-skinned black person. The power of racism, oppression and the social imbalance of skin-tone dynamics, which emanate from slavery and apartheid systems, influence both these concerns but create different power dynamics. These are key issues to tackle in building a black empathic approach within therapeutic relationships.

A black empathic approach organises and links the experience of internalised imagery and negative imagination and places it in the context of real lives. To achieve this, the therapist's early experiences of oppression on the basis of skin colour, hair texture, language and caste must be processed in the context of his or her exposure to white Western influences on his or her life. Within the relationship of therapist and client, these experiences must be taken into account to enable us to explore how we feel about each other.

A balance of philosophy and familiarity with black issues, combined with an understanding of the emotions evoked by racism, is an essential component of a black empathic approach. We can be challenged by our differences or the way we identify with each other. The pain and isolation of individuality can disconnect us from the collective challenge of racism. A philosophical and emotional approach to oppression can contribute to the development of theory that enhances therapeutic approaches to black issues. Training and supervision are based on these components.

Western cultural entrenchment engendered by oppression can render a black person speechless at times when he or she might benefit from upfrontness and the sharing of experience. Empathy requires sharing, forgiveness, impartiality and integrity, so it would be unhealthy to condone or collude with oppression by being silent or inactive in these conditions. It is therefore important to create ethical conditions of accountability for the way we respond to black issues.

When we consider a black empathic approach, it is important to remember that racism is a culture ingrained within other cultures. The indoctrination of racism globally has been thorough and adds another dimension to multicultural therapy. The power of a black empathic approach sits in the belly of this experience, and most therapists have the potential to truly harness this power if they reflect on their own diversity issues. Questions proposed by trainees and experienced practitioners have evidenced concern over these matters.

The development of a black empathic approach will help eliminate the need for clients to explain and justify experiences of racism. For black counsellors working with black clients, careful attention needs to be given to creating empathy from shared experiences rather than from subjective identification (the position of the counsellor's similar experience). This allows for empathy to be experienced in a deeper context of understanding my black experience together with yours and the experiences of others.

Training elements can be utilised to develop a black empathic approach, at the same time maintaining the boundaries of disclosure and over-identification (meeting the counsellor's need to be less isolated in his or her experiences). There are many challenges in the development and use of a black empathic approach. Therapists practising from the basis of Eurocentric training will find old ways challenged and discover new ways of communicating. In this chapter I have paid attention to ways that empathy can be viewed in the context of black issues. I would encourage readers to use the ideas presented as a model for their practice.

Pointers for therapists (including trainees and trainers)

- Begin the therapeutic relationship with a multicultural approach. For example, during initial sessions find out whether the client has made an informed choice about working with you as their black/white female/male therapist.
- Ask questions about what the client expects of you as a black/white female/male therapist during your meetings, as these inferences can affect the cultural nature of your relationship.
- Acknowledge diversity using appropriate disclosure. Explain that you are aware of similar (if relevant) oppressions but that you are aware you have different stories.
- Offer information about the development of trust and understanding cultural influences in the client's relationships and the therapeutic relationship.

- Use the assessment process to take some history of the client's range of oppressions by asking about his or her experiences of bullying, racism, sexism and other cultural oppressions.
- If appropriate, tell black clients about your awareness of how name-calling and second-class treatment have affected black people. You can explain that you may use your awareness of these issues to understand the problems they are bringing, but you will not expect them to talk about the issues if they do not want to.
- Consider the source of your empathic responses. Are they connected to black issues or are they defending against the effect of racism?
- Use personal development forums and supervision to explore what it feels like to work with black issues.

Part II

Recognition Trauma

The concept of recognition trauma has been used as a paradigm for the emotional process that unfolds when we explore black issues and the impact of racism. To move on from sharing and connecting in Part I, I have developed three additional concepts to help elucidate the impact of racism on trainees' relationships with each other and the exploration of black issues in their therapeutic work with clients. The concept of ancestral baggage in Chapter 4 identifies the unconscious aspects of the way history and social disposition have influenced black people. The concept of black Western archetypes presented in Chapter 5 draws on Jung's ideas about collective imagery pervading our unconscious processes. I have used this to assist with the process of understanding the impact of racism on the psyche. In Chapter 6 the concept of cultural schizophrenia has been used to draw attention to the complex cultural dimensions that often intersect with the mental ill health of black people.

4

Healing Ancestral Baggage

When people die, nature is the only hospitable place where their spirits can dwell. Their spirits, living in the other world, remember clearly the experience of walking on the earth. They remember the moments when they contributed to greater good and helped to make the world better. But they also remember with great remorse the failed adventures and the gestures that harmed others and made the world a less dignifying place. The more they see the more they ache, and the more eager they are to turn their attention to helping those still in this world, however, spirits need to enlist our co-operation and help.

Somé (1999, p. 54)

I use this quotation to explain the meaning of 'ancestral baggage'. Somé uses his African spirituality to understand how the ancestral spirit of humans may link to the psyche of the living, in a way that suggests how we may inherit a sort of cultural lag. Not every black person or therapist will subscribe to this way of understanding, but I find it helps to contextualise a number of the concerns presented by trainees and colleagues in their attempts to understand parts of the process related to black issues. I have created the concept of ancestral baggage to place attention on ways that individuals may be influenced by elements of loss and negativity linked to past cultural influences. This is my attempt to enlist the 'co-operation' that Somé mentions and extend the structural framework of a transcultural approach. I believe that a process of coping with cultural fragmentation and grieving is an essential element of this process. Most therapeutic approaches encourage exploration of memories and fantasies that link relationships to those who have gone before. This chapter uses the concept of ancestral baggage in a transpersonal way to describe how past influences on the lives of black people may impact current generations and the collective psyche of today.

Richards (1992) affirms the transpersonal dimensions of this approach: 'We transformed suffering into an opportunity to express spirit. And through its expression its existence was reaffirmed' (p. 25). Using Richards' proposal of reaffirming through expression of spirit, I am relating the transpersonal to the unseen, immeasurable and some-times unexplainable aspects of black issues in the therapeutic process. The concept of ancestral baggage is used to explain the emotional and transformative aspects of trainees' experiences as they become affected by and process the history of racism. Excerpts from transcripts of train-ees' discussions of black issues demonstrate their curiosity about the impact of the past on the present.

The concept of ancestral baggage is a way of understanding how the dynamics of former generations' relationships get passed on and affect black issues in the present. I am therefore suggesting that a black client's emotional situation may be affected by his or her upbringing and also by his or her ancestors' modes of response. This is a proposition about intergenerational patterns of relating that date back to ancient African kings and queens and to the slaughter and genesis of slavery. This may be viewed as an aspect of transference that has not been fully explored. We go through our individual life process and inhabit our own personal ancestral baggage. Learning situations that raise awareness of ancestral baggage provide us with numerous opportunities to rewrite the nega-tive aspects of these scripts and transform our lives. Psychotherapy and counselling is just one way of supporting the inspiration and insights that can contribute to this process.

The process of transformation and change that we engender either naturally or therapeutically puts us in touch with our inspiration. This inspiration is represented in daily worship and ritual, art and creativity, and the repetitive actions that make up our lives. We then, consciously or unconsciously, replay these actions through our historical and cultural reference points.

The questions below, posed by both black and white trainees, can be considered within the context of history, cultural heritage and ancestral baggage.

Why don't we leave the past alone if it appears to be irrelevant to the present?

Transculturalists challenge therapists who respond to cultural questions as though they were being given an additional problem. If this question were turned on its head, we might consider why we do not leave the present alone if it appears to be irrelevant to the past. It might then be possible to consider the function of fear and denial so often associated with the challenge of facing the impact of the past on black people engaging in therapy. The influence of Eurocentric theory that conditions our response to this question may need to be considered. Psychoanalytical approachs may view the past and family history as a key component in the therapeutic process, not to be left alone. On the other hand, therapists working from a humanistic stance may encourage a present-time, existential approach that would leave the past alone.

The 'don't go there' signal is ever present in therapeutic relationships, especially when minority issues are being considered. Past experiences of oppression that render individuals speechless when they process minority issues get stirred up. Once the silence is broken, individuals usually share an experience of being directly hurt by racism or of witnessing someone else being hurt by it. It is important, therefore, to be aware of how the counsellor's own denial in the present may prevent him or her from acknowledging the historical and cultural context of denial. The past will be irrelevant only if we refuse to contextualise the present. The following question, similar in context but more explicit, acknowledges the attachment of a negative connotation to working through the impact of the past on the present. The something negative that we fear but may not be fully conscious of can be conceptualised in a transpersonal way as ancestral baggage.

Isn't it negative to focus on the hurt of colonialism and racism?

Yes, it may be negative – but it is necessary. The therapist's role is to support clients through negative phases. Therapists and clients may choose to leave the past alone if it appears irrelevant to the present. This act of leaving alone can be explored in a self-reflective way. Am I in denial? Is the client in denial? Am I willing to go there with the client if she leads me there? Am I willing to address the past if the client makes reference to it or if I sense there may be links? Am I aware, informed or confident enough to discuss the cultural and historical context of ignoring the past? Am I attaching my own negativity to the client's experience? Do I feel confident about either considering the impact of racism on the client or exploring the hurt of racism? Therapists need to be ready to explore the impact of racism on themselves and their clients. Remaining in denial may keep both counsellor and client in an oppressive state of powerlessness. A wish to process this state is expressed in the following question.

How do we work with the problem of fear and mistrust related to the violence of racism?

Using the concept of ancestral baggage, we can presuppose that the impact of racism, and prejudice, can lay dormant in the psyche through generations or the lifetime of an individual. Therapists must be careful not to interpret lack of consciousness of this impact as denial. Trainees are likely to ask how we know the difference. The answer to this question may lie in the content of the therapeutic process experienced between the client and the counsellor. I have used the concept of recognition trauma to describe the awakening of hurtful experiences related to racism, which sometimes evoke feelings of guilt, shame and anger. Symptoms of recognition trauma emanate in a similar way to the awakening of feelings related to the impact of sexism and heterosexism. Helms (1990) uses a racial identity model to explain responses to awakened feelings related to racism. This model incorporates the people of colour ego status theory; it proposes that the white ego status goes through a period of immersion/emersion where a search for the meaning of racism and redefinition of whiteness may occur. In contrast, the immersion/emersion ego status for black people may create an idealisation of one's socio-racial group and a denigration of what may be perceived as white. In this process individuals use their own-group external standards to define themselves. I believe it is important to find ways to understand and work with these processes. Sue and Sue (1998) propose: 'Multiculturalism requires that educators and counsellors be aware of the systematic dimensions of racism and alienation and thereby attempt to understand the experiences, lifestyles, and values of students and clients' (p. 517).

This multiculturalist starting point is important in that it reminds us that racism has been systematic. This is where we can make links from the past to the present using the concept of ancestral baggage. Working through a phase of recognition trauma may be likened to the working through of Klein's 'depressive position' (Rycroft, 1968, p. 32), which is said to unlock embedded feelings related to the good and bad mother symbol. According to Klein (1986) the baby manages this position at about six months:

> Whether or not it can identify with an internalized 'good' mother to the extent that it can repair the damage done by its destructive urges to the 'bad' mother or whether it must flee the implications of the position – constitutes the nodal experience for the infant on which its subsequent relative normality or psychosis depends. (p. 115)

Klein's proposition that therapists can provide a container for repairing destructive urges from the past sits well with the healing process for racism. In a similar way, providing a therapeutic process to work through recognition trauma may assist clients to identify and externalise embedded feelings from the impact of racism. When traumatic experiences occur as a response to racism and prejudice, it is not easy to remain aware that both oppressor and victim may have internalised destructive urges, causing them both pain. An awareness of this in the therapeutic process may support the development of a black empathic process between counsellor and client.

Recalling my own process of recognition trauma, I became aware of grief related to denial of my own black history. The grief associated with this lost part of my identity seemed to lay dormant in my subconscious, yet it connected me to the everyday experiences of racism. From the recognition of my hurt and rage about these experiences, compassion emerged to help me to work with these issues as a professional. Ackbar (1996), an African American psychologist, relates to this grief as 'a post-traumatic stress syndrome', suggesting that we break free from this dilemma:

> Our formulation suggests that the blemish of these inhumane conditions persists as a kind of post-traumatic stress syndrome on the collective mind of Africans ... and though its original cause cannot be altered, the genesis can be understood. ... Our goal is to take us beyond the simple recognition of the trauma and to begin the process of healing our minds so that we can be free of slave mentality. (pp. i, ii)

Counsellors can help with this idea of freedom by not leaving the past alone and by providing a therapeutic process that can facilitate recognition trauma and the process of healing ancestral baggage.

During my working through of this process I found that one of the most difficult things was to break out of stereotyping myself as a black woman and face my need for help. This meant taking the risk of asking white colleagues to look out for me and give me more support in my work as a black counsellor trainer. I feared the risk of experiencing further racism or, worse still, white colleagues not knowing how to listen to and support me as a victim of the oppressor group that they belong to. Yet trust-building is a primary element of counselling. I had been working on my fears and feelings about racism with my white counsellors. That was a breakthrough in my life and work. Although we had agreed to address the issues together, I was faced with the challenge of making them aware of my frustration at their stuckness and their inability to initiate discussions about black issues in team meetings. I was trying to relinquish the role of the black expert. I experienced my colleagues' behaviour as a form of exclusion linked to personal and institutional racism. These repeated experiences of exclusion created insights. I eventually came to the realisation that none of us had had black issues included in our training. One of my colleagues used the term 'oppression burnout' to describe what she thought I was going through. This was a new concept for me and gave meaning to the ways in which recognition trauma can manifest. The term 'oppression burnout' aptly describes my past withdrawal from white groups and men as a kind of a last-straw way of coping with recognition trauma and an attempt to protect myself from further pain. The following question confirms the collective nature of these experiences.

How can I deal with the fear of lack of acceptance when relating to white people outside my culture?

Lack of acceptance is a feature of racism that causes black individuals to feel bad about themselves. Fear is a component of bad feelings and low self-worth. It is essential that therapists work through their personal and historical rejection and mistrust about racial dynamics in their client work, no matter how disturbing the dynamics may appear to be. In addition, fear and mistrust related to experiences of racism can be exacerbated when racism is ignored by both client and counsellor. Giving up when the going gets tough may repeat the process of abandonment and isolation that can be associated with the experience of racism. Somé (1999) encourages us to 'crack it open' and bring new understanding of what may be inside:

> In order to crack open something in yourself to allow you to be aware of the presence of ancestors' spirits, you have to walk into nature with your emotional self, not with your intellectual self. You need to open wide your heart so that you can become moist and drink deeply from the emotional echoes that you receive from the frown of a gnarled tree or the twist of a branch. Seen in this way, nature the dwelling place of the ancestral spirits is a vast field of grief. (p. 54)

Somé associates ancestral influences and fears of not being accepted with a type of grieving process. Aspects of this grief associated with ancestral baggage became apparent when I was transcribing the following discussions with counselling trainees. Their narrative reflects the traumatic impact of racism on the process of attending to black issues.

Black female: I can remember a question that came up. Why is it that black people are picked on or have such a bad image most of the time? This happens in America too. I mentioned something about imperialism, the history and slavery.

Isha: Was this useful?

Black female: Oh yes, it was very useful. It enabled me. I realise that it's not just white people that carry images of racism, who are racist; black people also take it on.

Isha: Are you talking about internal racism?

Black female: Yes.

White female: This can be the daily experience of black people. I am thinking about a client who tells me that when she went into a store in London, she was followed immediately by a security guard. She says people don't believe her when she tells them of this kind of experience, so I do try to be aware of what black people tell me about their experiences.

Black female: I was reminded that it is an experience that we live with every day of our lives.

Black female: One thing I have noticed is that white people are too scared to speak their mind because they are scared of being classed as racist. I get the feeling that it affects them to an extreme where they almost disinherit their whiteness. I don't know if I am explaining myself properly. They don't want to be part of racism and because they are white they automatically assume they have prejudice feelings. They conjure up this person who does not accept their culture and colour for who they are because they don't want to be associated with racist people. It's almost as though an element of people's whiteness can be lost through blackness. I don't know if this makes sense, but I have seen it.

Black female: During the workshop, I became aware and learned that black issues do not only affect black people. Black issues bring racism. I learned that there was racism between the English and the Irish. Far back, they were treated like blacks being discriminated. Also that this affects gender issues and sexual orientation. I learned a lot, that there are other issues with black issues.

White female: I always thought that I understood black issues and the culture, and coming from Ireland and our own history of oppression and colonialism, but I don't understand. Someone in the workshop said, 'You don't know what it is like to be black unless you are black.' That is one thing that I have really learned. Also someone said, 'Every day I wake up, I am aware that I am black and the colour of my skin.' This really had a great impact on me. It was such a powerful statement and I wanted to cry. That was something that I was not aware of, that people feel that way. For me in the counselling relationship, I have learned that if I have a black client, how they might feel. They would look at me as white, being in power, not Irish; they may not be aware of my oppressions. They could see me as being in authority and all the things that black people may have bad experiences about. I would need to be very aware of these as a counsellor and how this could influence our relationship. I never thought about it before. I was aware of cultures, but I know very little about other cultures. I would admit that I don't know and have to ask the client for help to explain a bit about their culture. I think it is absolutely imperative to have black issues workshops and cultural workshops on the training. My self-awareness has improved dramatically.

White female: For me it has got me onto the next step. It has been a slow process for me and I am just getting to a place where I am prepared to acknowledge and admit that I have got to. I think, for me it is about making judgements about people and it could be about all sorts of things, but for me I do focus quite a lot on my racism. And I know black issues are about lots of different things, but this is important; that's what I look at. What I have realised that the pre-judgements that I made about people every day I didn't notice them. Whereas before they just went really fast across my brain, now they kind of sit there and I really don't want to think about them. What I have managed to do this year is not just dismiss them. It has given me the courage to confront that in me. Sometimes I have felt very alone in this, and this may be part of the process of looking at something so personal and deep. What I have realised is that we are all at different stages of this journey. It's weird, I feel I can't look at anybody, I don't know why. So in a way there has been something about the safety of looking at this in the group that has been going on. It was said earlier, that we have seen that sometimes when black issues is put on the agenda and we have to think about it, fear has shut me down completely. I have seen that happen with my peers. Not only is it really difficult to get to a point where I can face myself like this that more care needs to be taken to support each other. This is about everything we are learning, but specifically about something that for me is so raw, so personal, that if I am going to face it, I don't want to do this alone. So for next year I would like to look at how to make it an even safer place, because the fear paralyses people. It almost needs to be like, it's ok to have these feelings, let's just get on and talk about it rather than it's not ok.

Asian female: I learned a lot during the workshops. Before going to the workshop I thought my knowledge about not issues but about blacks was adequate. I learned that many black issues apply to my issues and me as an Asian person living in white society. I learned a lot about colonising and the history of blacks and how that can affect the personality of an individual, how that personality can carry on through history. How we can lose our own identity and confidence and the blockage that we cannot go on, because I myself always looked at white people as superior to myself without consideration. I just accepted what they were saying because they had white skin and blue eyes. I learned that was not correct. At the same time I came across the reality of my own responsibility to get my place in white society; this means to learn more to see why I can't go on to integrate, to regain my confidence and move on. Also I learned that this is a mutual effect on blacks and whites, because I have many white friends who feel really guilty and they hesitate to say anything and support. In conjunction with my workplace and these workshops I learned a lot. The other thing about black issues that I learned here is oppression though history and that black people suppress other minorities. Maybe they are just repeating what happened to them in the wider society.

Isha: *I wonder if you can you link your responses to areas of your development on the course and whether you have evidence of what you have learned that links to your work with clients.*

Black female: I might get rubbed up, resentment, be annoyed if someone is very racist, or maybe I might understand.

Isha: *Any of these could happen and the feelings might be transference or counter-transference, so what would you do with them and how would you take care of yourself?*

Black female: Take it to my supervisor. I have to understand that my thoughts and feelings I am aware of and I have to be careful about not switching off. I am there for my client. So I have to work through it.

Isha: This question is open to anyone. Do you feel that the work you have done on the course has impacted the way you use supervision and the way your supervisors are with you?

White female: Definitely we have discussed cultural and black issues and the possibilities of not understanding someone because the culture is different, but I am looking at areas where people are too scared to voice these things. I know that I might find it difficult to talk to black people unless I know them very well or I am in a supervised group.

Isha: Why is this?

White female: It's a safe environment, the element is this group. If I challenge my thoughts it is safe to also receive other people's thoughts to what I say. In another environment it could be quite threatening.

Isha: What is the fear?

White female: The possibility of offending someone or receiving an aggressive response to offence when offence is not what is meant. So at least this is a place to resolve situations before you have clients.

Black female: I am not going to reply to that, but I am going to add a bit about what I have learnt from the black issues workshops. It is that black issues is not just about racism; it is to do with the way black people relate to other black people as well as how they relate to white people. For me in counselling situations as a black woman, what is going through my head, is my client thinking I am not good enough? I am wondering what she is thinking about me and how I can be there with her. In relation to how it affects my relationship with other black people, at times it is helpful. When a young black man comes to me and he is telling me about his respect, having young black people that look up to him, I find it easier to understand where he is coming from, because within my culture as the older child we have to set examples that young people follow. So it makes it easier for me to enter into their frame of reference, but there are times because of history, because of racism, and because of the way I have the experience of being black, I am wondering you know when I am with another black person, because I don't see black people in key posts very much. One of the questions is how did they come to be where they are, what qualifications? I know in my head that they have struggled. It has been difficult for me at forty-seven not to have reached a stage in life that I ought to have reached. I feel that my white contemporaries would have probably reached that stage. I am not talking about you, Isha.

I don't think I am stupid, although my education would have put me down and made me feel stupid. So over history that makes me wonder whether when I am talking to my white counsellor, was I to be open enough to accept this is really how I am experiencing this and not to feel threatened by this and to assume I am accusing her of racism, or for her to feel defensive about it.

Isha: Can I just come back to what you said in the beginning? Were you also suggesting that a client may question how you got to be a counsellor?

Black female: In fact, a recent client wanted to know about me, and I did not want to get into that with her. I told her I was married and a few things and I said she is open to fantasise about whatever. One of the things she said to me was, 'As a Nigerian' – I must have mentioned to her I was Nigerian – 'you have gone through a lot and you have reached maturity.' I did not add to or dismiss what she said; I just thought she could keep whatever fantasies that were hers. But sometimes I am left thinking, 'Did that mean she may have thought I was not good enough to be her counsellor?'

Isha: Was there anything that occurred in the black issues workshops to assist you to manage this situation?

Black female: To manage this I can help her to understand that she is not the only person who has these thoughts, just like in *Love's Executioner*, where the fat woman shares a sense of revulsion about being fat herself, it is here, there and everywhere. I can stay with her and let her know this is a real feeling and allow her to voice what is going on for her and how she is experiencing me. If it were to annoy me I would then take it to my counsellor or supervisor because at times I have been hurt by black issues and my therapist and supervisor have been really helpful. My supervisor is white and she says she experiences me as anxious and I don't feel that I am anxious in her presence, so I was wondering where that was coming from. So immediately, as a black person the thought of my race came into it.

Black female: Um...the fact that we are in a group together and we were able to share. In my group there were three black women and one white, and we were able to discuss these issues in a reasonable way.

Black female: I have had the experience of taking a black client to a white supervisor, who is clearly on one level aware of black issues, but I feel that because this person comes from a psychodynamic background she was a bit too ready to see what the client is presenting as a defence. I feel that the workshops have given me the confidence to go on thinking even if I can't always challenge this person verbally, that actually this is about racism; it's not a defence or anything else. I really have been given the confidence to hold on to my own thoughts and feelings about it, through the workshops and through some of the case studies that you have given us.

White female: The second workshop was very useful. It was interesting to see how people fitted into the two groups that were set. If you identified white, go into that group; if you identify as black, go into that group. It was interesting to see the number of what we wouldn't really consider as 'black' in quotes in the same group that I belong. If I were to explain that, I would say that all the people that came into my group saw themselves as members of the oppressed non-white group.

White female: I came into this course thinking that I knew a fair bit about black issues. I realise that I knew sweet F. all, but I have come out understanding things better. I don't know what it is like to be black because I am not black, but I can try to understand how people feel. From this I realise that I have been walking in the street not listening to what people in the street are saying and there are some really nasty people around, especially in my work environment. I never heard the racism towards black people, towards Asian people, and I am really disgusted, but I am glad that I have this new sense and I am more interested in understanding now.

The mention of disinherited whiteness, guilt passed on through history and a heightened awareness of everyday racism expressed through the narrative of trainees gives a flavour of the intangible context of ancestral baggage. As they engage in a reflective process about black issues, black trainees seem to feel more at ease to share their experiences and challenge inhibiting silences. The trainees' process of exploration demonstrates a working through of their recognition trauma exemplified in a new awareness.

Fletchman Smith (2000), in the introduction to her book *Mental Slavery*, encapsulates these trainees' voices when she says:

> I begin from the position that slavery was damaging for everyone concerned with it. As in all situations in which there are perpetuators and victims, it is what the victims do in their own minds with the horrors they experience that – to a large extent – determines

the future state of mind of that individual. This explains why some people have not only survived, but have thrived in spite of the experience of slavery. Others have not been so fortunate. (p. 7)

Using Fletchman Smith's understanding we could suppose that second- and third-generation people of African heritage whose communities have suffered slaughter and the internalisation process of racism exist in the wounds of the collective psyche and ancestral spirits. This Middle-Passage place of unrequited love and grief, inherited trauma and pain, a rootless place of ancestral baggage, may still have healing to do. Focusing on the emotional distresses rather than our heritage of great African achievements may seem like a negative and despondent reflection of African history. Needless to say, honouring great black leaders, mentors and those who have positively influenced community and personal life can play a significant role in healing ancestral baggage. Great leaders such as Mary Seacole, Phyllis Wheatley, Olaudah Equiano and Kwame Nkrumah, to name but a few who have influenced changes in attitude towards black role models, are examples of empowerment. Although these leaders no longer grace the world with their physical presence, we gain strength from their tremendous power of survival.

The experiences of black people have been carried into the present via songs, folktales, art and literature. They are within the rhythm of our music, the language of our stories and the images and symbols of our art. They are portrayed in the way we dress, our hairstyles, our walk and our talk. The experiences we carry over from the past are re-enacted in our everyday existence.

The negative experiences mentioned by some trainees and described by Fletchman Smith (2000) as 'not so fortunate' continue to impact the black psyche. These experiences that I call 'ancestral baggage' are the unspoken but evident effects of slavery and colonisation. They affect current relationships within black communities and between black and white people.

Peoples of Africa, the Caribbean, Europe and the Americas developed strategies for survival during the grave Middle Passage era, during which many slaves were hauled as goods and chattel. Slaves imitated their masters' ways and developed codes of conduct observed by their communities so families could survive the atrocities that were committed against them. It is rarely acknowledged that the families of white slave masters also developed self-preservation strategies.

The effect of many of these strategies can still be observed in our society today. One example is the substitution of European names for

African names, imposed by the slave owner and adopted by African families as they became fragmented, spreading across the world. The adoption of beatings as a means of control shows that slavery had a significant long-term impact on black families.

Distancing of families from their origins continues to disorient and fragment black family relationships. Fragmentation, compounded by capitalist inculcation to conform to stereotypical Eurocentric images of self, can create confusion. This confusion is often taken on as a feature of identity, and individuals believe in this identity as though it belonged to them. As a result, many black individuals have rejected their origins and adopted a Western outlook, which can create mistrust in their own authenticity.

Trust issues can be linked to past or present relationships and racism and may be influenced by ancestral baggage. Trust is not a blanket experience for the black client in the therapeutic relationship. It may contain elements from intergenerational and global dynamics that influence congruence and self-awareness. Therapists need to be equipped with the ease, experience and knowledge of black issues to facilitate trust among black people and across the cultures and dynamics of black and white. The use of only a Eurocentric approach may underestimate black clients' experiences and the impact of racism on them. Just as love can create a memory of lasting comfort, the wounds of racism may be so great that they create lasting discomfort. A wound of hatred that becomes permanent has to be managed along with the feelings attached to it. Deep wounds connected to the experience of racism can contribute to low self-esteem and, if they are not addressed, can lead to depression. It is vital that therapists become aware of the potential for black clients to harbour these symptoms, whether they are made explicit or not. This preparedness contributes to the development of good practice that addresses black issues. To assist reflection on the process of healing ancestral baggage, I have identified four areas for consideration evolving from trainees' discussions.

Denial and internalised anger

Some black people may not be aware of the impact that racism has had on them and their family. Defence strategies may be in place to prevent them from facing the pain of their experience. They may view the experience as something that has nothing to do with them, that is to do only with militants or radicals. Skin scrubbing, skin lightening and dislike of natural kinky hair and of African physical features can also be symptoms of these defence strategies. Individuals may also dismiss their African roots and the cultural heritage of their extended family.

Guilt, resentment and rage

Guilt is often subtly portrayed in the work ethic that we must work harder to be better than white people when we are already good enough. It is visible in patterns of overwork for fear of being seen as lazy or unable to provide. It is visible in the suppression of language, the practice of name-changing and the containment of dialect in attempts to assimilate. Black clients have reported experiencing resentment and rage on becoming aware of the violence and abuse of racism that they or those close to them have endured. This awareness can be followed by recognition of a loss of originality and a shocking awareness of their internalised pain and the role of their unconscious defences in the perpetuation of their own oppression. This is the process of recognition trauma.

Fear

Fear often accompanies clarity. People fear the enormity of the negative impact of racism. They fear isolation and rejection by peers as they gain clarity about powerful feelings associated with this experience. They may fear the seemingly irreparable damage and experience hopelessness about change. On the other hand, individuals become aware of ways to empower themselves with a positive black identity.

Clarity and empowerment

Clarity comes with a consciousness of the beauty and strength of African heritage and a vision that integrates a positive attitude to the black self. Empowerment is the sister of clarity because it prompts action and the individual learns how to re-establish pride in his or her identity.

In the therapeutic process self-esteem can be supported by drawing on the psychodynamic concept of transference to process ancestral baggage. In psychoanalytical theory unconscious processes can become apparent to the therapist in the transference. If an issue being discussed links to racism, the transference process attached to recognition trauma might then be viewed as a kind of Middle Passage grieving state, where ancestral baggage is being processed. Internalised racism can be viewed as a symptom of ancestral baggage that becomes apparent with a variety of defences such as displacement, identity confusion, low motivation, subservience, a highly image-conscious attitude and silent grief. These symptoms may emerge after a black person has suffered from a racial attack. Ackbar (1996) refers to these symptoms:

> Our progress is still impeded by many of the slave-based characteristics. ... The objective of the discussion is not to cry 'victim' and seek to excuse those self-destructive characteristics created by slavery. ... It is not a call to vindicate the cause of the condition, but to challenge Black people to recognize the symptoms of the condition and master it as we have mastered the original trauma. (p. 25)

Conclusion

The work of black scholars and psychological theorists such as Ackbar encourages us to get on with the business of acknowledging and dealing with ancestral baggage. How we engage with this issue depends on the therapist's willingness to attend to the transpersonal aspects that affect black issues in the therapeutic process. The concept of ancestral baggage has been explored in two ways: first, by presenting trainee counsellors' fears and concerns about working with black issues, which are embroiled with consideration of how trainees' personal experiences may affect their exploration of racism; second, by presenting trainees in discussion about their own process of understanding black issues. Their narrative reflects attempts to understand black issues in the context of their training and client work. This context was illuminated during the study. It became clearer as the study went on that the fears and concerns of trainee counsellors were linked to their past experiences and present acquaintance with the theme of black issues. I have used ideas from transcultural writers to clarify elements of ancestral baggage such as grief, proposed by Somé (1999), and the damaging effects of slavery, proposed by Fletchman Smith (2000). I have also discussed the relevance of recognition trauma, a concept that was born out of observations of trainees' powerful emotions linked to the impact of racism. The concept of ancestral baggage evolved from recognising the impact of the past on trainees' present responses to black issues. I proposed that this concept be used to understand experiences of diversity and the therapeutic process of black issues. Productive therapy occurs when this process has been acknowledged as an aspect of personal development for both therapist and clients.

Pointers for therapists (including trainees and trainers)

- Communicate information in a way that imparts a shared experience as well as an understanding of the experience.
- Encourage black trainees to develop empathic responses based on their experience of being a British citizen or knowledge of their ancestral homeland. Encourage white trainees to process the impact of their heritage and ancestry as members of the oppressor group (see Lago, 2006; Tuckwell, 2002; Dalal, 2002; Ocheing, 2003). Literature, music, artefacts and images can be used to connect to experiences of diversity and convey knowledge of a shared history.
- Encourage trainees working with settlers or descendants of settlers to explore the client's cultural history rather than just taking information about history.
- Create a foundation for the therapeutic process by addressing the client's history in the context of his or her personal or family journey to British society and its effects on his or her heritage.
- Ask clients about their family background. Use family photos or objects of cultural significance to explore geographical location, occupation and the lifestyle of their descendants. If relevant, explore the context of 'back home'. If you are using objects, get the client to tell the story of the object, its origins, journey to Britain and separation and assimilation experiences. Associate the impact of language and cultural differences. Significant points that have influenced the object's life can be discussed – for example, identity issues, being removed from its origins, transportation to an unfamiliar land, the experience of different ownership, the history of its value, its name and purpose.
- Pay particular attention to the experiences of black men and their differences from black women and white men and women. Develop a dialogue that assists them to share through creative expression.

5

The Black Western Archetype

Following on from Chapter 4's transpersonal focus on ancestral baggage, this chapter develops the Jungian concept of 'archetypes' (Jung, 1970) to explore some cultural influences on black issues. The link between cultural assimilation and the challenges of obtaining personal freedom is highlighted in a review of black issues in the therapeutic process with a black female client. The review reflects the use of an integrative, transcultural approach. With diversity work – and for black people in particular – the therapeutic process can be influenced by a re-enactment of what I would describe as the 'black Western archetype'.

The concept of archetypes arose from ideas about the substance of the unconscious processes of the human psyche. Philosophers, scientists and psychologists have been intrigued by what unconscious processes lie behind human experiences. In a similar way to ancestral baggage, archetypes are viewed as a phenomenon of the unseen and often unarticulated impressions and symbolic representations of the human psyche.

Jung (1970) perceives the archetype as essentially unconscious. The archetype is altered by becoming conscious and by being perceived, and it takes its colour from the individual consciousness in which it appears.

I have introduced the idea of black Western archetypes using what Vanoy Adams (1996) describes as Fanon's cultural context and what I perceive as the influence of racism on archetypes: 'Fanon suggests that the racist contents of the collective conscious are imposed by white culture' (p. 165). I am using this concept to develop an understanding of the link between culture and internalised racism.

According to Samuels et al. (1986), Jung perceives archetypes as certain psychological patterns that are inherited and can be recognised in the unconscious life of individuals. These patterns are perpetuated by the collective unconscious within social structures, and they are repeated everywhere throughout history. Archetypes permeate images of the self. They are said to be recognisable in outer behaviour, especially with universal events such as birth, marriage, motherhood and death, and they are reinforced by tradition and culture. Individuals become influenced by these archetypes that emanate from the collective psyche. For example, the archetype of the wise old man (Ellenberger, 1994) that sits within all of us becomes collective as we endow queens and kings, swamis, rabbis and priests with leadership.

Jung suggests that everyone possesses a shadow archetype that embodies the dark, negative aspects of the psyche. This archetype contains unmentionable thoughts and fantasies that manifest in dreams. Jung portrayed elements of his own shadow through racist imagery in his dreams, made conscious in his descriptions of Africans as savages. He believed that if the shadow archetype is made conscious, it has the potential to be modified as it connects to the ego status and collective consciousness. In recognising this potential, I am proposing that black Western archetypes can inhabit racist parts of the collective shadow, which become conscious through exploring individual shadow elements of internalised racism. This usually evokes the process that I have called recognition trauma, which can be worked through in therapy. Going along with Jung's hopes for archetype modification raises possibilities for transformation of the negative impact of racism through working with black issues in the therapeutic process.

One of the first questions that trainees asked about black Western archetypes was the following.

What kind of black Western archetypes are there?

A black Western archetype that has pervaded the lives of black men is the 'lazy black boy'. It can be seen via its impact on the history of underachievement of black boys in the British education system and the low status of black men in the labour market. Although employment law has begun to address equalities in recruitment, black men still struggle against this archetype by dropping out of the race for work or overworking at the risk of neglecting their families. The emotional aspects of this phenomenon have rarely been addressed.

The 'step and fetch it' archetype describes the black person who behaves in a subservient manner to white peers. This archetype, emanating from the historical role of the female house slave, has been played out collectively in the subservient roles of black domestics in the labour market. Behaviour related to this archetype often becomes apparent with symptoms of burnout from overwork and stress as a result of striving against institutional racism.

Negative archetypes portrayed in racist stereotyping of African-heritage people can impact the collective black psyche and black family relationships, causing internalised racism. Internalised racism can be likened to internalised sexism. In the dynamic of internalised sexism, a woman may act according to the role that she has been assigned by dominant male role models and patriarchal society. Black people may act according to the roles assigned to them by a society saturated in racism and racist images. They may act in accordance with white Eurocentric dominance inherited through slavery, colonisation and Westernisation and through living in predominantly white communities. For individuals, internalised racism can manifest in a variety of self-demeaning or self-harming ways, such as derogatory language about skin colour and self-image directed towards the self or other black people. In its extreme form, internalised racism can manifest in defences that distort concepts of identity and produce self-harm on the basis of skin colour. If these harmful elements are not addressed, they can result in low self-esteem and depression. Using an understanding of internalised racism and the concept of black Western archetypes, therapists can support clients to re-integrate positive images from their heritage and develop an identity congruent with our multicultural world.

Metaphorically speaking, the black Western archetype is an attempt to colour in Jung's concept of archetypes. This adding or addressing of the colour dynamic may present a challenge to the collective unconscious and negative socially conditioned responses to black people. I am therefore proposing that therapists work with the assumption that these negative elements have become part of the cultural nature of archetypes in the Western world, as a type of collective shadow. Dalal (2002) addresses this cultural permeation in 'The meanings of black' (p. 153) (being predominantly negative).

The concept of black Western archetypes has been used to engage with the question below, proposed by another trainee counsellor during my study (McKenzie-Mavinga, 2005). This question proposes an exploration of the archetypal nature of defences against painful experiences of racism.

How do I put aside my own political and emotional beliefs when working with someone who believes the negative stereotypes about himself or herself as a black person?

Defences built on archetypes are the substance of society's negative stereotypes. These defences can be worked through in the therapeutic process. To help explore this question, I go along with Jung's

(1970) proposal that ultimately the archetype should be exposed. In a therapeutic context this would involve therapists in naming the archetype as they reflect on their client work and assisting clients to explore and understand the way archetypes affect the unconscious.

> Only when all props and crutches are broken, and no cover from the rear offers even the slightest hope of security, does it become possible for us to experience an archetype that till then had lain hidden behind the meaningful nonsense played out as the anima. This is the archetype of meaning, just as the anima is the archetype of life itself. (p. 32)

Jung's perspective on the defences around archetypes gives clues to their pervasiveness and invisible influence. Likewise, defences around black Western archetypes can be perpetuated by stereotypes pervading both the Eurocentric black psyche and the Eurocentric white psyche. Vanoy Adams (1996) draws attention to Fanon's perception that '[a]s blacks partake of the same collective unconscious as the European...the black has taken over all the archetypes belonging to the European' (p. 163).

Fanon's awareness of his own emergence from the impact of racism gives us insights into the subtleties of working therapeutically with the emotions of this experience. Therapists must therefore realise that working with black issues in the therapeutic process is not about being politically correct. It is about challenging individual assumptions and prejudices and risking exposure to the often hidden territory that lies beyond oppressive stereotyping. Other trainees' concerns about negative stereotypes are explored below via a review of black issues in the therapeutic process that exposes the impact of black Western archetypes on a client.

Review of Therapy with Jacinta

Born in England, Jacinta is the oldest of four children in a Jamaican family. She is the only child not biologically linked to the stepfather who raised them. She was concerned about difficulties in her five-year relationship with a white female partner. She felt that the relationship was in conflict with her upbringing and her early dreams of a heterosexual family unit with children. She believed that her inner conflicts about her sexuality and the difficulties she was experiencing showing affection to her partner were causing stress on the relationship. She had 'come out' about her sexuality to her mother and one or two of her close friends. She felt that her sexuality had been accepted by them, although she had never introduced her partner to them. She also wanted to discuss her confused feelings about her identity as a black woman raised in a shroud of secrecy about her biological father. She was grappling with her low self-esteem, which had been eroded over her thirty years. As a defence she was re-enacting negative stereotypes about herself.

Jacinta suffered what I would explain as hiding behaviour linked to the experience of a negative 'gaze' and beatings from her parents. The 'gaze' can be viewed as a look with intent, which can signify a feeling towards another. It can be an all-powerful means of interpretation or conceptualisation and a tool of perception and influence. Akin to the mirror phase between parent and child, the literal gaze (Lacan, 1977) looks outward and at another person or an object. An inward gaze brings insight. 'This is a form of looking which goes beyond; which penetrates into deeper layers of the psyche' (Schaverien, 1995, p. 191). A kind of inward gaze occurs between client and therapist and this is an experience that may not have words, but is often linked to the transference. hooks (1992) uses several writers, including Foucault, Hall and Fanon, to summarise ideas about power and the gaze in relation to black people's experiences:

> Spaces of agency for black people, wherein we can both interrogate the gaze of the other but also look back, and at one another, naming what we see. The 'gaze' has been and is a site of resistance for colonized black people globally. Subordinates in relations of power learn experientially that there is a critical gaze, one that looks to document, one that is oppositional. (p. 116)

hooks suggests that black people have used the gaze both to their detriment and as a form of resistance to rebuild black identity. Attempts to restore the black gaze have been made throughout history. Examples of these are the Harlem Renaissance in the United States, the recognition of great black leaders and politicians, and the introduction of positive black images in the media and the education system.

A gaze influenced by the black Western archetype of a cowering 'step and fetch it' victim, induced by slavery, came to mind when I listened to Jacinta's story. She explained how as a child she cowered behind the front door when strangers passed her home and habitually covered her hair under a beret. I was aware of her lack of eye contact with me and the way she leaned her head to one side as though she were sad.

Our early sessions were spent evaluating the contradictions of her relationship and her inability to return the loving gaze of her white female partner. She expressed difficulty in showing affection and sharing her feelings within the relationship. Then we began to explore the dynamics of her family history and the therapeutic relationship between us as black women. Jacinta had deliberately sought out a black therapist to work through the trauma of her experiences. In the review she explained why she thought this type of therapeutic relationship (a black positive gaze) would be beneficial to her. We linked Jacinta's sadness to a certain look reflected to her by her stepfather that made her feel she 'did not belong to him'. She described the aftermath of the beatings, mainly administered by her mother. It seemed that she had experienced a rejecting gaze from both her parents. Normality meant that she had to face the humiliating silence of siblings and others in the home who witnessed the beatings but became voiceless. In addition to her everyday experiences of racism, she had internalised these negative family behaviours and become voiceless and unable to face her loved ones and her oppressors. I wondered about Jacinta's need to repair her relationships with her black mother, her rejecting stepfather and her white oppressors. I felt inspired to consider the impact of ancestral baggage on her psyche. My understanding of black issues in the therapeutic process, and an awareness of her family dynamics and the impact of racism and homophobia, enabled Jacinta to experience a new kind of coming out.

The transcript below outlines a conversation reviewing our therapeutic work over a period of two years. The shared experience of two black women in the therapeutic setting is intended to act as a model for therapists working with intersecting oppressions such as homophobia and racism. I asked Jacinta about finding a voice for her experiences and emotions. The dialogue is interspersed with brief explorations of trainees' questions relevant to the review.

Isha: Can you remember where in your sessions did you begin to speak about the beatings and what enabled you to begin talking about them and what happened at that time? It goes a long way back.

Jacinta: Yeah. I think I have spoken about it in little drips. I had mentioned it and not expanded on it too much really or gone into it too deeply. I think it was when you tried to get me involved in expressing my kinda anger by using the cushions. That made it more start to sink in for me.

Isha: Because it was physical?

Jacinta: Um because it was physical and I couldn't quite do it. (Laugh) I felt very uncomfortable. You know particularly around expressing my anger for my mother in that kind of way, in a physical way, or even to express it verbally. I found that very difficult but I think more that kind of discomfort brought the giggling, the laughter about the discomfort of trying to express myself that way that it came more and more to the fore.

Isha: So what was the next bit that it brought up 'cos you stopped after a while; it became embarrassing and difficult?

Jacinta: It bought something up about kinda still wanting to censor me, about not wanting to say anything negative about that particular situation in my past. It feels like this year more so that we have come more to cover the beatings more.

Isha: I remember that you raised something about beatings in your writing.

Jacinta: Oh yes, yes, there is a chapter in it where the little girl is being beaten by her step-grandmother. The writing, I am still thinking about it and wanting it to be more real. It feels like, yeah, it was hard to write it, it was hard to write that, even though it was hard to write that and um even now it feels like it's not real, like there is some grittiness to it. It feels like I am a bit distant from it.

Isha: When you were talking about the beatings to me, did you feel distant from it? Do you know why you actually brought it into your counselling sessions?

Jacinta: Um, (laugh) I think I was quite focused on the novel at that time and it felt like a particular part that I have had experience of. I can't remember if I felt distant in here but I don't know that I particularly pursued it or whether there was a gap and I went on to other things and came back again.

Addressing internalised oppression

Jacinta referred to a point in her therapy where we integrated some cushion work to help her locate powerful feelings that had previously remained hidden. It was my speculation that these hidden powerful feelings were the residue of internalised oppression and racial oppression. Alleyne (2005) addresses the intrusive and invisible nature of racial oppression:

> Much has been written about internalized oppression...which is the process of absorbing the values and beliefs of the oppressor and coming to believe that the stereotypes and misinformation about one's group is true (or partly true). Such a process can lead to low self-esteem, self-hate, the disowning of one's group, and other complex defensive behaviours in relation to one's group. Although this concept has been fully explicated in the works of the aforementioned writers, only a few...have dealt specifically with the concept of the oppressor within ourselves – the internal oppressor and black identity. Prejudices, projections, inter-generational wounds and the vicissitudes from our historical past are all aspects of this inner tyrant – the internal oppressor. They are kept alive through the transgenerational transmission of trauma. (p. 295)

The next question, about working sensitively with the internal oppressor, means placing theory aside to be with clients in the emotions of their black issues.

How can a therapist acknowledge the impact of negative archetypal influences in a non-theoretical, therapeutic way?

The impact of negative archetypal influences is likely to be unconscious and must be approached in a non-theoretical way. Although it is essential to the understanding of the therapeutic process, theory about black Western archetypes is proposed as a contextual framework for black issues; it is not intended to be quoted to clients. Wilson (1993) addresses this context:

> The appropriate reclamation of Afrikan history and culture will provide Afrikans with a realistic and supportive vision of reality, with self knowledge, self esteem, self confidence, self acceptance, and self control; with the ability to form empowering affectionate relationships. (p. 114)

Wilson's use of the word 'appropriate' is important here, for consideration should be given to the knowledge base from which the therapist responds. The therapist's cultural experiences and consciousness of the way archetypal influences affect relationships is essential background knowledge. A theory-based response may be useful only in explaining concepts such as internalised racism to help clients understand how they defend against or cope with oppressions. I have occasionally asked clients whether they are familiar with this term and discovered that its use assists them to understand their process and feel an empathic connection. In my discussion with Jacinta, naming the process of internalisation helped her knowledge base of the relational process, which became key to repairing her relationships. Informing clients appropriately can engage therapists. Jung (1970) proposes that archetypes be exposed. This approach can be applied to black Western archetypes and help to demystify the power dynamics of the therapeutic relationship. Ideas to support an answer to the following question about the process of black Western archetypes can be gleaned from the next part of the review with Jacinta.

How can therapists assist transformation from negative black Western archetypes to positive ones?

It is important to understand and expose the dynamics, conflicts and representations that negative archetypes can produce. Therapists can introduce the concept of black Western archetypes into their supervision and use opportunities to explore the process of their own issues and archetypal conflicts as a parallel process to their work with clients. Jacinta found it supportive to engage in a discussion about parallel process in her novel writing. This seemed to reveal the unconscious impact of negative archetypes and her internalised racism.

Isha: But what it says to me is that although it had been raised in here several times, you were also raising it in what you were doing outside, in your own personal life and your writing, one of your passions, but you were raising it in the sense of it being someone else in the novel.

Jacinta: Yeah, yeah.

Isha: So I am wondering if there was a link between us working on it and you writing it about.

Jacinta: Well I, (sigh) I can only say generally that now the bubble feels like it's er, you know I would have said that there was no autobiographical information or incidents in there. If you had asked me two years ago I would have said that the autobiographical material was very minimal. Now I am still working with it, it feels like quite a big

chunk of it is autobiographical. So I think we explore in here but it also comes through in my writing. The two are very interlinked.

Isha: It's all from inside

Jacinta: Yeah, yeah.

Isha: So what is it like realising that through the work we have done some of your writing appears autobiographical?

Jacinta: (Laugh) Well I was surprised that I didn't see it earlier. Although I would say that I did not want to see it earlier. You know you hear the clichés about people's first novels being about their experience and I wanted to ignore my experience. So it's still a surprise to see how much of it is from my own experience or to do with family or near experience.

Isha: So you are no longer as distant from it as you were feeling at the time.

Jacinta: No, yeah, yeah.

Isha: It sounds like you are more living it now. The two have come together in some way. It's come close and it's real.

Jacinta: I would say I acknowledge and accept it. I guess I wanted the writing to be more distant and it wasn't, but also I wanted it to bring more out of me.

Isha: What has brought more out of you?

Jacinta: Well the discussions we have had and you know this thing particularly around the beatings and hiding from that in this situation and the violence of that situation, putting it on the sidelines and trivialising. These sessions have brought it more fully to my, (pause) I can see it more and I can feel it more and see how it still connects to my thought processes, my fears about doing things and not doing things.

I have signified how important it is for therapists to engage clients in discussions that connect with the influence of history and disempowering defences. In Jacinta's therapy I challenged the way she trivialised her experience of beatings and offered a space for her to understand the defence system she had built around this. The following question, proposed in relation to black issues, invites discussion about the development of understanding when processing defences.

How can therapists understand denial, defensiveness and re-enactment of oppressive patterns?

As Wilson (1993) suggests, we must be clear that ignorance, shame and the unconscious play an important role in oppressive patterns:

> Simply because we choose to forget a traumatic event, simply because we choose not to learn of a traumatic history and a history that made us feel ashamed, does not mean that history is not controlling our behaviour. Simply because we don't know our history, and may not have heard of it, does not mean that history does not control our behaviour. One of the most powerful things that we have learned in psychology is that the most powerful forces that shape human behaviour are those factors that are consciously not remembered by human beings, that are unknown to the person, are those experiences that the individual can swear s/he never had. (p. 4)

Jung's (1970) work on the collective unconscious is helpful in understanding how negative archetypes can be internalised as defences and passed on from person to person – that is, by white people to each other and among black people of both African and Asian heritage; also between black and white people. He uses the image of a trickster to describe this process: 'The trickster is a collective shadow figure, a summation of all the inferior traits of character in individuals which sometimes appear as a corresponding projection on other social groups and nations' (p. 150).

When Jung informs us about the trickster archetype he reminds us that we are subjects of a collective 'shadow', which becomes personalised. The collective shadow, an archetype in itself, disintegrates under the impact of civilisation. Conflict occurs when symbols cross from the unconscious to the conscious and, apparently, fragments of the collective shadow get left behind in the unconscious. These fragments can become transferred into folklore and remain disguised. Archetypes are portrayed in folklore, myths and fairytales. They are often reflected in carnival images and mythical characters in African history. Wilson (1993) discusses the personal aspect of mythology:

> Mythology often can be seen as a form of denial of reality. If memory is too painful to be recalled, if recalling it means suffering pain, shame, guilt and other negative things, the individual may not only deny the reality of that memory and experience but may actually create a mythology in their place. (p. 28)

In Caribbean folklore, mythical characters such as *Douens* portray the transference of good and evil in cultural belief systems. *Douens* are said to be the spirits of children who have died before being baptised. They live in the forests. They have neither sex distinctions nor faces, and their feet are turned 'before behind'. They wear large straw hats and wear their hair in the current 'Rasta' style, with long plaits. They raid the neighbouring gardens for young corncobs, a special delicacy. Although they live in the forest, they come out to the villages, especially on moonlit nights, and lure children away when they come out to play in the moonlight (Ottley, 1979, p. 20). This interpretation of *Douens* is affected by religious archetypes of good and evil. The *Douens* character can be seen to represent the negative parts of adult emotion that project evil into the deceased unbaptised child or a means of controlling the wayward child who must be home before dark.

Like the *Douens* character, negative images and hatred reflected through racism onto others have been used to control and demean ethnic groups. Jung (1970) explains 'the shadow' of the inferior traits of others perpetrated in a trickster style like the *Douens* character. The trickster archetype can be associated with the experience of internalised oppression, and more specifically internalised racism. Black Western archetypes can be likened to the trickster as they act like an unconscious personality emanating from the hurt of the past. The original personality has eroded, and the stereotypical trickster re-appears via negative images of the self, which are reproduced over time in a multifaceted way.

Examples of these negative images are recreated in the stereotyping of black people portrayed as Golliwogs, laughing musicians with rolling eyes and gleaming teeth, cannibals and the tropical seductress. Hurtful rhymes and riddles such as 'Eenie meanie minee mo, catch a nigger by his toe, if he hollers let him go, eenie meanie minee mo' are examples of negativity interjected during my own childhood, because during that period they were culturally sanctioned.

Projection and internalisation of these images can create a developmental crisis within the minds of both black and white people and become characteristic of conformity to white supremacy. Whereas the white Westernised psyche copes with this crisis by normalising negative images, the process of negative identification and internalisation can create an identity crisis in black individuals.

Many black people continuously strive to maintain confidence in the face of these negative images. Some are aware of the damaging effects, whereas others unknowingly operate their lives as though these projections belong to them. Striving against the impact of these black Western archetypes is a constant drain on individuals whether they are conscious or unaware of them. Therapists can assist clients to understand denial and defences associated with these strivings.

Exposing black Western archetypes

Isha: So what is the impact of this work?

Jacinta: Well I recently did another talk in front of a big group of people. Now if I think about when I was four or five and I think I talked to you about wanting to hide behind doors from strangers passing our front yard and wanting to run inside and hide. Well you know that kind of hiding was you know for me was, I didn't feel, I felt like I had no right to be here, I had no right to be here. I needed to pretend I didn't exist. So I can see now where I can stand before people, people who I don't particularly know, and say more about myself and show myself more and my experience of myself. So that's an example of me kinda coming out a bit more in the world definitely and the writing as well. And just, I don't know just more of an appreciation of accepting who I am and just being in the world.

Isha: Can I ask, I mean you mentioned between the age of four and five, was that the only time you remember being beaten, at that age? (Long pause)

Jacinta: No, I don't remember the times; I remember a particular time when we were beaten, but I think I was older. (Laugh) It was a dangerous thing we were doing. We had a bathroom extension and our bedroom was on the lower half of this roof and we were sitting outside on the window sill pretending to be fishing on the roof. I remember my dad caught us. I don't remember the beating but we did. As I said I more remember my mum beating us, I don't remember my dad doing it so often, or at all. But I always associate her doing that with um, just the injustice of it. It just felt like she didn't listen to, (pause) one time I remember getting beaten was because our room was untidy. Yeah being beaten just because our room was untidy. That felt minor. (Laugh)

Isha: It seems to me that from what you said to me that after you had been beaten there was an aftermath.

Jacinta: Yeah 'cos if like it happened in the bedroom it was like embarrassing, it was shameful to have been beaten, then you would come down and go into a situation where everybody seemed not to notice that it had happened. They ignored you and would kind of look at you.

Isha: And that seemed to have affected the patterns in your life in terms of being out there and acknowledging yourself to people.

Jacinta: Well if I was being beaten and started to cry, if I was scream-ing and whatever the sound I was making and mum would say 'If you don't stop I will give you something to cry for', so it was always, well it's like I have this pain and I am crying because of this pain, but obvi-ously I shouldn't have this pain because you have just threatened me but I shouldn't show it. And to show anger towards her, that was also a no-no. You shouldn't show well anger towards your parents and resentment towards your parents because then you would be pun-ished again. If you showed any signs of rebelling or kicking against their authority, well that was squashed, crushed. So yes, so my way of dealing with things that were painful was never to show it, was never to let other people know that I felt like that. Kept it all in, kept it all down, and squashed it.

Isha: Do you remember any other particular circumstances in your life where you remember doing that and you just didn't show it when something was hurting you.

Jacinta: Well you know in my early teens there was my parent's divorce or first it was their separation. You know well, I didn't let them know about that. Well they were going on with their own stuff as well, but it didn't feel like it was a kinda safe place in which to express the sadness, the disappointment and the pain of them separating, because it was a very painful separation. And also with my mum and finding out who my father was. Her denial that he existed for lots of years I'd ask her every now and again and she would deny it. My not wanting to push to find out because it felt like it was painful for her and it would raise pain for me. So I kept asking her every now and again, but I wouldn't particularly act on it or push too much.

Isha: Do you think the beatings had anything to do with not pushing too much as well? You said you were aware of pain and feelings towards your mum.

Jacinta: Um, well you know I, by the time I started asking her we hardly were getting beatings at all.

Isha: What age were you then?

Jacinta: Well about thirteen, fourteen or fifteen kind of age.

Isha: You were forming your own identity.

Jacinta: (Pause) Well sort of yeah, (laugh) I didn't particularly see myself with any identity at all. (Laugh) There is a fear attached to that sort of difficulty, showing my mum difficult things or things I find painful or that I am angry about. It's very difficult for me to express that anger towards her. Yeah, I'm sure that beatings had something to do with it. But you asked about was I forming my individual identity, well that involved sexuality. That involved, but again, even those pleasurable things, they were kept back or the potential of those pleasurable things, they were kept back. I didn't want to be rejected or feel that other people didn't want me. It was always squashed back, they were kept back. My mum was someone who said that if you go out with boys you would get pregnant, so sex was not particularly healthy. Also wanting to be with friends she talked about as being in bad company.

Isha: Did she know them?

Jacinta: Yes she did, but there was still that element, going out with boys and it was bound to end up in pregnancy.

Isha: Those were your teenage years.

Jacinta: Um um.

Isha: It sounds like that what you are telling me is that the beatings impacted on future relationships.

Jacinta: Um yeah, yeah, (laugh) with anybody.

Isha: And your friendships as well.

Jacinta: I don't know if that particularly is because of the beatings or because of my character, that I would only show certain aspects of myself towards my friends. You know I became a good listener. I would encourage them to talk, but not show myself. I wanted to keep their friendship. The way to keep their friendship was not to show myself. I think the thing with the beatings was that my mum felt like she was the centre of my universe really. She was the person that I was dependent upon and beating felt like rejection. Afterwards I wanted to get her approval back. Get something back, not have this wedge between us. I did not want to face rejection from anyone.

Isha: That theme of rejection and not showing yourself seems to run right through your story.

THE BLACK WESTERN ARCHETYPE 109

Jacinta: Um um, and I do remember us talking about you know, I used to, before the teens try and suss out how mum was and mould my behaviour according to how she was. So if she looked pissed off, I would not piss her off, or if she was irritated, I would try not to irritate her. I kinda took it on board that it must be something to do with me, why she was er. (Laugh)

Isha: Why she was angry.

Jacinta: (Laugh) Yeah, yeah, yeah, but you know I tried to mould my behaviour according to how she was.

Isha: You had bad feelings inside when she was unhappy.

Jacinta: Yeah, yeah, and there is a feeling of wanting to protect her.

Isha: Is that feeling there now?

Jacinta: Oh you know, that idea of trying to express my anger and resentment there is always that element of being disloyal, or if I say to you, in my head it feels like a disloyalty to say anything negative, and that is still the case even though I will say it.

Isha: And is it because you are saying this to me or just because you are saying it and it could be to anyone?

Jacinta: It could be to anyone.

Isha: So has it then remained a kind of a secret?

Jacinta: What?

Isha: What happened to you with the beatings?

Jacinta: What, to my mother?

Isha: No a secret for you. You haven't spoken much about it before you spoke to me.

Jacinta: Yeah, it's come up through our contact, 'cos I did do counselling before and I don't think I mentioned much about that situation. The counsellor was very good, but he was white and he was male; that was why I wanted a person of colour.

Overcoming internalised racism

Isha: So you think there is something about me being a black woman that has assisted you.

Jacinta: Yeah, yeah, very much so.

Isha: Do you want to say what it was that I said or did that was about me being a black woman?

Jacinta: Before I knew you I guess I thought there would be more of a common experience if I went to a black woman for counselling. I don't know if that is particularly true, because I read your book about 'Searching for Mr McKenzie'. I think I liked that book because it was about a search for a father. That was one of the things I wanted to look at. But there is this thing about if you mention about violence within the black family, within a white context or outside of a black conference it seems to be open to being stereotyped. So it feels like I am not always free to say what I really want to say. That's another thing that kinda stops me from saying what happened. Coming here and you actually teasing it out and you, by saying that this situation does matter. It's always been there and I keep coming back, keep coming back to it in our sessions, but also trying to trivialise it and make it some minor experience. Well again it's a common experience to lots of black people I know and they seem to be alright with it you know, the usual saying that well 'I had it but it didn't do me any harm'. It felt like I am making a bigger issue of it than it is and highlighting it more than it really needs. But through these sessions it has come through repeatedly even though I say it's trivial. In these sessions I have known that it is a big issue for me and that it needs to be acknowledged. I have started to acknowledge it.

Informing and educating

As Jacinta became more aware of her defences and process of internalised racism, I became more aware of the archetypal elements in her story: the cowering, being silenced by beatings that affected her close relationships, her silent tears and holding the pain inside. I became more aware of my role as a kind of messenger reflecting black issues from my own experiences and learning that these were useful to her process. This raised a concern similar to the one addressed in the next question.

Is it the therapist's job to inform or educate a client about black Western archetypes?

One could ask whether therapy has an educational function. The therapist has a responsibility to engage clients in a process of self-understanding, self-awareness and self-change; this is education. If it is the therapist's job to respond to the client's story, relationship patterns and life processes, then understanding the impact of black Western archetypes intrinsically becomes part of this process. Leifer stresses:

> An Afrikan-centered educative approach in addition to defining and designating certain states of consciousness and forms of behaviour relative to the needs of Afrikan peoples must engage the client in full analysis…The participant in Afrikan centered therapeutic and educational encounters discovers how he has been unconsciously conditioned by a Eurocentric system to respond habitually and unthinkingly to its social cues to Eurocentric authorities and social context which induce him 'to perceive, think, feel, and behave in certain ways'…. (Leifer, qtd. in Wilson, 1993)

Wilson goes on to suggest that 'a Eurocentric consciousness displaces and represses, imposes on its Afrikan hosts the dream states of sleepwalkers and somnambulistic wanderers in the dark of night' (p. 111). The next part of the review highlights my efforts to assist Jacinta to awaken to the reality of her unconscious conditioning – as Wilson puts it, to awaken her from her 'dream state'.

Isha: *I remember when you told me that you were concerned about giving it (the beatings) attention because you have friends who have said that beatings have not done them any harm. I remember that I said that you are not your friends and asked what did it mean for you? I remember there was a little difficulty because I challenged you for trivialising your own situation and even though you were bringing it you were not giving it much time.*

Jacinta: Yes let's move onto the next thing, (laugh) but yeah if I keep bringing it back so obviously it means much more than I give it credit for.

Isha: *Even now I can feel how sensitive the issue is and how important it was for me to connect with you, it seems, as a black woman on this issue. What you said to me about beatings being common in black families, I know that. It is knowledge that I bring to my experience as a counsellor, but hearing you now confirms that my knowledge of that has been important. Not just my knowledge of a stereotype, but also allowing it to be something that we explore.*

Jacinta: Yeah, yeah.

Healing black family relationships

Isha: I am also remembering that when I used the term abuse it had a big impact on you.

Jacinta: (Laugh) Yeah, yeah, 'cos that such a very strong word. Again at the time I would say it did not describe me. I am not one of those NSPCC children or the children you see occasionally on the television or in my work. But also just thinking about the use of that word, well maybe it does apply to me. The other thing is thinking about my mother she has both elements; she is a lot more complex than I want to make her. (Laugh) I want to make her simple, to be loving always, I don't want her to be this other side which is aggressive, violent, or I can't quite acknowledge that all the time or settle with these two kind of extremes of being with her. But I do feel like that when I apply that there has been abuse and violence done to me, then it feels like I am accepting my experience but I am also accepting my mum as she is. I am not trying to idealise her, I am making her more real and making my experience more real for myself. That can only be good 'cos if I keep denying that even though I have not talked to her about her abuse, our relationship has got better. Through our counselling sessions I feel at some point I could talk to her, whereas there was no way I felt that I could approach her. There is now the possibility of me opening to questioning her or finding out more about her own experience. Hopefully maybe at some point it won't come out as blame, it will be something to explore as well.

Isha: It sounds as though your listening skills have developed as well. Through this experience you feel more able to listen to your mother without the pain getting in the way and that will benefit you. You will have a closer connection.

Jacinta: Yeah, yeah, we will have a fuller relationship definitely. You know the fact that I can talk more about my father that has come out of these sessions as well. There is still the fear of hurting her but not the rejection so much. She hasn't you know, my experience of her is that she has not rejected me despite different things I have been through and she has been through. She has not rejected me. Yes there is a lot more possibility.

Isha: How does it feel looking back on this journey today?

Jacinta: I just feel richer all these things I have been pushing away or squashing down. My life is more interesting. You know my sense of being myself is more interesting. It's not such a sense of dryness, more colour. I just feel fuller.

Isha: I remember in your final sessions you were talking about noticing the colour and the brightness outside a lot more as if something had suddenly opened.

Jacinta: Um I was thinking the other day my anxiety is about will I end up alone and all that business? But now I feel if I can go through life and have an open heart that has become as important. You know not being closed down and I think that if I can achieve that, if I can stay open that would be great.

Isha: Are there any other significant points in our relationship that have really worked for you?

Jacinta: There is the point that I feared that I wasn't interesting enough for these sessions, to come to you. The anxiety of not being listened to. I feel like I can bring anything now. The fact that we talked about it helped.

Isha: That was a point where we were connecting about what was going on between us.

Jacinta: Yeah, yeah, (laugh) we talked about my concerns that you might be bored. Talking about that helped to draw me more in.

Isha: I was wondering whether it was significant that I just waited for a particular time. I remember at one stage and this was to do with the boredom thing, I decided to want you to address things and bring things. In the early days you seemed to want me to give you ideas what to do and take the lead. I remember at one stage addressing that and saying that 'it's down to you', which you seemed a bit uncomfortable with. I haven't done much of that, but when I have done it's had quite an impact. It's sort of, in a sense letting you know that you are the one who is powerful. You can decide to show yourself without me having to draw it out of you.

Jacinta: (Laugh) Yeah and you know these sessions, I have wanted you to, I don't know if you call it giving away your power or something, but wanting it to be someone else, you to draw me out. You used to say that I am talking about my mum when she couldn't always come for me at school. That sense of wanting someone to come for me instead of always going to them. Yeah, I have always wanted that, but here (laugh) every now and then you reminded me that I am autonomous and I have to bring myself in. These sessions are about not hiding.

Isha: *That was also significant of the work we done together, about not hiding.*

Jacinta: **Yeah, yeah.**

Summary of review

Jacinta's story demonstrates the possibility of working therapeutically with the dualities of internalised oppression and assisting black clients to develop psychologically nurturing concepts of what it means to be black.

Using an integrative, transcultural framework that included knowledge of the historical context of African Caribbean families and the concept of black Western archetypes helped my understanding of Jacinta's situation. Jacinta was impacted by her mother's secretiveness and violence towards her. As a result of this she hid from adults as a child and felt unable to show affection to her female partner (ancestral baggage). She was writing a novel that featured a child being beaten, and through her therapy became conscious that her own experience was embedded in her writing (black Western archetype). She suffered denial of her birth father and a negative gaze from her stepfather, coupled with the pain of the beatings. Being ignored by the family and the burden of shame and embarrassment caused her to believe that she 'had no right to be here'. Having no right to be here is also a symptom of internalised racism, a trickster of the black Western archetype.

In Jung's (1970) terms, together we 'exposed' the archetypes. As her therapist I held out the challenge of her ability to show herself to me without any threat to her physical or emotional being. This included sensitivity towards her as a black woman. Shame and embarrassment related to her past were tentatively acknowledged during the interview, and she confirmed that my ability to reflect the significance of the beatings was important in her therapy. Holding out hope of her empowerment and ability to develop the role of initiator in the intimate communication between us as adults and as two black women played a significant part in her recovery. Her low self-esteem and difficulties in her relationship with her mother, her lover and herself were repaired. I have listed below some therapeutic pointers from the review with Jacinta. These pointers can be considered when understanding a therapeutic process using concepts such as internalised oppression and the impact of black Western archetypes.

Conclusion

Black Western archetypes within the collective psyche perpetuate models and mythologies of the colonial era. Black families may either support these models or continually struggle to avert them. It is therefore necessary to process racial stereotypes and internalised racism in the here and now and transcend to a deeper level of awareness and communication about them.

Sameness can often be taken for granted when we work with the contradictions of diversity. By presenting a review of Jacinta's therapeutic process, I have shown that black therapists are challenged to work with the contradictions of our shared experiences, particularly our experience of racism, while acknowledging our differences and our responsibilities as professionals. Trainees' questions have been explored in the context of the discussion with Jacinta. It is hoped that therapists using Eurocentric models to develop their understanding of black issues in the therapeutic process can gain ideas for their own work. We are challenged to pay attention to the pain and disempowerment behind the impact of racism. The process of exploring this problematic dynamic can be recognised across and within other diversities, such as gender, sexuality and ability.

The concept of black Western archetypes has been offered as a means of understanding how racism as a cultural phenomenon imposes itself on the psyche. In describing the therapeutic process with Jacinta, I have referred several times to the relevance of the gaze and its implicit link to ancestral baggage. It is my hope that the intention behind a negative gaze can be deflected and that a distorted mirror can be reframed.

Pointers for therapists (including trainees and trainers)

- Provide the opportunity for clients to choose an appropriately experienced, gender-, race- and sexuality-aware therapist.
- Develop an understanding of intersecting oppressions such as homophobia, racism and gender oppression.
- Become informed about the impact of heritage and cultural history influenced by slavery and colonialism.
- Be willing to address and process the transferred dynamics between therapist and client and use the process to empower the client.
- Gain an understanding of archetypal stereotypes that may be re-enacted within the black client's behaviour.

- Accept difference or similarity between client and counsellor in a non-collusive dialogue.
- Sensitively challenge the client to explore his or her upbringing in the context of his or her cultural background and living in Britain.
- Gain knowledge of and work with an understanding of interracial, inter-gender and same-race and same-gender experiences that affect the therapeutic relationship.
- Be prepared to explore social oppression, family oppression, internalised oppression and oppression within same-sex and opposite-sex relationships.

6

Cultural Schizophrenia

Following on from the concept of black Western archetypes in Chapter 5, this chapter introduces the concept of 'cultural schizophrenia' as an offshoot of the mental health label 'schizophrenia'. I relate to this concept as a discourse linked to the silence of institutions that compounds the experience of mental distress and the multiple challenges faced by black people caught in the revolving door of the mental health system. I am using the term 'cultural schizophrenia' with reference to the unconscious or conscious splitting-off of communication about black issues. In the context of mental health professionals and trainers and trainees in counselling and psychotherapy, I am viewing cultural schizophrenia as though it is an unseen institutional phenomenon that ultimately silences the clients themselves. Although this is a two-way problem, in that every individual learns to set up his or her own survival systems, the institutions of psychotherapy and psychiatry must be more aware of cultural exclusions and work to eliminate them.

Watson (2004), in her research on the training experiences of black counsellors, found that '[m]any of the counsellors used silence as a means of "survival" and as a way of escaping from the racism they perceived in their training group work' (p. 43). I am familiar with silence as a means of survival. It is common in my work as a counsellor trainer and in my own withholding in times of fear. In addition to my early experiences of abandonment, my silence is like a watchful gatekeeper over the impact of racism as I have learned to protect myself. I must therefore experience a willing listener, someone tuned in to my cultural dilemmas and oppressions who can help reinforce my own process of finding a voice.

As an example of cultural schizophrenia I present a discussion with Angela, who experienced a mental health crisis and found gaps in the responses from health professionals. Her story epitomises a kind of cultural schizophrenia within mental health professions. As a result of this, her experiences are compartmentalised. In the first part of the discussion Angela focuses on her mental health experiences and treatment.

In the second part she shares her background experience as an African Caribbean woman. The following question indicates that this trainee counsellor is curious about the history of black people in contact with the mental health system.

In the past why were black people not offered counselling and instead sent to mental institutions and put on medication?

Over the past fifty years, concern has been growing about the over-representation of black people in the mental health system (Fernando, 1988; Kareem and Littlewood, 1992; Moodley and Palmer, 2006). Many black people were detained under section 137 of the 1983 Mental Health Act. This Act gave police permission to arrest anyone who appeared disorderly in a public place if the police suspected that he or she was in mental distress. Many individuals detained under this Act were diagnosed as 'schizophrenic' and remained in psychiatric care for long periods. Overuse of these laws produced concerns about misinterpretation of cultural expression and misdiagnosis of black psychiatric patients resulting in institutional racism. I would therefore suggest that institutional racism is a component of cultural schizophrenia.

Angela, a middle-aged African Caribbean woman who came to Britain from Grenada, was admitted into psychiatric hospital twenty-five times over a period of thirty years. Diagnosed as schizophrenic, she was given electric shock treatment and medication. Angela discusses her fears of Obeah (which I discuss below), her faith in God and how she continues to survive a system that she feels has never really listened to her experiences as an African Caribbean woman in Britain. Some questions presented by trainee counsellors are responded to by modelling a discussion with Angela. During the discussion I become aware that Angela, a first-generation settler, does not raise the issue of being a black woman in Britain. With my support she finds her cultural voice. Angela uses poetry to share some of her experiences and her relationships with her doctors, supporters and peers. In the following poem she reflects on how it all started:

My Fate. By Angela

I wish to share my fate with you today
And hope it wouldn't put you out of the way
For many of us have trod this way before
But look now I can assure you not too far to go

I suffered depression in an acute way
In and out of hospital, I couldn't stay
Until my confidence was taken away
But God was with me day by day

Now I am here today my dears to share
My success story in a quiet way
So don't give up the battle I hope you'll agree
Because we can get rid of this dreadful malady

Mine happened 21 years ago you see
When my marriage broke up I had to flee
Three children to bring up on my own you know?
That took some doing, I was on the go! Go! Go!

Before I realized I ended up in hospital
The doctors couldn't find my cause
To treat my illness it took some years
With hard work and bitter tears

Look now I am a living example to all
A slip is not a fall, get up and crawl
Crawl to your feet 'cause we're not weak
God will do the rest, just do your best

Angela: I have been into psychiatric hospital over twenty-five times in thirty years.

Isha: When was the first time?

Angela: The first time was nineteen seventy-one.

Isha: What did they offer you?

Angela: They just gave me tablets and I would have done much better and had less relapses if I had counselling. I had a little counselling in the later stages, about three months with a psychologist and a month with my GP's wife. That was the time I was in hospital for six months. I was in a depression. The doctors gave up on me. They had given me electric shock treatment and they told me they have done everything. The CPN [community psychiatric nurse] and social worker gave up on me. During that time we had a meeting every morning with the other patients and the doctors where we could talk and say what we feel. Then an Indian doctor called Herbie said he could take me on. He worked with me and we talked for a few weeks and it helped. One of my biggest fears was Obeah. He explained it as an influence that the person had on me. I was in a quandary not knowing much about Obeah whether to believe that this had happened to me. That put me on a guideline that if it is just an influence then that could be different. It was the stress of my marriage that brought this on.

What is Obeah?

Angela refers to the influence of Obeah, an African spiritual practice that has been something of a taboo subject in the Western world. Although Obeah is akin to Shamanism, Westerners sometimes view Obeah as though it were the shadow side of healing, as its powerful magic can be imposed on someone to affect their well-being and life situation. I have worked with several African and Caribbean clients who have expressed concern about the negative effects of Obeah on them, as though they have been punished or cursed. Richards (1992) offers some perspective on the experience of Obeah:

> Obeah reflected the unnatural state of slavery; evil fighting evil. But it also reflected the African belief in spiritual priorities, spiritual realities, spiritual relationship, and the intimate connection between spirit and matter. Out of the context of the traditional order, discipline, and morality, African religion often became distorted, less communal in nature, and characterized by more frequent use of spiritual powers to serve personal ends. ... Its use by us against our own can only be controlled when we create viable and harmonious African societies, in which the slave order no longer predominates. (p. 17)

Isha: So where did you get your information about Obeah?

Angela: I was brought up hearing about it. My husband and mother-in-law threatened me at the time that they would do me in, you see. Then I learned that he sent my garments down to his mother and the mother and a neighbour did whatever they do. So that is what triggered me off. So I felt convinced at the time. Even up to now I am not sure, and I think oh no this thing can't take me, because it could have been the stress of my marriage.

Isha: So you were not sure whether it was the stress of the marriage or Obeah?

Angela: Even now, I still, I can't, I can't, naa this ting can't take me. Yet when I am ill I am convinced it is happening, for the experiences that I have when I am ill. The experience is demonic.

Isha: What kind of experiences? Can you describe them?

Angela: I get very paranoid. The television will be speaking about me. Thank goodness in a way. What the telly is saying, it is not frightening it is good things. I think, how could the telly know this about me? I could see myself in the programme. I think, is there a camera around? And that sort of thing. But mainly, because I was brought up as a Christian, my performances are more religiously based. I get extremely religious to the extent where I actually cast out demons out of the other patients in the hospital. This is what is lacking in the mental health, time and attention; it is such a stigma to this illness. You counted as nothing. You are just there. They are keeping you alive, by giving you food. They make sure that you have a tablet. They used to wake us up to give us Mogadon, sleeping tablets. Eleven o'clock you dead asleep and they wake you up to make you sleep.

Isha: (Laugh) That's crazy.

Angela: So we used to laugh at these things. But I had a lot of fun in the hospital as well. When I get the giggles, you know when I am on one of my highs, laughing and joking and things. One of the roles I played when I am ill was a nurse. I used to go around nursing all the others and they leave me to it. One thing I wasn't happy about, they used to separate me from the others.

Isha: Do you know why?

Angela: Because I was too sensible. The sister would say, we need you here but please come as a visitor, not as a patient. They did a risky thing they would ask me to hand drugs to the others. They would say, be careful of John, he is schizophrenic.

Isha: Is that what they told you about yourself?

Angela: No, the first diagnosis was schizophrenia, but I discovered from other schizes that I wasn't. Then they decided that I am manic-depressive. I am manic-depressive but lately I don't get lows any more, I get highs.

Isha: You get highs.

Angela: Yea but it was the opposite in the initial stage. I go right down to rock bottom and there was no alternative but to come back up, you know, to the core of my being. I tried to throw myself in front of a car in Marylebone road, but I really had lost track of reality. I was really gone. At the time I decided to try rolling in front of the traffic. I was seeing people and I thought I was the only one in the world.

I thought God! I can't live on me own like this, no one to give me food, nobody to open their door to me. That is what was in my thoughts. So I thought I better go and join wherever the others are.

Talking about treatment

Angela's experiences of hopelessness and hitting rock bottom meant that she relied on medication to keep her safe. Discussions about medication with clients can be supportive. Most of my black clients reported not knowing why they were on medication and had felt unable to question and explore their treatment. Not discussing treatment can further disempower mental health clients and perpetuate silences, adding to a client's mental health oppression and the discourse of cultural schizophrenia.

Isha: Were you on medication at that time?

Angela: Yes I was. I had the depo injection Thursday and Saturday, I still end up in hospital. They took me off that, it seems as though these things didn't work anymore. I had a slight one a couple of weeks ago. I was in hospital a couple of weeks ago, I had a slight one and they put me on lithium. So that's what I am on now.

Isha: So does lithium work for you?

Angela: Well I have just been on it for a couple of weeks, we will see, it's supposed to keep a balance. I was happy with what I was on anyway. Amphetamines and Stelozene.

Isha: They are not supposed to keep you on the same medication for too long are they?

Angela: They never review me that is another thing again, lacking. They never review me for years you know you just go repeating prescriptions. There is so much they need to pick up on.

Isha: So when you first went into hospital, they told you that you were schizophrenic, but they didn't offer you any counselling or other therapies.

Angela: No. Nothing, nothing.

Isha: How long after this did they give you electric shock treatment?

Angela: About ten years later.

Isha: Why did they decide to offer you that treatment?

Angela: Because of the depression. I only had three, and then they stopped. They never give me any explanation as to why they stopped. Even this present doctor asked me why they stopped the lithium and I couldn't answer. I just went along with them.

Isha: So they didn't explain it to you?

Angela: Nothing, no explanation. They tried me on many other tablets. Those days I was naïve and I didn't know what was happening to me. I just go along with what the doctors say and just gave myself over to them.

Disempowerment

The disempowering nature of a mental health diagnosis can be compounded by cultural schizophrenia. In Angela's situation, she is unaware because she has 'no explanation' about her medication, so she goes along with things. Like many mental health patients, she feels incarcerated by the diagnosis, by the institution and by the medication, yet this is her place of refuge. Cultural schizophrenia is functioning as the institution withholds information, and Angela becomes unconsciously silenced, adding to her silence as a black woman.

Isha: Can I ask you what age you were when this was happening?

Angela: Thirty-three.

Isha: You were very young and at no time at all did they offer you any alternative.

Angela: No, nothing. What helped at the time was when I went to the group. I used to take over the group, because no one else would talk. They were that ill and withdrawn and afraid to talk up. After the meeting they would say to me that I talked for them.

Isha: So you were helping them?

Angela: I was helping them indirectly. I gained therapy for helping the geriatrics. The sister would ask me to go for this patient, hand this to that one.

Isha: So when they gave you electric shock treatment did they ask your consent?

Angela: No I heard from the other patients that it worked for them. But there was no explanation about it. They gave me three and just stopped. I don't know if it was the anaesthetic that was harmful.

Isha: What was it like when you had it?

Angela: You don't feel anything. You are a bit numb and forgetful when you come out of the anaesthetic.

Isha: Why did they give it to you three times?

Angela: I don't know. They didn't say in advance whether you were given a course. No explanation, you are just, you know, you are just there. I brought myself to where I am today. I must give myself the credit. I didn't just sit down waiting on them. I found ways and means of doing my own thing outside of hospital. ... About ten years ago I started up my own self-help group. There were about twelve people. We opened a bank account and we were called CRED – Christians Recovering from Emotional Distress. I used to stick posters in the paper shops. I was based at Camden Black Sisters. They gave us a room one evening a week.

Isha: What did you do?

Angela: I brought the group together. We shared experiences and organised outings to theatre shows. You know to get them out, because I know what it is like to lose motivation and everything, you don't even want to clean yourself. I experienced lying in bed for two weeks at a time, just barely sipping some tea. I sleep day and sleep night, that's how bad it was. I work two weeks and spend two weeks in bed. I don't know, my bosses really liked me to put up with that.

Isha: So when you stayed in bed for two weeks how did you end that?

Angela: I went, I used to literally feel the depression lifting, like a weight on my forehead. Then I would take little steps and force myself to get to the bathroom. Then I would cook and say at least I cook a meal for the children. Most of the days my daughters would cook for me when I was like that. Then there was a time I was really, really depressed. I used to go to the day centres and see worse ones who are really ill. You can see the distortion on their faces. I looked at myself and asked myself. What are you doing here? Just smoking and drinking coffee day in and day out. Well the labour exchange was not too far away and I decided I don't care how depressed I am, I am going to find a job. I looked on the board and I saw a job 'assistant needed' at Middlesex Hospital. I never hide my condition from them. They arranged for an interview and I told them about my history, that I suffer depression and

from time to time I need to go into hospital, so it would not be a shock. They took me on that basis. I asked them to give me a chance and they took me on. I said, 'Thank the Lord.' That helped to lift that particular depression.

A sense of empowerment

Angela attempted to re-engage with aspects of her life, as a black woman setting up a support group and finding work. During Angela's struggle to transcend her depression, she would sometimes be taken back to the security of the hospital; at other times she felt in charge of her own admissions.

Angela: They kept me on and when I was not well I stayed off and then went back. I had a nasty breakdown, one of the worse ones in 1982. I walked Marylebone Road, about a half a mile to my workplace with my nightdress on. I was sensible enough to do that. Some of the girls there, it brought tears to their eyes. My manager took me to hospital. Then I realised that I couldn't cope anymore with working, and trying to raise three children. I asked my boss for early retirement. He agreed and started the ball rolling. I got early retirement and thank God I was getting a pension from them. The first breakdown was a blessing in disguise, I got a brand new three bedroom flat in the West End, so it wasn't in vain. I benefited from my breakdown, but there was too many re-occurrence, partly due to me because once I am well, I stopped taking my medication, because I felt that I didn't need it I am fine. That was the worst mistake I have made. I had many relapses that wouldn't have happened if I had stayed on it. Now I am sensible enough to stay on it.

Isha: Do you think that you got used to the medication making you feel better, it made you stable? So if you didn't have it then you wouldn't get used to it. So when you came off it you had a relapse.

Angela: I'm not even sure that it is the thing that helps me. I think it is my will power that keeps me. When I am swallowing it, it's just to be doubly sure. I feel deep down that I could do without it and control myself. Some of the times when I go in I didn't need to go in, I just wanted to take a rest. I go to the doctor and say I am getting symptoms; I pack my suitcase and get my admission letter. Many times I took myself into hospital, all the way down to Epsom.

Although many times Angela returned to hospital care voluntarily, in the poem that follows she describes her experience of compulsory detainment:

The Charter Clinic Hotel (Chelsea).
By Angela (1995)

Little did I know if someone had told me so
That I would be placed in this paradise
The Charter Clinic you know is especially so
What a privilege in disguise
The outside of the building is not appealing
But as you step inside you would realize
It's a haven in disguise
But it's not only that
'Cause the Doctors and Nurses are wise
Even it you don't realize
They done a perfect job on me
Even when I once tried to flee
They held me down as a bully
When I tried to escape
I thought I was about to be raped
They gently took me back inside
Now I must show my gratitude
To all at the Charter Clinic Group
And hope that one good day
We all will shout a good hooray

Isha: So you took yourself and how many times have they taken you in?

Angela: Quite a few, maybe six. I have been sectioned a couple of times, because I used to run away from hospital. I used to think they are holding me here against my will and I don't want to be here so I run away. So when they get me they section me. I even try to run away from the illness and go to Scotland in a nursing home with some books and do some writing to make it go away, but it happened on the train.

Isha: What happened on the train?

Angela: Paranoia, I missed my stop and feared that I was followed. I just got off the train at the stop beyond Gleneagles and called for the

police. That was something that they commended me on, because I know when to call for help. I asked the police if they find a cure for cancer because I believe that I have a theory that will cure certain cancers. He said, 'No not yet darling.' He took me to the police station and by the time they got the minister in the nursing home to come from Gleneagles to Perth, I ran away in a field. They sent the ambulance after me and took me into hospital. I was so paranoid.

Acknowledgement of Black Issues

Angela maintains her sense of self and the multidimensional aspect of her situation. She understands that she needed specialist help. In her depression and her experience of treatment she feels supported, and yet things are done to her. It appears that she was grappling with the intersecting identities of her African Caribbean heritage, her mental health diagnosis and her role and self-esteem as a mother. The impact of cultural schizophrenia meant that these aspects of her life situation remained unsupported. The following question raised the issue of how to help with this.

How do you help with issues of identity and a sense of being black in Britain?

I am aware that Angela has chosen to share her story with me as another black woman, but she has not yet acknowledged herself as a black woman. As I sense the importance of this, I take the risk to acknowledge Angela's identity. It becomes clear that initially she denies any experience of racism. She mentions that she started a support group at the Camden Black Sisters centre, and it transpires that she is aware of her need to be understood in the context of her experiences as a black woman in Britain. She uses my prompt to talk about her early years back home in Grenada.

Isha: So do you think that was the best thing that could have happened for you to go into the hospital or do you think something else would have worked for you?

Angela: No at that time it was the right thing. A hospital is very good for me. I find my ground there. I feel secure and safe there. I look after myself, but I am treated special. In all hospitals I have been treated well. The food, the way they talk to me, as a sensible person and not an idiot walking around like a zombie.

Isha: So most of the time you were on medication or using your own kind of therapy. Do you think they treated you well as a black woman? What do think helped you in terms of you being a woman from the Caribbean.

Angela: I can't say I experienced any prejudice. There were lots of whites and blacks as well. On the whole I have never experienced it in this country. I am not denying those who have, because I have seen it happen to others. Personally no, if there were I slight it, I overlook it, I look on it as a fool. They haven't travelled; they don't know what it is like where I come from. Another thing I would like mental health to do towards black patients is to find out our background. We need black psychiatrists who know our background, for instance, when they put me on lithium and I asked to go into hospital two weeks ago, I was stressed out and I was getting a bit paranoid and I was stuck in the house on my own. It was midnight, I was in bed and the phone line jammed and I couldn't get help. I got worked up and I asked my doctor to send me in hospital so I could be well. I know I wanted to be well to travel in three weeks' time. He asked me, how are you going to get there? I said I would take a cab, so I went there. It was a Chinese man. They don't know my background, he doesn't know my personality, that they should go into. I've always been a bubbly busybody, now they taking all that and put it into one thing and say I'm manic. They leave no room for who I am and like I'm talking to you with excitement. That's me, but they go put that she is high; they leave no way to wonder what sort of person she is.

Splitting off black identity

It is clear from what Angela has revealed that as a result of cultural schizophrenia and institutional racism there has been little space for her black identity. She buries her black identity to keep safe from racism. Klein's model of psychopathology emphasised the defence of splitting in individuals as a natural approach to assigning objects into parts that are all good or all bad, in a form of denial (Davies and Bhugra, 2004). It seems that through lack of acknowledgement of her cultural background, Angela has been denying her cultural self. In her next poem she acknowledges the professionals who begin to see both sides of her:

At My Appeal (sectioned 1995).
By Angela

To you my dear Madam and Sirs
Who took the pain to listen to my cause?

I wish to say a big Thank You!
For reviewing my case and setting me free
It was a painful ordeal to sit before thee
Listen to lies that got me angry
But I kept calm as it would go against me
If I had rebounded in the panel would you agree?
Never-the-less I think of you as I would always do
Who see the both sides of the coin before you make up your mind?
To lift my ban at this terrible time
My God richly bless you three
And may his light shine upon thee
Especially the lady who sat before me
Good-bye dear Lady and Sirs
I trust this would not re-occur
THANK YOU!!

Listening to the cultural dimensions and differences among black people without homogenising can present a challenge, for it is this very homogenising that can create the conditions for cultural schizophrenia. Therapists need to approach this aspect of black issues with an open mind, so as not to perpetuate stereotyping. Curiosity about differences among black people is posed in the next question.

Is a black person born and raised fully or partly in an African/Asian society different from a black person raised in the Western world?

If we consider the differences and similarities between Jacinta (Chapter 5) and Angela, we see that they are both African Caribbean women, though they originate from different islands. Jacinta has a Jamaican heritage, but she was born and raised in England. Angela was born and raised in Grenada and came to England as an adult. They were both affected by aspects of immigration, either as first- or second-generation immigrants. They were differently impacted by their upbringing, yet both were subjected to harsh physical punishment by their parents. What they have in common is the loss of their cultural voice. Differences influenced by black people's origins cannot be taken for granted. Being open to differences in the history and cultural experiences of black people challenges cultural schizophrenia and helps to personalise their experiences. In the next part of the interview Angela shares her particular experience of growing up in the Caribbean, specifically Grenada.

Angela: I was brought up at the back of a counter. Since five years I am working, I am sixty-five now. I have sixty years of work. In Grenada as a child, after school I was behind the counter, serving customers. I do me homework on the counter. I was in Grenada for twenty years. I am always active and I have been working up until three weeks ago, so I cannot accept retirement. I am tuned in from youth. Mama was always saying, 'Eh eh too much playing, get busy, do something.' That's me.

Isha: Do you think that has anything to do with why you get so tired?

Angela: Well I don't get tired now. I am bursting with energy and I got to use it up, but if I start using it up, they say I am getting high.

Isha: They don't understand the background.

Angela: They don't understand backgrounds. That's why I say we need black psychiatrists. Some of the things they ask you about your background, how you were brought up. I wouldn't say I was a happy kid, there was happy moments, but I wasn't a happy kid, because I got a lot of beating from my parents, and names. I got a beating from my first husband, and then my father gave me such a beating in the street and humiliated me, because I had a boyfriend and I was twenty years old. Is not Obeah, is all these things pile up. Then you see I couldn't talk. From mum she would say 'shh'. They tell you what to do, but you can't answer. 'Is the yellow dress for Sunday school.' 'No I want to wear the pink one.' 'No is the yellow and that's it.' They do all your thinking for you and not allowing you to develop. You see, well poor soul. She tried her best and she just inject it into us. Sometimes I was very bitter towards her. I would say, 'You cause me to be who I am today, you partly are to blame,' but I said, 'I forgive you because you tried your best.'

Isha: So Angela, how did you get to understand that all this contributed to what happened?

Angela: Because I am a great thinker I sit and meditate and work things out mentally. How this affected me in my late thirties because I was never able to talk, I had no one to talk to and I was a chatty child, never able to say mum I am hurting. I had no one to turn to, when I am hurting, I just say my little gentle Jesus prayer and curl up. It was there festering for many years, it had to come out. What I would have liked to be a nurse and couldn't, now I am nursing people.

Isha: And that's how you are healing.

Angela: All what I wanted to be, my writing, I never knew I could write. I wanted to be like Michael Scot who I was in love with at thirteen and be first. He became a doctor; I heard he died a few years ago. Had the capacity to study, but I couldn't study because I had to sell. Before I say 'six and four ten', somebody wanted a pack of cigarettes, somebody wants a loaf of bread, so I couldn't get down to studying. I'm not a great reader. I couldn't be bothered with manuals, just show me how to work the thing. I never read a book from cover to cover. They call me scan reader, piece here and piece here I read the back and the front and I think I know what is inside.

Isha: Maybe you do. That's how I read sometimes.

Angela: I wish I would be able to read, as my daughter does.

Isha: So now you are writing.

Angela: I have written my autobiography, which needs polishing up. I have not had a very good response from three publishers that I sent it off to. So I have been advised to send it to America.

Isha: Do you think that coming to England from Grenada has something to do with how you felt, in addition to your unhappy childhood?

Angela: No that was ok. I accepted it almost immediately.

Isha: What is it that helped the women who came to your group at Camden Black Sisters?

Angela: I think because my experience was much worse than theirs.

Isha: The conclusion that you came to about the Obeah was that it didn't really happen.

Angela: Sometimes, and sometimes yes.

Isha: Did you ever go to see anybody about Obeah?

Angela: Yes, five baptised women, my husband got to do me that. That is what they told me in Trinidad.

Isha: So did he tell you what to do to turn it around?

Angela: Yes, but I wasn't sure if I believed. He took one bracelet, and he tell me he will mount it on a different bush and bath with it. And take a hops bread and put certain pepper, I think it's a chilli pepper and put it in the crossroad in early morning. I said, 'If you believe in God, then God will take care of that.' So I just throw away the bracelet

and get rid of all the paraphernalia. I say it is God or nothing. I can't be worrying with this Obeah. God is stronger, that's how I goin' now.

Isha: And a lot of this is your own inner strength.

Angela: Yes, yes. So now I tell them now, you can't harm me I am immune to these things. I been through it and I come out successful. It was when I was weak and naïve and thing. All you can't do it again.

Discussions about mental health diagnosis and treatment with black individuals can be empowering. Therapists can contribute to healing the loss of cultural voice by being aware and not colluding with denial or splitting-off of cultural background, as in Angela's situation. Spiritual and transpersonal experiences such as Obeah need to be explored from the client's viewpoint. I have no personal experience of Obeah, and although I am willing to discuss it with my clients, I am aware of my limitations in this area and I have referred clients to people who specialise in Obeah.

Why have I experienced difficulties asking my black/Asian clients about their experience of being black/Asian and how it might relate to the issues they are bringing?

Cultural schizophrenia creates loss of voice in therapists and clients, making it difficult to talk about black issues. The challenges of engaging with the racial context of therapeutic relationships are not always obvious, as they can be unconscious. It would be reasonable to associate the fears and blocks of cultural schizophrenia with the impact of black Western archetypes on the collective psyche. Responsibility for transcending this malady lies with the therapist and his or her personal development issues. Loss of voice associated with cultural schizophrenia may be linked to ways that racism can render therapists speechless. I see cultural schizophrenia as an institutional phenomenon that can permeate training. To counteract this phenomenon, the silences of cultural schizophrenia in training, supervision and personal therapy need to be broken. For Angela the consequences of not addressing silence may have compounded her mental health situation. After thirty years under the influence of cultural schizophrenia in her mental health treatment, she concludes that her discussion with me has broken the silence.

Angela: Yes, you know how long I have been trying, I tell a bit here and a bit there. We going to talk more. I get out a lot there to one person and this is a blessing to me that you know most, because this is

great what we doin' now, because nobody ever give time. The doctors don't know me, for thirty years they don't know me. They don't know all that I tell you here. No.

Isha: I think if they knew this and listened and wanted to know in the first place, you may have recovered sooner.

Angela: That's what I am saying. They don't know about people's background, they don't know what they suffer or suffering. All they know is they give you a label, you are schizophrenic, you are manic-depressive, they give you tablets.

Isha: They treat the symptom, not the cause.

Angela: Yes. That is what I am saying. If I had counselling in the initial stages, I wasn't going to suffer that much. I didn't know there was such a thing as counselling in the sixties and seventies.

Isha: I really appreciate talking to you and I would like to use some of the poetry from your book, you seem to be inspired by writing.

Angela: Yes, I think that to be manic-depressive is a privilege because I have got something to give. I think it is a chosen illness too.

Isha: What do you mean by that?

Angela: Highly intelligent people get this, but you have to know how to use your intelligence. People like Spike Milligan, Winston Churchill, Robert Burns; I love to read about them. Their stories inspire me. I spend a lot of time in the library browsing, this is why I want to find creativity and develop my writing.

Conclusion

This chapter has focused on a culturally specific conversation and questions relevant to black mental health. I listened to Angela for as long as it took for her to feel excitement about being able to share more than she had been able to in thirty years of her life as a mental health patient. Internalised racism was apparent in her initial denial of any experience of racism. Institutional racism is later highlighted within Angela's knowledge that 'they don't know what it is like where I come from'. Angela shares that at first she was labelled schizophrenic and came to her own conclusions that her 'depression' was different from the diagnosis that she was given. Cultural schizophrenia in her treatment as a mental health patient caused a lack of attention to her cultural background, her isolation as a child, domestic violence and her life as a black single mother in Britain. It became clear that these elements of her story form the backdrop to some of her troubles, and she recognises the need for cultural reflection and a space to share these aspects of her background. In the discussions she frequently refers to being on her own with no one to turn to. It appears that she has experienced repeated disappointment about gaining a culturally safe space and enough attention to be 'a black woman' from just one significant person in her life. She is relieved from her fear of Obeah, but her facilitation as an African Caribbean woman in Britain within the mental health system appears to have been neglected. Angela speaks of repeatedly placing herself in the hands of the mental health system, then running away, only to be returned to forensic incarceration. I wonder what she was running away from. She gains recognition through the jobs she is given and by supporting others in similar circumstances. She explained that her relief comes from her faith in God, her poetry and returning to her homeland, Grenada. For Angela, 'Every barrier is a bridge'.

My study (McKenzie-Mavinga, 2005) showed that reasons such as fear of getting it wrong, ignorance and lack of training contributed to white trainees' difficulty in opening dialogue about black issues in the therapeutic process. These fears germinate the seeds of cultural schizophrenia. The impact of cultural schizophrenia was evident while I was writing this chapter. Suggestions that there was too much dialogue in this central chapter made me conscious of a pressure to silence Angela's voice and replace the silence with Eurocentric ideas. But I have challenged my internal oppressor and given space to our voices, so often compromised by the processes of cultural schizophrenia that impact black mental health.

Pointers for therapists (including trainees and trainers)

- Develop an understanding of depression and mental ill health in the context of a black individual's developmental process, heritage and social status as a black person in Britain.
- Try to distinguish between the client's distress, mental health issues and distress caused by institutional racism in therapeutic or psychiatric care.
- Support listening relationships with black clients by becoming informed about African and African Caribbean customs and cultures

and about internalisation of both positive and negative images of
black people.

- Be aware of the black client's graduation towards feeling safe enough
  to discuss being black.
- Do not generalise, as each client has his or her own unique experience
  of being black.
- Whether black issues are discussed or not, assume that all past and
  present stresses and anxieties worked through with black clients
  support the development of their African/Caribbean/Asian identity.
- Support black identity development, as this is important to mental
  health and well-being.

Part III

Finding a Voice

The title of this part speaks for itself. 'Finding a voice' expresses the challenging yet liberating experience of becoming un-gagged. My study assisted trainees to open a dialogue where there had been silence. I discovered from our discussions that their silence contained many powerful emotions attached to experiences of racism. Fears about responding to racism in the therapeutic process and concerns about experiencing racism were expressed. It is becoming more common to see case material that includes black clients or black therapists in psychotherapy and counselling literature, but it is rare that we are privileged to listen to and understand the voices themselves. Part II opened a process of exploring black issues by focusing on ways of understanding and supporting unconscious elements of the therapeutic process. In Part III space is given to the particular experiences of black women breaking the bonds of silence and black men speaking out as wounded warriors, sharing their personal experiences.

7

Breaking the Bonds

In this chapter the experiences of black women finding their voices through group work are presented. In Chapters 5 and 6, the individual processes of black women were shared. We saw how Angela, a mental health patient, shared her experiences through her poetry. In this chapter creative writing as an aid to exploring black issues in the therapeutic process in groups is examined. I build on aspects of group support and the facilitation of black women breaking through the boundaries that keep the expression of their fear and anger at bay. The impact of racism and internalised oppression is described through their writing.

Writing has always been a tool for sharing experience. Freud and Breuer recognised that creative writing, which predated psychoanalysis, was nevertheless a valid way of understanding the mind. Group process has been a means of personal development and resolving community issues for centuries. Black women have always gathered to celebrate their achievements, share their grievances and support their concerns. Using shared writing to explore the historical impact of racism and patriarchy means that they can work through experiences that may have affected them over long periods of their lives. In the group, black women's voices are listened to through their shared experiences and evaluation of hidden feelings, reflecting their struggle for cultural empathy. Issues of isolation, the search for self and the black female gaze are addressed in the context of healing the deep hurts of racism. The benefits of this externalising process are affirmed as a kind of 'rite of passage' in the following quotation:

> Then we know that the oppression-of-self which is the final task of all oppression is in operation. For this reason, I affirm categorically the right of Black women to speak out of their many realities and be heard out of the variety of their experiences and locations. And it is for me there that Black women's writing attains its agency. (Boyce Davies and Ogundipe-Leslie, 1995, p. 7)

Many black women carry the inhumanity of racism and sexism at the same time that they are being grossly overworked and underappreciated. Hidden feelings about these experiences form the bonds that keep black women in a place of silence.

There are many stories to tell, and each one must be listened to lovingly, for words to express the self have been dressed in the unfamiliar. Affection has been confused with sexualisation, and many black women have had to barter for real love.

The objectification and mutilation of African women's bodies created ancestral baggage and black Western archetypes dating back to slavery. Their families were torn apart and their sexuality plundered by slave masters and mistresses. At the same time black men were being emasculated and denied their role within the family. This predisposition gagged Africans and forced many of them to silence their pain.

As an unconscious process, Lorde (1984) recognises the risk of suppressing our feelings: 'To refuse to be conscious of what we are feeling at any time, however comfortable that might seem, is to deny a large part of the experience and to allow ourselves to be reduced to the pornographic, the abused and the absurd' (p. 59). Lorde also reminds us that slave narratives often repeated the important message that the survival of black people depends on their ability to repress their feelings. The sustained brutality committed against black people and their fragmentation throughout periods of slavery and colonisation created a socialisation where hurt and grief over separation from loved ones were difficult to express. I call this process of fragmentation 'transatlantic trauma'. Of course, there are powerful feelings attached to these historical experiences. Lorde (1984) affirms these feelings of the African American woman:

> Every black woman in America lives her life somewhere along a wide curve of ancient unexpressed anger. My black woman's anger is a molten pot at the core of me – a boiling hot spring likely to erupt at any point, leaping out of my consciousness like a fire on the landscape. How to train that anger rather than deny it has been our major task of life. (p. 17)

So how do we 'train' that anger and grow through the powerful emotions of life?

The influence of black Western archetypes produces unrealistic models of our self-expression based on European codes of conduct. Often when black women do not conform to these models in expressing our powerful feelings, we are accused of being 'oversensitive' and 'aggressive'. As a result, some black women avoid the expression of anger, for fear of isolation, rejection and labelling by the mental health system. Our anger gets transferred into campaigns to eliminate racism and sexism and the quest to rescue our families from the destruction of capitalism. There is a risk of anger dominating our lives rather than love, sometimes causing us to deny our need for each other and our shared traditions and stories, and thus to bring black women into a group is an act of empowerment and love.

Lorde (1984) affirms that consciousness and sharing from a black-woman-centred approach creates an opportunity to express without the distortion of white racism, sexism and homophobia. The absence of this opportunity can perpetuate the myth that we are all the same: 'For not only do we touch our most profoundly creative source, but we do that which is female and self affirming in the face of a racist, patriarchal and anti-erotic society' (p. 59).

Although most people are aware of multiculturalism in Britain, this society continues to be conditioned by racism, patriarchy and anti-eroticism, and we have only begun to scratch the surface of this. Listening to the voices of black men and women is an act of empowerment and a challenge to this conditioning. Only recently a black trainee shared with me his observations of white trainees' suspicion when the class grouped for an exercise and naturally fell into separate black and white groups. The white group expressed concerns that the black group might be talking about them. It is highly likely that this could happen, as the study demonstrated that black trainees focused some time on their white peers instead of themselves. One black trainee raised the following question for her white peers.

Do white people acknowledge the pain and suppression that lead to today's anger carried through generations?

I have experienced white therapists expressing fear at the anger of black clients and black clients sharing their experience of withholding their stories from white therapists. On both sides there seems to be a lack of trust, and for white therapists a lack of empathic response to black people's powerful expression of black issues. If this is what racism does to the mind, then where do black clients' stories get told?

The following description of black women sharing through writing shows that using our own cultural reference points, we become facilitators of each other's black issues in the process of healing. In a group situation we are faced with our different yet similar wounds. It is these contradictions that create the conditions for healing. As we enter into the dynamic that separates us, we enter into the dynamic that bonds us.

The group that I present was attended by six women from mainly African and Caribbean backgrounds. A few of the women had inherited other cultural mixtures, but all of them identified themselves as black. We began by discussing the act of writing and all that it meant to them. There were issues of secrecy and disclosure. Some women were raised in communities where nothing was sacred; others where they would be scorned for 'washing their dirty linen in public' if they told their stories. There was the issue of shame to write about and deal with – black female shame.

The women were encouraged to rewrite their personal story in their native language and to include unexpressed feelings of anger and fear that they associated with their experiences. Their stories become collective through sharing, and isolation disappears as the group take ownership of their powerful feelings. I asked the women questions about exploring emotions in their writing. They were starting a journey on which they were expected to write about everything and share with others. In the group they were encouraged to break their secrecy and use the shared help available to express issues of disclosure and shame.

As Beka shared some prose that she had written, we helped her recognise certain angry feelings that she had not specifically identified in her work. Women in the group also noticed that there were voice changes when she verbalised her anger. She lapsed into Jamaican patois, her mother tongue. Beka was aware that she did not use her mother tongue in situations where she was in the minority as a black woman, such as while she was at work. She switched into patois when she felt a degree of familiarity in the group. This method of censoring had been passed on by her parents. The realisation that strong emotions such as anger were attached to her voice changes was a revelation for Beka. The group's sharing of their own experiences of language and emotion supported her new awareness and self-expression. This was a useful way to locate and explore patterns of concealing feelings such as anger. The subtext in writing is similar to the subliminal context of unconscious processes.

Exploring the subtext and subliminal process

We found that within the subliminal process lay oppressive messages about being black and female. This is what Cecile, who was a trained counsellor, had to say:

Cecile: When I was growing up in Jamaica, I grew up in a very protected environment. I come from the country. I come from a very close family group. My parents worked hard. I had mother and father in the house. That's not always the case at home. I was fortunate that we grew up like a nuclear family and I had a very good education before I left home, which continued here. I am putting this in context. I left boarding school in Jamaica and came to England. I realise later on in my life, that I was never exposed much. I would leave boarding school at the end of term, and go to my aunt before returning to the country. That was as much of the exposure. Especially if you are a girl child, they wouldn't let you out of their sight they think that you are going to get pregnant. Therefore, I realised that I was not really exposed at all. So when I went back to Jamaica, there were some areas in Kingston called Shanty town that I visited. I had heard about these areas before but never seen them. So as a black woman returning home I have a responsibility to really go and meet and talk with people in those areas. I may have been more fortunate and had more privileges but they are my people and part of me. I wanted to meet them on their territory, on their ground and not from some lofty heights up there. I asked could I help in any way. They looked at me with suspicion because my accent is different and they said. 'You come from foreign eh?' I say, 'No man I come from Jamaica, I come from down the road.' They say, 'Yea but yu travel, no tru?'

Cecile has an awareness of internalised cultural messages and identity issues about being a black Jamaican woman who has lived part of her life in England and returned home.

The women were encouraged to work out how some of these internalised messages have turned into behaviour and attitudes that have become harmful to them. They were also supported to research the link between these attitudes and their ancestry. This work is more extensive than traditional European therapies because it pays attention to a whole spectrum of influences that reach backwards into the women's social heritage.

Inherited oppressive messages are linked to all areas of womanhood, including spirituality. The discussion revealed that some of these messages were hidden between the lines and in the subtext of the writing. Below are some excerpts from the discussion that followed Cecile's remarks. Cecile spoke about her experience of oppressive messages as a black woman. She had been experiencing low self-esteem, and this had affected her career. She spoke about influences in her relationship to literature, identity issues and her awareness of internalised cultural messages in black women.

Cecile: On my diploma training, a black woman used to streups her teeth [to purse one's lips and make a rubbishing sound by sucking air through teeth]. And a white woman said that she was offended by it. The woman denied that she ever sucked her teeth and changed her body language. Then after the meeting, people came and told her that they thought the woman who challenged her was terrible. I couldn't believe what I was seeing.

Isha: They were colluding with her.

Cecile: They were colluding with her. She was very upset and in supervision I told her that I have seen her do it and more importantly to understand what this is about. For example when my mum sucks her teeth, what is she saying; I can't be bothered to talk. Going back to slavery again...

Cecile links the other woman's experience to her own family experience and identifies internalised cultural messages. A discussion about the suppressed voice ensues:

Isha: You were not allowed to talk. You would be in trouble.

Cecile: Exactly, we were not allowed to talk, we would be in trouble. And what I notice with black people is that sometimes they are not talking and you can read something on their face. With my sister and me we do a small glance at each other and we know what we are talking about, we are both thinking the same thing. Sometimes you see somebody kicking their lip up.

This excerpt shows how empathy and experience can be shared without speech. But is there an ancestral link here? Slaves found various ways to communicate messages to each other when they were watched by their masters.

Cecile: This woman was obviously embarrassed about it and tried to deny it, so again, I went back to what was it about, where did it come from?

Isha: *Did she talk with you about it in the end?*

Cecile: **No, even after all that discussion, she said she was not aware of it, and I don't believe her, she must be aware that she does it at home. It's too much of our culture for her not to be aware of it.**

Isha: *You don't believe her, but you have brought this to her awareness by challenging it, and it's also a common expression, so it's not just about her one doing it.*

Slipping into patios myself, I attempted to bring Cecile's attention to a possible link with her own issues. Cecile's writing connected her with other black women who reflected some of the oppressive behaviours that she was familiar with and had begun to work through herself.

During the group sessions we used some of these examples to relate to the personal experiences of the women. I asked the women to make up a humorous story about the experience of 'The Woman Who Streupsed'. This helped to highlight some of their own subliminal messages and place these in the context of their own history.

We decided that the woman who streupsed had a vexation that was being triggered by the dynamics of the group she was in. She was trying to conceal her powerful feelings with a habit that had been passed down to her by her ancestors, and so she was unaware of it. By examining this process we discovered many habits, idiosyncrasies and behaviour patterns that the women had become conscious of.

We went on to write about the anxieties and stresses that lay behind these behaviours. Then we traced the experiences that had caused the anxieties. Cecile revealed that her issue of not being able to talk had deeper implications as she had always felt that she was not listened to by men.

In the women's writing it became clear that deeper feelings were not written down. This happened for various reasons, including fear, taboo, lack of awareness and sometimes the editing-out of issues they felt concerned about sharing because they were about their black identities. This is like being in a submissive role as a writer. Finally, we made links with characters from folklore, stories and the women's ancestry. We discussed the folklore character Diablesse.

Besson (2001) describes Diablesse as a 'she-devil'. She has a cloven hoof hidden under a long frock, and she frequents cemeteries and crossroads. Diablesse has been wronged by men, so she is greatly feared by them and adored by women, especially those who have roving husbands. She lures young men who make advances to her after a dance and encourages the victim to follow her home by pointing a light in the distance. As they follow her, the light recedes and she leads them to a precipice. Then she suddenly transforms herself into a huge hog and with a shriek disappears from sight, leaving the victim to stumble over the precipice. Men who are aware of her true nature listen out for the sound of her hoof and carry walking-sticks so they can cross them and ward her off. The character of Diablesse also has a biblical basis in the temptress Eve, who as Diablesse holds the evil wishes of wives who want to punish their neglectful husbands.

Stories of such folklore characters have been passed down through generations of storytelling and shared experience in African and Caribbean village life. Some of the women had grown up with these stories. The women likened Diablesse to their feelings of anger and revenge at betrayal in their relationships with men. Mythology preceded psychology and also preceded adulthood. Our therapeutic process of re-telling folklore from black history was transformative. Hartill (1998) suggests that '[a]ll mythology, every fairy tale, expresses the truth of transformation and change – and that therein lies the chance of our own renewal, our making new' (p. 49).

The women were encouraged to visualise stories and rhymes from their past and endow the characters with their own emotions. The stories were based either on recall or on fabrication. The process was transformative in that ancestral cultural baggage was acknowledged. The shame and embarrassment of disclosing their negative behaviour patterns was alleviated. Developing these issues through creative writing seemed a natural process for the women. It gave them a focus for their issues and a useful passage to their emotions. Working with the subtext and subliminal messages can be likened to working with the unconscious in the writing. This is what Cecile had to say about her progress in the final group meeting.

Cecile: For a number of years of my life I have allowed myself to be in the submissive housewife role. Now I have woken up. I got out of bed and shook myself and said Cecile, what the hell do think you are doing to yourself? You cannot be of any value to anyone else unless you value yourself more. And slowly but surely I have began to work on myself, reclaim myself, take hold of my internal power and I articulated to my partner that I will never be any good to you until I can take care of me. ... It has to do with deciding to no longer assimilate. It is time to be accepted for me. What makes me angry is when my colleagues say to me, 'I don't see that you are black.' When they say this I am being done a disservice although I know it is their way of saying to me 'You are ok. Cecile.' It is very racist. I used to start feeling very angry and I functioned well as a professional but the more I interacted with white people from a personal level, anger built up about what has been done to our people and continues to be seen as unimportant. When you think that you have worked through stuff, you discover that you have more to work on. If I go at the racism with a sledgehammer it will not work, so I will continue to chip away at it now I have become more aware.

Lorde (1984) summarises the connection between us and the transformation process as we write together: 'Within these deep places, each of us holds an incredible reserve of creativity and power of the unexamined and unrecorded emotion and feeling. For each of us as a woman there is a dark place within, where hidden and growing our true spirit rises' (p. 36).

Unexamined emotion and the technique of description

Through identifying emotional patterns within the writing, the women became aware of their unconscious processes and, as Lorde put it, their unrecorded emotion. At this stage the editing-out of personal information becomes a thing of the past. The women were encouraged to write in an uncensored way and include their whole experience. Every woman arrives at a point where she can no longer hide herself; she is opening up. Messages about not sharing, not crying, being the strong woman can no longer be harnessed within the psyche. The unsaid and unshed are revealed. The act of self-disclosure in a safe, confidential setting becomes a priority in the group process. We must not underestimate the detrimental effects of isolation that some of the women experienced.

Some of these black women had been beaten, ridiculed or starved into silence. In the group, silence is transformed into description. We found that description opened up the raw elements of black issues, and sharing helped the women to associate similar experiences and reflect their goodness to each other. I now identify three phases in the group's process of writing about black issues:

1. *Sharing thought and fantasy,* the production of free-flowing thought. The women are encouraged to write anything that comes to mind, no matter how outrageous it may appear. One group member, Judy, presented an example of thought and fantasy. She wrote about her feelings of loss and family disintegration. Her family had grown out of

the habit of meeting every Sunday for a family meal. Judy also wrote about her wish to be like Diana Ross, who has a family yet travels the world as a star and always appears flamboyant. Diana Ross expresses herself through her writing and shares through song, gaining public attention and admiration from thousands of people wherever she goes. We discussed issues of family loss, and I encouraged the women to engage collectively in their own fantasies about Diana Ross.

2. *Inspiration (or 'inspirition')*. Self-knowledge is disclosed during dis-cussion about the writing. This is where feelings, the senses and description are given attention and the women tap into their ability to develop their stories. Writing about loss of family inspired Judy to talk about closeness and cultural heritage. She felt more able to talk about issues of identity, whom she wanted to be like and how she can be a more authentic self. (I have used the term 'inspirition' to describe the developing link between spirituality and ancestral heritage, by which we gain insight and create new ideas and images in our minds. The feelings and emotions complete the picture that helps us connect to others' experiences. This stage connects us spiritually through empathy.)

The discussion that started with Judy's wish to be like Diana Ross progressed from inspirition to an examination of what kind of images about our personalities and lives we try to project onto others and how we attract attention for feelings and emotions. So issues of confidence, assertiveness and depression became paramount. The group worked together on strategies to ask for help, get attention, break isolation and get closer to family and friends.

3. *Publication*. Sharing personal writing with others was the mode of publication used in the group work. I suggested that the women use description to emphasise the skin characteristics and physical features of the main character within their stories and read them out. The shift from inspiration to publication is similar to the shift from uncon-sciousness to awareness. This shift is brought about by group relation-ships and attention to the writing process. I had an expectation that each woman would make the shift, because in my experience the act of disclosure and naming our identities helps to break through the oppressions. Publication requires the individual to be explicit.

Shared reading in the group brought to light the issue of oppression based on differences within the black community and within the group of women. On becoming aware of this issue, Judy revealed her suspicion of me as the facilitator. She linked this issue to an experience of psychological abuse as the darkest child in her family. (This oppression is usually called 'colorism' or 'shadism'.) The oppression continued through her working life, and her relationships with other black women had been conditioned by feelings locked within her about this experience. She also became aware of her fears that I would reprimand or ridicule her in the group, as she had experienced in the past. To avoid being drawn into this dynamic, I was compelled to attend to my own wounds from being ridiculed as a light-skinned black woman by darker-skinned women. Not facing the truth about the divisions within our communities maintains our disconnection from each other.

Publication brought about a shift in the group dynamic about colorism. The group supported Judy to break through her difficulties about being noticed. Isolation linked to the effects of internalised racism seemed to be her underlying issue. We discovered the powerful dynamics of difference within the group and between Judy and myself as the group leader. Understanding the dynamics of difference can break the barriers of isolation. Not much has been written about isolation as a defence or colorism. Isolation is usually an indication of mistrust as a result of past hurt. Isolation is also a common issue for people who experience colorism and mental ill health.

Isolation, blocks and mental health

Each woman was given an opportunity to break through her isolation. As she added the experiences of others to her own, the silences were broken and the group worked collectively on the issues. It was common for these women to feel blocked owing to the intensity and volume of their issues. Most of the women were not used to having time or attention to evaluate the black issues in their lives. There has been little time to locate the joy. Their lives have been conditioned by attempts to mask the pain. They have grown used to conforming. They have lived in fear of annihilation, and their beauty has been interpreted using European stereotypes such as straightened hair. Makeup products such as skin lightener have been marketed to make them more female and less black. It has been difficult to stay clear in thought through the tiredness and striving to be accepted beneath this masking. For some this has led to confusion and mental breakdown.

The women in the group were encouraged to share unedited material and write about blocks rather than bulldoze through them, so we used their writing to explore what the blocks were about. Much of the emotional material and terror were harboured within these blocks. I am familiar with this process in my own work as a writer. I rarely feel that my writing is worthwhile. I get distracted easily, I am often faced with my isolation and I know the terror of speaking out. Relief comes with the awareness that others who read my work find affirmation, share in the challenges and connect empathically with my experiences. My own blocks are the emotional channels to my writing. I am aware that these blocks can lead to emotional distress and bouts of depression, but some of my most creative writing has happened when I have been unwell. I call this a 'creative depression'. Things usually open up at some point because I have stilled myself. Feeling too sick to write, I sometimes feel that I am close to the edge of madness. Since I have worked closely with black mental health patients, this is a familiar experience. I wrote the poem below in a writing workshop that I attended:

If I do not express myself

I defend
I deny my sisters,
For a time, we are afraid.
It is not the end
We pass through it
And create another masterpiece

>   Isha McKenzie-Mavinga
>   (2005)

Some of the women had experiences of the mental health service that had impacted their lives. Medication, depression and being shut up for life were subjects of their writing. This was revealed in descriptions of attack and fears of annihilation. Some of the women believed that they were driven mad while in psychiatric care. Others believed that they were depressed by the oppressions that they had experienced throughout their lives. Mental breakdown was a common family experience. They had little knowledge of the treatments they had been given and of the long-term effects of medication. I continued to encourage the women to write about anything. They revealed through their writing that they had rarely been given opportunities to discuss their mental health issues. Some of the women had previously felt helpless in their contact with statutory organisations. Many of them had immediate or second-hand experience of racism or domestic violence and serious injury or the murder of someone they knew. These experiences lay at the core of their distress, and they had been harbouring a lot of fear as a result. Given the rate of black-on-black homicide, these issues are not to be taken lightly.

Mother tongue

Finding a voice to express the language of oppressions can be a challenging and contradictory task. In the quotation below Maya Angelou (1998), writing about 'Art for the Sake of the Soul', shares through her writing the contradictions of oppression through language and the need for positive reflection of black people:

> Some White people actually stand looking out of their windows at serious snow falling like cotton rain, covering the tops of cars and the streets and fire hydrants and say, 'My God, it sure is a black day.' So black people had to find ways in which to assert their own beauty. (p. 133)

The contradiction presented by Angelou demonstrates the hurt and confusion suffered by black and white people as victims of racism and as members of the oppressor group. Making global links with their writing, I encouraged the women to explore the different languages that they had experienced during their lives. I placed an emphasis on language because I know that language is one of the ways in which black people and immigrants in Britain have been oppressed. During the process of slavery the tongues of our ancestors were psychologically tied. Slaves were not allowed to communicate in their native languages. They were not allowed to use their African names. Some became distanced from their origins. Their communication was conditioned by enslavement, but they found ways to express themselves. Colonisation and assimilation have perpetuated the suppression of language. The black woman's search for self is embroiled in language differentiation. This was highlighted in Cecilia's and Beka's experiences.

A range of languages, including Spanish, French and patois, were shared in the group. I view language inhibition as a signifier of the women's repressed voices. Some of the women recalled the times when they or their parents arrived in Britain. They were encouraged to reflect on times when they were made to feel their speech was not good enough and ordered to speak proper Queen's English. They were also encouraged to identify symbols and metaphors and reflect on the language, giving their writing a voice. In doing so, they were able to explore between the lines. This was another way to overcome their fears and share and express the black issues that had not been written.

Metaphor and liberation from fear

Fear can be contagious: if one person shows it, others will follow. Fear can lead to prejudice, challenge, power, rebellion, revolution, madness and even death. There is great fear of expressing fear. Discouraging the expression of fear can lead to more fear. We dress fear up to make it presentable; we disguise it with laughter, embarrassment, smiles, game playing, shyness, hesitation, lateness, avoidance, irrational thoughts, sickness and strange behaviour sometimes mistaken for madness.

Exploring metaphor was a useful way of locating fear in the group, like the censoring of language in Beka's experience. We approached fear in two ways. First, I asked the women to underline places in each other's texts where fear might be hidden, and then I asked each writer to create metaphors for the fearful experiences that had been highlighted. This enabled the women to face any possibility of unexpressed fears in their writing. As Lorde (1984) puts it: 'For we have been socialised to respect fear more than our own needs for language and definition, and while we wait in silence for that final luxury of fearlessness, the weight will choke us' (p. 44).

Metaphor is a playful way of confronting an issue that a woman may be well rehearsed at distancing herself from. In the group she is playfully encouraged to face and express her fears in the context of her life. The women were encouraged to use the full range of their cultural experience and language. There are many folklore tales and invocations that link culturally with fearful experiences. The women were encouraged to invent their own metaphors for fear. After this exercise, they were encouraged to explore their fears more deeply.

Healing and the final draft

Working deeper brings us to the final draft. The final draft must include details of each woman's attempts to challenge and change the role that she has become accustomed to after the experience that made her suppress her feelings. So the group can then reflect on each member's process of empowerment.

Women were encouraged to tell their story using memory. This helped them to link history with the present. The approach also helps the women to heal through common experience. Isolation is broken, and they are encouraged to look outward towards positive relationships in their lives, rather than solely inwards towards their pain and depression. It works because lyric, verse, invocation, ritual and oral traditions belong in the heritage of black women. Her search for self is affirmed by her ancestors and their methods of storytelling to heal their pain.

Applying this approach to other types of groups

Before closing this chapter, I want address one final point, raised by another trainee, about the racial context of this work.

What can a white therapist offer a black woman?

Work with black groups often raises this type of question from white therapists. I am aware of their concern that the exclusivity of this work can make them feel shut out from black issues. Lago (2006) takes an introspective approach to this question. He emphasises the importance of white therapists getting in touch with their deep-seated racist impulses in preparation for work with black people, suggesting: 'If we are to overcome the internal racist within us, and find release from the guilt, fear and shame that bind us, we need to meet the "shadow" side of our psyche and begin to integrate the acceptable parts of ourselves' (p. 209).

It is also important for trainees and trainers to approach this question in the light of the language that white therapists use in their work with black clients. Other cultural and minority group issues and concerns must be considered while bearing in mind the specific context of black issues that have been shared.

Writing as a tool for healing can be useful for anyone within diverse settings. It is the contradiction of that difference that can provide a 'Who am I?' question for the individual. Through writing it out, the status quo can be challenged

Conclusion

It is clear that the process of therapeutic writing has helped black women towards a greater understanding of themselves and their coping skills. Writing has worked as a tool for reflective process and a means of externalising hidden messages that create low self-concept. Through the group process of exploring black issues, the black women became more visible. I challenged the women to exaggerate and make up whatever they could not recall. The women exchanged the bad experiences for joyful ones. Through fantasy writing they became aware of how much control they have in managing their own stories. We invented and wrote about rituals that help to eliminate pain. The sharing, acknowledgement and guidance that happen in a group make it work.

An experience shared becomes the common language of oppression and expression.

Marion Bethel (1995), in her research on black women's creative writing, seeks out evidence of the importance of this approach:

> For me then the act of writing is an act of resistance, a drive towards self-knowledge as I locate my voice in relationship to my community, the Caribbean, Africa and the world. As a woman, writing is part of my refusal to be completely trounced by male dominated culture; as a black person it is part of my resistance to being fascinated and tyrannised by the brute power of European and Euro-American Philistinism. (p. 78)

The exercises shared in this chapter are not exclusive to therapeutic work with black women. They can be used with mixed-race and mixed-gender groups. I have presented the work with black women to show how working actively with a shared experience functions to assist healing. In diverse groups there needs to be a common theme to generate collective empathy. The disposition of black women's groups shows that there is likely to be collective empathy present, as the group begins with the shared experience of race and gender. In other circumstances the starting point will depend on the group's significant factors.

Organising select groups raises questions about discrimination and openness to sameness and difference. In any transcultural setting, the facilitator needs to be aware of his or her cultural heritage and the oppressions that may influence the group dynamic. The majority of participants, whether black or white, male or female, will have been influenced by British culture, whereas each group member will have his or her own personal history of racial and gender issues to share in his or her writing. Ways can be found to assist each person to present his or her own history and developmental experiences.

In this chapter the search for self began with the black women's connection to each other. Building identity is an essential part of this search. In this chapter I have focused on writing as a way of finding a voice and speaking it out. An emphasis has been placed on what has not been said or heard and how the unconscious copes with the duality of racism and black womanhood. It is clear that links with history are important and that the subtext of black women's experience needs to be supported and considered in therapeutic work. Feelings such as anger and fear have been identified and located within the context of oppression and internalised oppression. The uniqueness of the reflective process and engaging with black-on-black experiences among black women has been highlighted.

For the women involved, writing became a way of clearing the mind. With each new writing experience came a new bout of awareness. The women expressed feeling more centred and confident. The lid had been raised on stored emotions and the healing initiated. Out of raised awareness came the striving for self-understanding and a wish to reframe their identities. It could be said that in this group the black women returned their personal and collective 'gaze' through writing. It is clear that responses to black self-image have become distorted by a negative gaze installed by racist patriarchal responses from the 'eye of the beholder', a process normalised by education and upbringing. The effects of this negative gaze can be considered endemic in the relationship dynamics of black people in the Western world.

In the same way that writing makes conscious a dialogue with the self, it is self-conscious. It is a way of understanding the internalised self and our relationship with others. It is a journey from the unconscious to the conscious and a journey from silence to language. It is also a journey from ignorance to recognition and from the margins to the centre. It is an opportunity for the black woman's subjectivity to be transferred from the sole attention of her family to her own self-discovery.

Pointers for therapists (including trainees and trainers)

- Provide support without homogenising by exploring similarities and differences.
- Be aware that there may be a cultural context to any unconscious processes when black women share their experiences.
- Develop an awareness of the social and historical context of black women in Britain, Africa and the Caribbean.
- Support disclosure using creativity to encourage metaphor, mythology and storytelling.
- Be open to the expression of pent-up fear and anger owing to lack of space and support to share and express strong feelings.
- Black therapists need to process their own oppressions, internalised racism and recognition trauma so that they can be fully present without over-identifying with black clients. This will also help them work with white clients who express racist ideology.

- White therapists need to work through their oppressions, racism and recognition trauma sufficiently to facilitate exploration with black clients and their black-on-black experiences.
- Encourage clients to use writing or recording in one-to-one therapy and group therapy. Explore past experiences of writing and expression through creativity.

8

The Wounded Warrior

In Chapter 7, I presented the voices of black women processing their experiences. The focus in this chapter is the process of listening to the voices of black men. In British society the role of black men is underplayed, and they are vulnerable to the negative mythology that perpetuates racism towards them. This is why I have entitled this chapter 'The Wounded Warrior'. Given that men are outnumbered by women in the world of therapy, it is strikingly apparent that black men have been less represented in this work both as practitioners and as clients. I have worked on training courses where black men have slowly disappeared, have been failed, or have left the course because they have not been heard, and I have had black male clients who preferred not to engage in Eurocentric approaches to therapy. They wanted reasoning and advice. Through my own processing as a black woman, I am learning to acknowledge their pain on their own terms and to address my naivety about their development processes and their needs. I have discovered the importance of paying attention to the significance of black men's individual experiences as portrayed by themselves and not through Eurocentric, white or black female interpretations. We must be aware of our social conditioning and of the impact of stereotyping on black men and allow them to share their histories and sexualities without sexualising their stories. To that end, the particular nature of black men's experiences is portrayed in this chapter through interviews with them about their work and their creative expression.

First, I share a brief discussion with Arike, an experienced psychotherapist and trainer who has battled against institutional racism and hopelessness. He shares insights gained from his facilitation of group work with black men in a high-security mental health hospital. Based in Trinidad, LeRoy, an elder and artist, challenges the concept of energy and space to include observations of our placement in history and the present. He uses paintings to frame and reflect images of key moments in the artist's consciousness. Through regeneration we are challenged to understand as spectators and heal the collective consciousness. The eyes of the artist and the presence of ancestors contribute to healing what LeRoy describes as the 'warring soul', and this act consequently opens doors for future generations. Byron, also based in Trinidad, is a musician who shares his experience of discovering healing through the drum. He expresses the importance of feeling the rhythm from within the African experience and the development of black men supported by African male role models. Byron's search for his identity takes him to the United States and into some reflection on his personal identity.

Although black men have contributed to the development of psychological theory, their stories are rarely presented in the literature. Fanon (1986) pioneered the psychological liberation of the black man by portraying the search for appropriate mirroring through his own experiences in the book *Black Skin, White Masks*: 'I cannot disassociate myself from the future that is proposed for my brother. Every one of my acts commits me as a man. Every one of my silences, every one of my cowardices reveals me as a man' (p. 89).

To emerge from the silence intact is a feat in itself. Black men are inventors, fighters and great leaders who have contributed to magnificent kingdoms and initiated revolutions; however, their role in the black family was made virtually impossible during slavery. The impact of this is still apparent. Given this history, it is not surprising that providing a space for black men to be who they are is a relatively new phenomenon. Distress pervading the black male experience in Britain today indicates high levels of violence and harm to each other and their over-representation in prison, hospitals and psychiatric care.

The question below, raised by a white male trainee, identifies some of the personal and institutional difficulties that perpetuate the lack of appropriate services for black men. The trainee is clearly challenged by his lack of connection with black men, and he is concerned about black men's anger from the impact of slavery and his own internal racism.

In working in a mental health setting, why do I find it more difficult to make a connection with black males and find their violence more disturbing than I do with Asian males? Could this be a huge, justifiable anger existing from slavery and my white guilt?

In response to this question, I am presenting the voice of Arike, an African Caribbean male who experiences the black man differently.

Arike is a person-centred therapist who has worked with black men over the past few years. He responds to the needs of his clients with an awareness of negative projections and connecting through his own experience as a black male.

Arike: **We have to involve ourselves quite differently in what could be called a European approach. At the same time it feels like I don't know what I am doing. On the other hand I am leaving myself open to whatever comes.**

Isha: With all that comes at us, quite often we forget about just 'being'.

Arike: In mental health, what we are operating with a lot of the time is spirit.

Isha: A lot of black people respond better to other methods of healing like music, body work, dance, drumming, writing, everyday activities rather than someone in a counselling role who is using a criterion by which to connect. So how do we counsel each other as black people influenced Eurocentrically?

Arike: As a counsellor I am the outsider in Broadmoor [a high-security hospital]. When I started the work I am doing with black men, the relationships between the men were not being addressed; they were just dealing with things as they are. In the middle of loud voices going on between staff and patients, that moment of connection from an outsider, a black man, saved another from an increased dose of medication.

Isha: The altercation was not seen as one black man trying to connect with another black man. There are many black men who have arrived in Broadmoor in similar circumstances, for social problems, petty crime and displaying anger, being viewed as having a problem with authority; therefore he is not safe and needs to be in the mental health system.

Arike: I am addressing the natural anger at situations out of our control. Some of the men are angry, but don't act it out. I am angry every time I enter the hospital, at what I see. The number of incidents that occur as a result of patients released from psychiatric care scares the staff, so there is the issue of not allowing mental health patients across the board to be responsible for their own lives. The additional thing with black people is the criminal justice system. Reports suggest that African Caribbean people are seven times more likely to be incarcerated; this may influence the mental health system.

Isha: Most people that I have had contact with who are involved with the mental health system talk of their fear of the black client. They are trying to counsel with the fear up front and this stops their empathy with black clients. They are working outside of the real connection.

Arike: **They are working with their projection.**

[In Kleinian work, projection is viewed as an unconscious defence against something unbearable. This concept is usually associated with the defence of splitting, where individuals transfer the bad feelings into some other place (Klein, 1946)]

Isha: I often see the fear in white people's body language when I am presenting a transcultural workshop. When I ask them about it, they say they fear being attacked because they might get it wrong. So we have come full circle back to training.

Reflections

I am aware that this discussion drifted away from the focus on black men. I have begun to generalise, using language such as 'most people' and black 'clients' as opposed to the specifics of black men's experiences. I have transferred the focus onto white people, and this is easily done when I am distracted by my Eurocentric training, the emotional crisis that interferes with me as a female onlooker and my empathy towards black men. During my study, it was evident that defensiveness during discussions led to the focus being transferred onto the needs of the white trainees. In the following interviews I intend to be more vigilant of this, for the black man needs to have the space for his own story and the expression of his own emotions, including anger.

Although the source and expression may differ, the anger and violence of black men is no different from the anger and violence of any man. As Wilson (1990) suggests:

> To be a sensitive Black male, no matter how innocent, law-abiding, all American, patriotic, altruistic, and loving, is to see the dilated pupils of fear in White women's and old men's eyes, to witness the defensive clutching at pocketbooks, to see yourself reflected in the mirrors of others' eyes as a mugger, thief and rapist. ... Only the careful presented façade, the meticulous expression of non-aggressive, non-assertive body language ... can alleviate to some tolerable degree the fears and suspicions of others. But this diminution of fear and suspicions in others bought at the too-high price of self-annihilation

is always tentative, delicate and is easily rent at the smallest misstep or the tiniest deviation. (pp. 37–8)

And what of the guilt experienced by the white trainee? Dalal (2002) postulates that white therapists are faced with the reality of their privileged position in society. If the therapist has not dealt with this guilt in his or her therapy, then it may be bubbling away under the surface, and defence mechanisms to avoid it may be activated. This can cause the therapist to become overwhelmed and incapacitated and may lead to overcompensation and a colour-blind approach.

Following on from this, the next question generates further discussion about the black–white dyad. There is no question about the influence that slavery and colonisation had on the division of men. Just as capitalism influenced the labour market, so the divide between privileged white men and black men became greater. However, although black males fall victim to society's racism, they are, as LeRoy suggests, responsible for 'charting their own ruin'.

Why do black males struggle in society, in general, in comparison to white males?

Refocusing the gaze away from the reflection of white men as representatives of all men is essential to stepping into the experiences of black men. Fanon (1986) sees the reflection process as integral to the black man's struggle. He portrays his own engagement with the gaze as a reflection of his blackness: 'I try to read admiration in the eyes of the other, and if unluckily, those eyes show me unpleasant reflection, I find that mirror flawed' (p. 212).

The following interview, which took place in Trinidad, reflects the expression and imagery of LeRoy, painter, poet and Obeah man. To LeRoy, Obeah carries connotations of a spiritual leader who promotes the black man's responsibility to himself and his community. LeRoy suggests that showing an interest in the creative abilities of black men can support the articulation of their concerns. He expresses his concern about disconnection from his black brothers. LeRoy portrays through his art messages of past and present. He analyses responses to his artwork using symbolic representation of mirroring to the spectator and the black-on-black gaze. He alludes to the inner source of internalised oppression and suggests that consciousness can be gained through realisation of this reflection, using a 'space to contemplate'. LeRoy shares his wisdom about the influence of Africa and healing the black consciousness. He tells me that he finds Jung's writing inspirational to his art and has a wish that his art will influence in the ways portrayed by Jung (1930/1950) in the following quotation:

> We let a work of art act upon us as it acted upon the artist. To grasp its meaning we must let it shape us as it shaped him. ... he has plunged into the healing and redeeming depths of the collective psyche ... where all men are caught up in a common rhythm which allows the individual to communicate his feelings and strivings to mankind as a whole. (p. 196)

Isha: Expression of some of the intergenerational problems for black individuals in Britain is sometimes attributed to loss of a sense of home. This can be due to immigration status, difficulties returning to homelands or loss of an inner sense of cultural heritage due to assimilation. You said that you felt at home. Do you think that being conscious of feeling at home contributes to our individual and collective healing?

LeRoy: Well it is a settling of self and the environment of self and some amount of healing, you know where you can feel at home with the space. Like I say it has to do with consciousness because when we are unconscious irrespective of how at peace we may appear, that appearance is fraudulent, because that consciousness is definitely a result of great struggle and sacrifice. Its rewards cannot be measured in terms of material things. It has to do with feeling and caring. Bob Marley talks about as long as there is disrespect, there will be war. Not just going out and shooting bullets, it's war within the self. For example last week we had several horrendous crimes in our space and today I may appear a bit down. Today I am visited by a very down feeling of giving up, like if there is no hope. I have these visits off and on; I am a human being. So I am doing battle so that I won't give up. I think what is the point of all this, what is the point of this interview? What is the point? So there is a warring taking place right now.

Isha: Yes, so when the warring is taking place that means you are not quite at home?

LeRoy: I am not at home, I am sick, I am out of balance, and I'm out of sync with myself, which is to be in consciousness when you are in sync with self. I am out of consciousness, my moorings are unleashed, I am drifting, and nothing now will give me solace at this point, so I am sick. Everything hurts. I was telling you about the crimes last week. A woman seventy something years old invalid, in Pampers, sick, lying on a bed was raped. That is a real sickness that man could violate all

sense of decency, all moral or ethical value. He definitely isn't a being any more.

Isha: *And this violates your sense of home.*

LeRoy: Yes. It violates. A young woman in Moval [a small town in the hills near to Port of Spain, Trinidad] who people talk about as being central to the activities of Moval, she has a little parlour [food stall], people depend on her. Somebody go in there and shoot point blank in her face. It is the shooting in her face that bothers me a lot. Here's this black woman and here's this black man. He didn't see himself in her, he didn't see himself shooting himself, he didn't see his mother in her, he didn't see Africa, he saw nothing. He just shot her, for what? If it was money, how much money could she have in there? A problem of unconsciousness is objectification, which underpins a history of self mutilation and massacre of black peoples. We have a responsibility to arrive at a consciousness which keeps our original identities intact.

Reflections

Fanon (1986) talks of consciousness in terms of relinquishing the self as object but echoes the hopelessness attached to finding the black self through the gaze:

> I came into the world imbued with the will to find a meaning in things, my spirit filled with desire to attain to the source of the world, and then I found that I was in the midst of objects. Sealed into crushing objecthood, I turned beseechingly to others. Their attention was liberation, running over my body suddenly abraded into nonbeing, endowing me once more with agility that I thought lost, and by taking me out of the world, restoring me to it. But just as I reached the other side, I stumbled and the movements, the attitudes, the glances of the other fixed me there, in the sense in which a chemical solution is fixed by a dye. I was indignant; I demanded an explanation. Nothing happened. I burst apart. Now the fragments have been put together by another self. (p. 109)

Like Fanon, LeRoy understands the need for a reflective space within the self-healing process, a space that reflects black history and puts the fragmented black self back together. He expresses his anger and hurt at black-on-black violence and lack of positive reflection. This is a growing concern in Africa, the Caribbean and Britain. The projection of experience through art, the evolution of the black gaze and the presence of ancestors are portrayed in LeRoy's paintings.

LeRoy: That painting we have up in Aripo, a very large blue painting about eight foot square. It is an impression of the Middle Passage. When examined you can see all the rubble and the mash-upness of the spirit of Africans who were thrown overboard or took their lives and their spirits dwell there. I believe strongly that this links Africa with the Africans. It's part of continuity in a chain of events, which must be taken into consideration so that we can fully appreciate the full chain. If one link is missing we do not have a chain.

Isha: Is that painting part of a series?

LeRoy: Yes, it is part of the El Tucouche series. I produced it in the Douens series. I was showing the rising up out of the sea. I was showing that the spirits were in limbo, all the disembodied limbs and so were pulling together and a stairway was built to float up to the top of the sea, so all the work is about that regeneration, it is about reclaiming oneself or sovereignty. Trekking towards one's El Tucouchea. In the first series I looked at man, and I concluded that we have fallen from grace. So you establish an apex of thought, an ideal, and there is where your God and your ancestors are. We have fallen from that for whatever many circumstances; enslavement is only one of them. What about enslavement of ourselves? Our own injustices against ourselves. We don't want to look at that at all. It is important. The people who enslaved did so because we had already enslaved ourselves. There used to be black people, but not anymore. Not that there are not black people. Our whole race is destroyed and subjugated into a term black people. But when you start to hear Africa, you know that you are arriving somewhere. Therefore to carry that is responsibility and calls on your sovereign energy. It calls on the tensions that you didn't even know you had. It's amazing when you actually work on yourself the discoveries you make.

The question of how to work on these issues has also been raised by trainee counsellors.

How do we heal the pain left by the legacy of slavery, colonialism and racism etc?

First and foremost, therapists must provide a space to listen to and understand the particular nature of black men's feelings and how they experience themselves. Byron, a Trinidadian of mixed African and Indian heritage, begins to address this question, understanding his acquaintance with the drum as a means of recovering his natural ties with his heritage. Byron's healing experience is firmly linked to his role model/teacher, another man of African heritage, who might easily be seen as a therapist. The following discussion also took place in Trinidad and centres around Byron's healing through his discovery of the drum.

Isha: Tell me about yourself. What is your background, your mixture, where you were born?

Byron: I was born here in Aruca, in the east of the island. Christened in the Catholic Church, you know. I was born illegitimate; my father's name is not even on my birth certificate. These taboos run real deep in this country; people don't like to talk about it. I grew up in Patna village; Patna is named after a city in India. I grew up what we would call a little red nigger among coolie people. Everyone was Indian and I was a little light-skinned nigger. So I grew up Catholic among Hindu people. So that was an experience by itself. Mum's grandfather was Chinese and Spanish of Venezuelan background. What we call the 'cocopanio people'. These are Venezuelan people who came to work on the sugar plantations. It was an experiment, a sort of indentured labourer type thing. The drumming is natural to me. Mum told me that since I was a child I was very rhythmic. She said that as a toddler I would be rocking in the crib, in time to the music. I don't know for some people there is the nature versus nurture argument. Mum herself is very rhythmic. I remember as a child in the sixties, I would be banging 'Klim' buckets and what have you on the table and so on and she would come and roll her fingers in time to the music.

Isha: But you were also exposed to the drumming here, the pan, etc.

Byron: Yeah, you hear rhythm. My grandmother would take all the children and shake you and they would make all these mellow sounds. Hip umm bimm bmmn hipm um bim bimmun. And they shake up the little baby and the little baby is giggling to this rhythm that it is feeling. As a little toddler you standin' up watchin' your family and cousins rockin' to rhythm, and they hearin' the sound in the background. Think that is how the children here grow up. If you watch kiddies' carnival they are learning to gyrate their hips in time to the music. It is encouraged here. It is culturally induced.

Isha: But then you discovered the drum as a healing instrument, that rhythm actually meant healing in your life.

Byron: Yeah, in fact most of the drummers here we play flatan and we tend to hit the edges a lot and you develop technique over time. Same thing in West Africa. For me I will not be playing much in the local Betz village in competitions and so on. Most of the guys here they come from poor black working-class families and there is a particular image and stereotype that goes with traditional folk drummers in this country. I grew up with a very rigid, somewhat authoritarian, strict Catholic mum, so she never wanted me to stray too much and play drums with the guys on the block because they would take drugs. Well all my life I have never done any drugs and don't take any alcohol, so in the end it sort of protected me. It's cultural conditioning, self-hate and thing, but I have noticed that more of my African American sisters are getting involved in drum and dance for their own emotional healing. It's their own way of fighting the racism and sexism and other forms of oppression that they are suffering every day of their lives. A few of the brothers are getting involved, in the south, you know and those who hang out with Caribbean guys and guys from West Africa. They are very conscientious about getting involved with anything to do with the positive aspects of their ancestral culture, but it's not enough.

Isha: So these healing properties of drumming, what about the drumming that you are involved with here in Trinidad?

Byron: Yeah, Jaja [Byron's teacher] is a hard-core student of the drum. He is very experienced; he has been working this part since he was a child for twenty something years now. I got my calling in ninety-five; I realised that I had to do something about the natural rhythm that I had inside of me. Jaja had to go through all sort of social pressure here. His type of rhythm is somewhat different to traditional folk rhythms that most of the guys play. He literally creates different types of melodies on the drum skins, musical intonations and what have you. His music is very therapeutic when you listen to it.

Isha: What makes it therapeutic?

Byron: It's the tonal quality. A lot of our folk rhythms here are high-intensity rhythms. He doesn't play his drums very loud. If you observe the animal skin is a natural thing and drum comes from the trees, which is also a living thing. So apparently the organisms in your body respond to the energy and the cells of the drums. Drums can be used for intimacy, for creating war and also for healing. Right now I am a humble student making serious progressive attempts to learn how the drums can be used to heal. I discovered that when I am drumming, my friends tell me that I am completely different when they see me drum.

Isha: Meaning what?

Byron: Well I'm smiling a lot. Rhythm helps heal me of all my old pain, especially with issues with my father that I never really got a chance to know, all the old rage and anger. I like high-intensity rhythms, I have been an intense person, I am a little bit more mellow now. It's like sexual erotic ecstasy for me.

Isha: Nothing else is important at that time, just sex.

Byron: Yes, yes, yes, yes, pure sex taking place.

Isha: You are totally in the present.

Byron: And with Jaja now his rhythm is much more melodic and it's helping me to calm down even more.

Isha: That's listening to his rhythms?

Byron: Yes and the silence between the notes.

Isha: Yeah, yeah, I understand that.

Byron: He is allowing some sort of creative genius to come out.

Isha: Uh hum, uh hum.

Byron: And he tells me that within me he sees the makings of a master drummer.

Isha: Uh hum.

Byron: And he knows what he is talking about.

Isha: Yeah, of course.

Byron: So I think it has been an honour for him to allow me to be part of his ensemble of seven because there are hundreds of drummers who would want to be part of his group. He is renowned overseas, especially in Europe and Japan.

Isha: So in terms of the student, you would also be in Eurocentric therapeutic terms, you would be known as the client.

Byron: Yes, yes, yes, yes.

Isha: Because he informs you with his rhythms and then through that you work through a process of your own and you become connected to his drumming and rhythms and also your own drumming and rhythms.

Byron: Uh hum, uh hum. Yes, strangely enough, musicians talk about it. Sometimes when you close your eyes and shut off your ego, because the ego wants attention, the I, the me, look at who I am, we men want to show off and see all the beautiful women in front of us worshipping us. When you close your eyes sometimes and you get into the melody that you are playing and you cut yourself off from everyone else a creative genius comes out and you start playing different. So it takes a tremendous amount of insight and discipline to be able to open your eyes and see all these people admiring you and yet give off that love emanating from your heart and your hands onto the skin and people get that vibe. In fact I know I have a drum calling because people tell me that when I play something moves them.

Byron describes his empathic connecting state through the drum. Sule Greg Wilson (1992) describes the spiritual and uniting connection to the drum, even though each individual has his or her own identity:

> Each Drum family, or orchestra comes from a certain ancestral line, nation, or 'tribe' as such has its own traditional language. Each drum in an orchestra, based on its shape, construction materials, size and playing technique was developed to speak a particular voice, to sound as its people, to speak their energy and their forebears. (p. 51)

Black men as equals

In this part of the discussion, Byron talks about his understanding of the dynamics between black men and black women gleaned from his reading of feminist literature. He is clear that for men to heal, they have to work on themselves and that their relationships with women are dependent on the women's ability to listen differently to them. He places an emphasis on women's influence as parents and lovers, and Byron is challenged to think about his relationships with other men, including his absent father. Fanon (1986) implies that this introspection is a process of emerging from internalised oppression:

> As I begin to recognise that the Negro is the symbol of sin, I catch myself hating the Negro. But then I recognise that I am a Negro.

There are two ways out of this conflict. Either I ask others to pay no attention to my skin, or else I want them to be aware of it. I try then to find value for what is bad. ... I have only one solution to rise above this absurd drama that others have staged around me ... to reject the two terms that are equally unacceptable and through one human being, to reach out for the universal. When the Negro dives – in other words he goes under – something remarkable occurs. (p. 197)

Racism and oppression can be likened to the drama that Fanon identifies. We now move on to the drama of homophobia and a question about sexual minorities raised by another trainee.

How are black gay/lesbian/bisexual/transgender people treated in their own community?

This question is a curious and contentious one, because the invisibility of black gay/lesbian/bisexual/transgender issues is rarely discussed. This lack of discussion creates minority oppression within an oppressed group. In Britain, people are beaten and killed because of their homosexuality. However, in most African and Caribbean countries, homosexuality is illegal, so there are no laws to avert homophobic attack and sometimes there is punishment for not being straight. The legalising of homophobia underpins a strong overt hatred towards gay people in black communities. Asking Bryon about his relationships with other men opens up his experience of sexuality in the Caribbean.

Isha: So let's progress a bit into the area of men and how you feel about Caribbean men especially.

Byron: This is a very complex issue. First of all, for the record, I am straight. I am a hot-blooded heterosexual male who has had a few homosexual encounters when I was younger and in my teens and I look back with a smile. I was born through the womb and I may die inside the woman. I always say this with a sense of humour.

Isha: Very few black men will speak openly about their sexuality.

Byron: Uh hum, uh hum. As you can see I am a red-blooded heterosexual male who is addressing my own internalised homophobia and because of my unaccomplished relationship with my biological father, he left home when I was two years old, we still have some of our relationship to thrash out. I grew up with my single mum, who had four children to support. As you know in this country from Jamaica all

the way down to Guyana the culture is very sexist, chauvinistic and homophobic. That could be endemic all over the world.

Isha: There are no examples of people in Trinidad trying to look at the oppression of homophobia.

Byron: Well gay men in this country right now are considering themselves socially illegalised and some of them are in the legal professions. They are oppressed and the mainstream heterosexual homophobic media understand some of the problems. People are willing to come out of the closet to discuss. Sisters like bell hooks in the US from her writing and brothers from the Oakland Men's Project are helping us to understand African American and other minority brothers' issues, such as violence in the home and homophobia. I looked at these issues and I couldn't run. I looked at how my Catholic mum had to suffer in the sixties when she had me as an illegitimate child. ... One of the things about my mother was that she never abandoned me, so I have a love–hate relationship with women. ... The rage and anger that I have is that women have not been studying men with the same compassion, the way I have been studying them.

Isha: Are those books just male bashing or an attempt to get women to empower themselves.

Byron: No, no, what it has done, feminism has highlighted the shadow side of men, that the devil is a he, but the devil could have been a she. What I am doing on my own since nineteen eighty-five when I became aware, I am discovering the shadow side of women, I am beginning to see woman as bitch and manipulator and even through that I have a lot of compassion, I realise that women cannot hear what men are not saying. When I articulate this to women about men as victim and powerless, they feel guilty and react because men have not told them this. They don't realise that men fear the damage that women can do to them emotionally. I live with my mother and she still holds the matriarchal domineering woman. I see my mother's darkness and I could understand why she couldn't live with a man. In spite of all the love that she projects my mother hates men, but I have the insight and compassion gained from life experience to understand why she is doing this. I am angry about the social double standards about equality because women are still not treating men as equal. I am fed up of having to objectify women and take the initiative risking rejection. Women do not understand rejection the way men understand rejection. It's part of the unfortunate reason why men have been conditioned and socialised to objectify women, because it's easier to be rejected by an object than by a human being. Over ninety-eight per cent of the moves I have made to women, I have taken the initiative. This is what patriarchy has done to set us against each other.

Isha: I don't want to harp on about how we feel about what you are saying, because I think what you are saying is really important. It's not new, I have heard it all before, and I can also understand the passion and anger that you are now faced with.

Byron: I was taught how to be a man from a female perspective; it does not work. I find myself having to be masculinist to get my point across. I saw my situation as a challenge. I was the result of a quick fuck. I saw the men in my family as confused, not aware of their sisters being abused by men, alcoholic fathers, and women being abused. I am very proud of my family and I believe in equality of women and I want to be the best family man I can be. There are a lot of things that we have to unlearn. I cry in front of women, I cuss and I scream, I don't fix things, I don't drive a car. I still believe in the sanctity of marriage, but from a different perspective.

Isha: So let's think about the healing of men.

Byron: Men have got to go through their own awakening; it's rather unfortunate that the same psycho-spiritual dynamic keeps repeating itself in Trinidad men of African descent. So many of us did not have role fathers. But we can't keep on blaming slavery and colonialism and turning to our historical past for answers. From my perspective you see the truth in the faults and you drop it. It's done with me. I am going to do something about this.

Isha: It's in the past.

Byron: Yes. So I have had to forgive my grandfather for what he did to my father and forgive my father for what he did to me. I have for-given my father, he hasn't forgiven himself. For men to heal, men have to start working on themselves, which means healing their own griev-ance that they have with their fathers and with their mothers too. A lot of women don't hear from men, you will be surprised to know the amount of rage and anger that men have towards women. They call them whores, cunt, bitch.

Isha: Yes, that's very clear. Even the way you fuck shows that you have anger towards us.

Byron: Yes, hard hard hard, I don't fuck, I make love, but when I look at women I smile, I think blessed are you and the fruit of your womb. The vagina, its pussy power, we can't do without it. I say Thank God for my mother. Men have to come to terms with these things. A lot of men do not talk about the abuse that they have suffered and the rage that they feel towards their mothers. There are many men who have been sexually abused, emotionally abused and ritualistically abused and many of them were abandoned by their mothers. And they don't articulate this to you because you don't ask the right questions.

Isha: *They are scared.*

Byron: They are scared because most people don't want to get into their stuff; that's why they run from psychotherapy. That's why they run from the mirror. Most of us are afraid of our own nakedness. We have concerns about the size of our penis; we cover our bodies; we make love in the dark. If I know a woman is into romantic novels, I think she is not committed to personal growth, so I leave. If a woman is not interested in personal growth then why stay.

Isha: *So you are continuing the oppression by staying?*

Byron: Yes, so for most of us it's a human problem not gender problem; people have to be willing to go within and they are scared. That's why we are afraid of the silence and afraid to look at our history. The psychosocial dynamics of our history since we were born, because heaven knows what we would discover because we would have to transcend being a victim, where we would have to blame someone else. It's men, it's women, it's Jewish people, it's white people, it's patriarchy. A lot of people are very comfortable being a victim, so we choose someone else to be responsible for my happiness. It's a familiar pattern, that's why marriage is this way.

Isha: *So if we take the onus off of men and women, how can men help men heal?*

Byron: First of all we have to talk to each other. Historically and socially we were conditioned to compete. We have to look at our sporting infrastructure. I believe in cross-gender sports where women can understand being part of a team. Women can then understand how men can cuss each other on the field and then be best friends. I tell my male friends our whole life was one of competition. Who is first and last, who has the bigger penis, what type of car do you have, who has the better looking madam, how are your kids. We were socialised to compete for your love. We heterosexual men do not have genuine friendships. Do you see the stupidity of all this?

Isha: So what does beauty mean to you?

Byron: I became aware that there is a damage that men have been doing to women and those women have been doing to men. So I can say on behalf of my father and my forefathers and for women to say the same that I am very sorry for the things we have done to you. It's a whole set of re-education and the stereotypes have to be unlearned. Being a pro-feminist man ideologically it does not mean that I have to give up my masculinity. If a man is not assertive he is not going to get respect. One of the calypsonians made a song 'Women Don't Like No Soft Men' and people took it to mean a soft penis, but this is what it means.

Isha: So when you say that it is time for men to apologise to women and women to apologise to men, is it also time for men to apologise to men? So it's cross-gender and inter-gender talk?

Byron: Definitely and also to our gay brothers and sisters too. It's interesting a lot of heterosexual men are appalled at gay relationships, but we love anal sex with our women. So it's double standards.

Isha: And that's the bit that seems most appalling.

Byron: Although some heterosexual organisation is trying to create theory to justify that anal sex with a woman is different to anal sex with a man. People create a philosophy to justify what they are doing. A woman asked me could a man love two women at the same time. I answered yes, but not with the same intensity.

Isha: Yes and it's a philosophy, it's not necessarily a reality.

Byron: I don't have all the answers.

Isha: No, but what you have to say is important, what is the black element in relation to black men?

Byron: I don't think you can say it's a black element. It's a human element. We are all chauvinists and skin colour and class issues have an impact.

Isha: What about the emasculation of black men?

Byron: Here we go back to where I began, our whole conditioning etcetera, loss of fathers and the way we have been socialised primarily by women.

Conclusion

In this chapter diversity issues that concern black men's voices have been presented, throwing some light on the importance of considering their cultural heritage, creative healing experiences and how greater attention can be paid to their therapeutic needs. Arike's situation encapsulates the issue of black male anger at the inconsistencies and inability of the mental health system to listen to black men's voices and accommodate their particular emotional needs. LeRoy contributes to the black voice from his experience of never having left the homeland, Trinidad, yet understanding the context of slavery and the Middle Passage and its prolonged negative impact on African communities. He interweaves his experiences as an African Caribbean elder into the reflective process of his art. LeRoy proposes that the black voice has been distorted but that through the reflective process of art, history can be healed. LeRoy suggests that consciousness can be gained through a process of reflection, so that as the individual becomes conscious of his or her cultural heritage, blackness drops away to be replaced by becoming African. Byron suggests that without the right questions, black men will not open up. This challenges the consciousness of a predominantly white and female therapy field. He shares his process though the drum and by re-thinking his black male identity. It seems clear that engaging with his black male sexuality is an important part of Byron's identity development. From my conversations with these three black men, it is clear that therapists must take into consideration the global and historical context of black men, which includes their mental health and their male sexuality. Therapists must question their ability to lend an ear holistically during the therapeutic process of black men. You will see that I have challenged my own ability to stay with the process of engaging with black male issues, for as a black female, I am also bound up in my Eurocentric influences and experiences of mental health and sexual oppression.

Pointers for therapists (including trainees and trainers)

- Engage with the cultural and creative expression of black men. This supports mutual reflection of their experiences.
- Female therapists must work through and step out of their fears and prejudices about black men so as to be better equipped to connect with them.

- Be open to engaging about relationships and sexual issues without sexualising black men.
- Avoid the pull to interpret black men's experiences using female or Western experiences and concepts.
- Take time to learn about the developmental process of black men and what being a black man means to them as a group and as individuals.
- Black male therapists, be aware of your similarities to and differences from clients, both male and female, black and white.
- Show that you are interested in the black man raised in matrilineal families and be willing to explore the implications of male role modelling.
- Be willing to work with the impact of heterosexism, patriarchy, homophobia and oppressions towards the black male.
- Be willing to explore black men's experiences of relating to each other.
- Do not make assumptions; find out about him and reflect his experience, not yours.

Part IV

A Bridge from Fear to Transformation

Parts I to III reflect a parallel journey to the therapeutic process. I have presented the catharsis of sharing and connecting to the emotions and concerns that came out of my study (McKenzie-Mavinga, 2005). Part II reflects on ways of understanding and exploring the sociological and cultural impact of black issues. Part III elucidates the process of finding a voice and understanding the impact of racism. It is usually expected that some form of transformation will occur. To gain an understanding of how to respond to black issues during the therapeutic process, training and personal development must also take place. Part IV therefore pays attention to ways of assisting this process. In acknowledgement of the fears expressed by trainees in the initial study, I have called Part IV 'A Bridge from Fear to Transformation'. Therapists, trainees and trainers are encouraged to create therapeutic models that challenge the marginalisation of minority group experiences. Emphasis is placed on the need to contradict a Eurocentric one-size-fits-all approach to clients that may run the risk of perpetuating racism and other oppressions.

9

Therapeutic Style and Approach to Client Work

This chapter explores different approaches to working with the impact of Eurocentric theory on therapeutic responses to black issues. Drawing on the concepts presented earlier in the book, I provide examples that help build culturally specific explorations during black issues work. The chapter has three sections. It begins with excerpts from an interview with Beryl, who uses what she has learned in her black therapy training to challenge the impact of slavery and denial within the black family. Four key points are drawn from Beryl's work. The chapter goes on to explain how Joyce, who trained in Britain, describes the experience of connection through language and draws on her practice in Jamaica to explain the context of bereavement and HIV and AIDS. We then move to a discussion with Dr Pat about the integration of traditional African approaches. The chapter concludes with proposals for the development of therapeutic styles that address black issues in the context of both difference and sameness.

Richards (1992) emphasises the importance of adapting to meet the needs of black clients. She identifies the link between language, need and circumstances in the development and transformation process as 'Nommo': 'Anyone who teaches black people successfully must use Nommo to teach. Nommo manifests itself in our ability to transform language. To give it new life. We create and change our language according to our need and circumstances of the black ethos' (p. 41).

Using Nommo to address black issues in the therapeutic process means adapting and developing our approach to include the historical and cultural settings relevant to people of both African and European heritage. Therapists need to develop their awareness and find a language to address geographical and sociological influences on their clients' personal development. Clients should not be denied opportunities to explore these aspects of their personal development. Wilson

(1993) suggests that mythology can be created by lack of awareness or denial:

> Mythology often can be seen as a form of denial of reality. If memory is too painful to be recalled, if recalling it means suffering pain, shame, guilt and other negative things, the individual may not only deny the reality of that memory and experience but may actually create a mythology in their places. (p. 28)

Beryl: 'Beating Is Not Like Stubbing Cigarettes Out'

Concerns about working with Nommo were raised repeatedly by trainee counsellors.

How can I creatively bring history and heritage into my clinical work with black and white clients to explore issues of shame, belonging, alienation and identity?

I use Beryl's experience as an example to clarify the process of black issues in this question. Beryl finds that her black therapy training enabled her to remember her roots and usefully work with the shared experience of racism. She unfolds the nature of a black empathic approach to this question and describes how a greater understanding of her own personal issues contributes to her understanding of the families she works with. Beryl questions her experience of Eurocentric training and the therapist's capacity to listen to cultural messages. In her approach she delivers insights using intuition and spiritual guidance that arise during her self-development and her social work and counselling practice. Having recognised the cultural and spiritual changes that needed to happen, she soared above her psychological chains and discovered tools within this experience to assist others. The stigma of childhood beatings is uncovered and placed within its historical context. This brings together past and present and helps to interrupt internalised negative messages.

Beryl worked with an elderly woman who had been physically violent to a young girl from Jamaica whom she had adopted. She was beating the girl with a cable. As a result of these beatings, the girl kept running away from home, and the mother had called the police, not realising that doing so would lead to a police record. She could not understand or believe that these 'two licks' could make the child so angry with her. She was saying that she herself had endured far more than this as a child, and she genuinely could not believe she had committed a crime. There is much controversy about harsh discipline in African and Caribbean families. Beryl avers that the approach to beating children goes back to times of slavery. She says:

> It's a question of looking at why people used to beat their children, the way that they beat them, and I know there is a big debate on how we use the word 'beating'. Lots of people say, 'Well, we say "beat", but it's not like stubbing cigarettes out or stuff like that', but it is still the same. For me it's more important to look at where it comes from and what we are going to do about it. Going back to that case, it's about how the system has got her a criminal record. The situation was perpetuated by the woman's shame. She could not let her other children know she had a criminal record because they would have been very angry with the girl.

Beryl asked the woman whether she had been beaten as a child, and the woman's facial expression changed. Beryl said to her, 'By your facial expression, I can tell that the beating you received was so bad that you can't even talk about it.' The woman replied, 'Yes.' As far as she was concerned, the beatings she was giving the little girl were nothing compared to what she had suffered herself. In addition to supporting the woman, Beryl had to convince her boss, who was white, that the client was not just a wicked woman who beat a child. The situation had to be viewed in the context of her history. According to Ackbar (1996):

> Our formulation suggests that the blemish of these inhumane conditions persists as a kind of post-traumatic stress syndrome on the collective mind of Africans...and though its original cause cannot be altered, the genesis can be understood....Our goal is to take us beyond the simple recognition of the trauma and to begin the process of healing our minds so that we can be free of slave mentality. (pp. i–ii)

Ackbar's theory provides a useful framework to discuss the experience of beatings in black families.

His sentiments about the traumas of slavery may not apply to all individuals and should not be used to homogenise the emotional context of clients' stories. However, it is necessary to remain open to the idea that the traumatic conditions of slavery may have affected the cultural dimensions of child-rearing in African and African Caribbean families. Just as the British Empire took on the role of colonial parent, the dominance of Eurocentric theory as the assumed parent of psychology and psychotherapy can sometimes silence both black and white therapists and clients on the issue of beatings.

Beryl's approach challenges Eurocentric dominance, and she acknowledges the therapeutic benefits of Nommo using her knowledge and experience as a black woman. She was able to turn the woman's violent attitude towards her daughter into an exploration of the woman's own personal experience of being physically violated – a situation so painful she had been rendered speechless. I would see this element of transformative process as recognition trauma. It was through Beryl's association with the woman's experience that she could see more clearly where she was working well as a therapist.

Significantly, in terms of the silencing mentioned above, Beryl was the only therapist I interviewed who spoke openly about beatings. Some of my clients have shared experiences of beatings that have clearly affected relationships in the black family. The collective and individual silence about beatings could be seen as another aspect of re-enactment of the past, as in the concept of ancestral baggage. Slaves were subjected to more beatings and brutality when they showed their emotions and complained or retaliated. Beatings and whippings have been justified in the name of culture. Beatings are a scary thing to speak out about, yet it is important to do so. Violence in the black family is as significant as any other critical event in family life; therefore, it is important not to cut off from clients at the point where beatings are acknowledged. It can be more helpful to place the violence in a historical context and not to isolate the experience. In this way the violence can be challenged and the client supported.

It may be argued that it is not within the therapist's remit to challenge or change a person; however, we cannot deny that the connections we make through therapy become part of the collective healing process. Just as a therapist involved with the perpetrator of violence has a choice to collude with violence or challenge it, as members of the same community we have a moral duty to challenge self-harm and harm to others. If we do not commit to our moral duty the effects of ancestral baggage are ignored. Clients bring what is currently bothering them; they come with stuff handed down from the past, and they may choose to use the therapeutic process to heal past as well as present experiences.

To support clients to explore black issues and violence, therapists need to have gone some way towards retracing their own history. If the therapist works with spiritual dimensions of the psyche, a space prepared using prayer and ritual may be needed. Sounds, smells, language and familiar objects can assist clients to connect with their rich heritage. Ackbar (1996) suggests that therapists need to be proactive in the transformation process: 'Psychologists and sociologists have failed to attend to the persistence of problems in our mental and social lives which clearly have roots in slavery' (p. 3); 'The chains are very heavy and our interconnectedness requires us to free each other and ourselves' (p. 43).

Why am I not accepted where I come from, and why am I pushed to think that black is bad?

Ackbar's suggestion that we must free ourselves and each other is important here. The question above expresses a negative consciousness that perpetuates internalised racism and damage to the collective psyche. To repair this attitude, the sociological reasons for this mindset have been addressed in the context of racism, black Western archetypes and ancestral baggage. In therapeutic work with black clients, the reflective process needs to be conscious of black Western archetypes and a vision of personal freedom. To change this negative mindset, wisdom, knowledge and positive reflection of black identity are needed.

Internalised racism has been summarised as the unconscious process of turning in hurt that happens as a result of racism. Unprocessed or undischarged trauma from the impact of racism on the psyche can perpetuate other dormant internalised oppressions, causing depression and low self-esteem. Therapists need to be aware of these intersecting oppressions. Attitudes and behaviour that result from experiences of sexism and manifest alongside attitudes and behaviour associated with racism are an example of intersecting oppressions. Internalised racism can be reinforced when the hurt of racism is not acknowledged or expressed. The hurt may not be acknowledged or expressed owing to a lack of awareness or the lack of a supportive environment for this expression. Just as most women are affected by sexism, it is likely that a layer of internalised racism inhabits the psyche of most black people. The experience of racism in Britain has caused a psychological backlog of low self-esteem. Feelings of powerlessness can cause black clients to deny or forget the richness of their heritage, inhibiting their ability to recognise and articulate self-worth. Therapists can initiate positive approaches to black self-development that can counteract this backlog. White therapists can draw on their internalising process of other oppressions to understand how racism can make black people feel powerless.

Can we work with unconscious material that links to the social dilemmas of racism? Can we place Eurocentric props aside and work with our spirituality?

The delicate subject of racism is ever present in therapy with black clients, whether it is mythologized, expressed metaphorically or not addressed at all. It is also likely that racism is not the only aspect of oppression that clients are not conscious of. Defence mechanisms may spread their protective shield across any or all oppressions. It may indeed be detrimental to resurrect experiences of racism in the therapeutic process without seeking prior permission from clients, just as we might seek permission to address any other violent or abusive experiences. Oppressions from the past are just as important as oppressions operating in the present. Beryl worked with both past and present oppressions, at the same time including her spirituality and liberating herself from the restrictions of Eurocentric approaches. These are her concluding remarks:

> I got good results, but I always felt that I was not getting it right because of what the book said. Then you, Isha, actually said to me, 'Who actually writes the recipe?' This had so much meaning and made a lot of sense. I did not have very much confidence. I doubted myself all the time that I was not doing this well enough. That led on to a black therapy course and then I realised that what was being taught was what I was doing. We had been taught in the Eurocentric way. I work intuitively. On one occasion I lit candles in a counselling session, because I had a strong urge to do this. At one stage I would not have done this, because the book doesn't say you can do this in a counselling session. I learned that I could trust my own intuition.

Four elements essential to working with black issues in the therapeutic process were highlighted during my discussions with Beryl.

(1) *The element of isolation.* Beryl explained to me that she had suffered racism in her work and left her job experiencing low self-esteem. The low self-esteem caused her to feel negative about herself and her potential to progress in her life. As a result of this, she lost confidence in her ability to find work, and even though she reached the interview stage in her job search, she avoided attending interviews. I suspected that she had become afraid that failure might impact her already low esteem. She managed to get another job when her cousin broke the isolation and she felt supported and encouraged. However, she 'dived in', as she said, 'at the deep end', and it seemed that she was unsure whether she could cope.

(2) *The element of educational oppression.* This element registered for me in the way Beryl explained how she had experienced the word of Eurocentric books as the only word and the rules by which she should work. It seemed that she had internalised a subservient approach to learning and had experienced little support to value her own ideas. For black learners this omission can exacerbate internalised racism. Realising her ability to integrate her experience and personal skills made it possible for Beryl to create a safe learning environment for her own students. Once Beryl had found a job where she could set her own limits and challenge the cultural misunderstanding of her colleagues, her self-esteem was raised. On becoming empowered she discovered her connection to others who also suffered from low self-esteem. Drawing on her personal experience and these skills supported her development of a black empathic approach that she was able to contribute effectively to the healing of other black individuals.

(3) *The element of violence.* Many people who suffer low self-esteem have been victims of some sort of physical or emotional violence. If physical violence has been experienced but not acknowledged, it is likely that emotional violence has also been experienced. People who have experienced verbal abuse, put-downs and consistent undermining of their personalities may suffer prolonged emotional violence without directly experiencing physical violence. Racism is a form of emotional violence that can be caused by the internalisation of negative images, negative language about skin colour or adverse experiences that distort the reflection of an individual's identity.

Beryl disclosed her ideas about violence and challenged the cultural messages that perpetuate violence. To empower others, we need to address our own wounds from physical and emotional violence, including the emotional violence of racism. Patterns of violence become patterns in our lives. We have only to look at the high levels of black-on-black killings to understand how physical and emotional violence can create destructive human behaviour and damage our gaze. In Chapter 8, I mentioned that LeRoy said the murderer 'did not see himself in her', the victim. Richards (1992) suggests: 'In turning on himself, he turns on those closest to him. ... Wade Nobles defines insanity afrocentrically. It is when a person of African descent does not understand that killing another black person is not homicide, it is suicide' (p. 48).

(4) *The element of internalised racism.* The process of internalised racism has been described in many ways in this book. In the above quotation, it is identified with the killing of self. Individuals carry

attitudes, behaviours and symptoms that manifest in the ways in which they manage ongoing experiences of racism in their lives. Beatings, killings, rapes and self-mutilation are woven into the messages that have been internalised from the experience of racism and other oppressions. If therapists prepare themselves appropriately, therapy can play a role in shifting the internal hurt that racism imposes on human lives.

Beryl was clear about the need to understand violence in the context of history and work this into a collective approach to healing. She used her knowledge of cultural violence and created an empathy with her clients, at the same time challenging theoretical systems that need to be revised. Ackbar (1996) affirms the therapist's role in this unconscious process:

> The process of human slavery is ultimately a psychological process by which the mind of a people is gradually brought under the control of their captors and they become imprisoned by the loss of the consciousness (awareness) of themselves. ... The challenge for those who choose to be healers of black life must be the removal of these psychological chains. (pp. 30–2)

Removing the psychological chains is a feat in itself, for as we develop a racial consciousness, the dangers of over-identification and homogenisation become greater. Richards (1992) acknowledges this process as 'oneness': 'The fact that a people's experiences and historical circumstances are shared over long periods of time in the setting of culture makes them one, and their oneness creates a commonness of spirit' (p. 2).

Identifying with others through our experiences is what connects us as humans. It is also common to assume that we are all the same because of our human nature. Eurocentric models of therapeutic process lean towards individuation yet do not pay enough attention to differences. Eastern and African models of healing may place a greater emphasis on sharing and community-building, so individuation may not be viewed in the same context. Our connectedness as black people often attracts curiosity from white peers, as in the following question.

Is over-identification more likely between a black counsellor and black client than between a white counsellor and white client?

For therapists this question can be a double-sided one, bearing the mark of 'oneness', as Richards suggests, while risking over-identification. So how do both black and white counsellors use their experience to create a balance of connection, understanding and empathy within their like group? This trainee's concern is expressed as though bonding between a black client and a black counsellor might be weightier than bonding between a white client and a white counsellor. We must be wary of underplaying the dynamics of the white client–counsellor relationship, as this is rarely explored in a racial context. The therapeutic relationship between a black client and a black therapist under scrutiny might then be seen as abnormal.

In the next section, using an excerpt from an interview with Joyce, who has used her counselling experience both in Britain and in the Caribbean, I explore the black-on-black therapeutic process for its learning potential.

Joyce: 'Language Is a Really Important Part of Black on Black Therapy'

Joyce, a Jamaican psychotherapist trained in Britain, described how a shared historical experience combined with an understanding of difference contributes to her work as a counsellor. She described how cultural empathy works. Within the phrase 'Uh hum' lies the importance of not having to explain and knowing there is a shared heritage, yet as therapists we must not take this shared experience for granted. The impact of language and the therapist placing language in its historical context is discussed below. Language is as important in Britain as it is in the Caribbean. Returning to the experience of back home and developing humility towards others with a similar background has become a core condition in Joyce's work and within the process of transcending our differences as black people. Emphasis is placed on messages that were learned in our developmental process.

Joyce: My therapeutic approach is a humanistic, person-centred approach. It comes naturally to me as I do not have to get into a therapeutic mode, I can just be myself.

Isha: *Can you tell me about your work with black clients?*

Joyce: In my approach I value my people as human beings. I get in touch with our oppression. It's not just the oppression of our history, it's the oppression of present-day society, and it's about our oppression from our men and the oppression of the system and the expectations that are put on us. When I get a woman who comes to me and her problem is relationship, it's usually about other people's expectations of her, the messages she has been given by her mother about the kind of woman she is expected to be. I do get some women who come to me and boy are they angry! I'm telling you! I mean like they are just so angry. It really is about getting in touch and finding what the anger is about. Invariably the anger is not about what they come and tell me it is about. It is far more deep rooted. ... The third area is about bereavement and one of the values is like this. I remember a young woman saying, 'When I come to you and when you say "Uh hum", or if I say "Uh hum", you know exactly what I am talking about. I don't have to explain to you.' And she said, 'That is one of the values of us working black on black, because you do understand what I am saying.'

> We will need this 'secret language' as long as we are colonised in a society that is dominated by an alien cultural group. (Richards, 1992, p. 42)

Joyce: Whether I work with black women in England or in Jamaica we share a history that not all black people share. It is a myth that if you are black then it is okay that we all share the same history. Black people in Jamaica have a history of slavery that not all black people share. Even other black people that share slavery have not experienced it in the way we have in Jamaica. So because we share the common history we have a starting point, which may be different if I am working with someone who resides in Jamaica.

Wilson (1993) emphasizes the significance of cultural history in therapeutic relationships: 'History is no casual thing that one picks up while passing through school. It becomes a part of one's total orientation towards the world' (p. 28).

Joyce: Now you see I am coming to the edge of my chair because I am becoming exited as I think about 'Uh hum' because it is such a powerful expression, it says such a lot. Because when I am talking to someone who is in distress and they say 'UH HUM!!!!!!!' I know that they know that I understand what they are saying. If I am listening to someone and I say 'Uh hum', I know that they are saying 'Yeah, well, maybe, maybe not.' It is a powerful expression.

Isha: The suppression and expression of language is a really important aspect of communication rooted in our history. The phonics of language has the meaning, not just the word itself.

Joyce: Yes rooted in our history.

Isha: Language is a really important part of black-on-black therapy.

Joyce: I think so. Yes, language plays a really important part. The way we use the language. I remember talking to someone in Jamaica who said that one of the barriers could be people not understanding the language. Going back to the Caribbean if you do not understand the language, being black on black would not help. Even as a black therapist, having been trained in England or the States, going back to the Caribbean, if you do not understand the language, you are lost. If you are seen as a black middle class coming from up town and you are going to go down into the inner-city communities which are commonly known as the ghetto, where people live in very close contact. Sometimes they use expressions down there that they understand very well and if you live in Jamaica and you don't even live in those areas, you may understand. However, if you are coming from abroad, even if you are a black person and if you don't understand the language, that can be a barrier to you going in there to offer help to those people, because they see you as different. So even within the culture, one has to be very aware of language and how language is used and interpreted.

Isha: Do you think this was similar for you in England? Black therapists in particular were seeing people in the inner cities that are not familiar with counselling. Then along came some odd social work type people who did not really know their language, and didn't speak it because we have been educated by the system to think and talk in a social work type way and can't hear what is really being said.

Joyce: Yes I think some of that is in England too. We would be talking about different phrases, different words that are used by black people in inner cities.

Loss and bereavement

Isha: You spoke about the healing issues such as anger, bereavement and oppression; I would be interested in hearing about this work and the importance of working black on black in those areas.

Joyce: As a black therapist being trained outside of the Caribbean and being away from the Caribbean for thirty-six years, most of my life.

Isha: Uh hum!!!!

Joyce: I found that when I went back I had a lot of learning to do.

Isha: What did you have to learn?

Joyce: Okay, working with people on issues of bereavement, I know the textbook way to go about it. As black people we have our rituals, I wasn't in touch with some of the rituals. I know about the importance of food. I know that the whole village comes out in mourning. I know that you don't have to personally know the family to come to the funeral, that if you don't go to the funeral, that it is seen as disrespectful not to come. Everybody is expected to be there. There are some things I didn't know about. The rituals where they pass a child over the coffin to keep the spirits away. Also rituals where the closest person wears red underwear to keep the spirits away.

Isha: Red underwear – I have not heard of that one.

Joyce: They paint the house red; others repaint the house if they don't paint it red. They move the furniture out of the house, to confuse the spirit when they return; they will not know the place because it would have changed.

Isha: So this was to deter the spirit from returning?

Joyce: I also needed to know what nine nights was about.

Isha: So you didn't know?

Joyce: I know how it happens, but I didn't know that it was about releasing the spirit on the ninth night. So I had to go back and relearn those things. I just knew that it was one of our customs and that it was very important. I also knew that having a wake was very important, but I had not gone into why. Why do we do those things?

> Our funerals have traditionally been rituals...family and friends are called together...until the family is transformed once more into a sacred community bound by a common experience, then cleansed, energised and raised briefly to spiritual heights through their ability to experience and express the suffering within....Crisis understood communally. (Richards, 1992, p. 31)

Isha: So here those things were done ritually, but not understood?

Joyce: That's right, that's right.

Isha: Going back gave you the content and understanding of it.

Joyce: Exactly, yes, yes. It's also about respecting the culture and that the need to know is important so that I can increase that respect. I don't think it is my client's responsibility to tell me these things. I need to find it out for myself so that I have a very clear and focused understanding when I am working with my clients.

Isha: Is it also a parallel for you because you have done that work yourself, therefore you are a good role model for the clients?

Joyce: If you go in with humility, our people are warm and caring and loving. I am not painting a rosy picture because I want to deny the elements of violence and corruption that surround us.

Isha: That is humanistic, you asking them to tell you about the runnings. In person-centred counselling you don't step on someone else's toes, you give them the opportunity to do it themselves, with your support.

Joyce: That's right, that's part of what I am saying to you. I think that I may have been born with some special skills that I develop as I go through my life, because I do not know where the real Joyce ends and the training begins. It all just feels a part of my being.

Isha: I was thinking of when you spoke about your difference and about overcoming the fear of being different, from whatever perspective it is, overcoming your difference from other Jamaicans, and their difference from you as a black person. ... Within us we have our individuality and our different life histories, even though some of us share the common areas of, for example, the experience of slavery in the Caribbean. So I think that transcending these areas of difference as black people is one of the key issues. Unless they get close to us and accept our differences by supporting us to define ourselves, therapy with white people can do little to help us transcend our differences as black peoples. We have to put our fear aside and work together in order to do this.

Joyce: Yes, fear has been one of the things that stops us from doing a lot of things, including documenting.

> The loneliness and vulnerability that comes from the removal of your chains and trying out your new legs is considerable as was the wilderness experience for the Hebrew children and Christ. ...The reminder of the security and companionship you knew as a captive is constantly thrown in front of you. (Ackbar, 1996, p. 40)

Isha: You were saying that you are working with HIV and AIDS workers. Is there anything you wish to say with regard to this area of work?

Joyce: Jamaica is still a homophobic society. I chose this area to work in when I went out to Jamaica, because this is an area that carries one of the greatest stigmas and a lot of people do not want to be associated with it. I had skills that I thought would be useful in terms of counsellors and training. So what I do is help them to develop courses and train friends and facilitators in small groups. And so it's a developing area in Jamaica and it is going quite well and there are a bunch of very dedicated people. I have a lot of respect for the people who work in that area because it is difficult and it is charitable. I would like to see that as black therapists that we become more supportive of the area of HIV and AIDS, because in the year two thousand, all of us will know someone who has been infected or affected.

Isha: So in terms of the level of homophobia that is exhibited in the Caribbean and supported by patriarchal societies internationally, how do you facilitate those workers to break through homophobia and work in this area?

Joyce: Promoting the message that HIV and AIDS is not a homosexual disease, because a large percentage of those infected in the Caribbean are heterosexuals.

Isha: And so the homophobia is just built on mythology really.

Joyce: Uh hum!!!!!

Isha: When you promote that idea you are doing a form of facilitation and is it that you challenge them, therefore they look at it differently?

Joyce: No, it's not like that, because the people that I facilitate in the supervision they are senior staff and they work with others out there and do the challenging. The other people need challenging about things that have been said like 'HIV and AIDS is a punishment from God'.

Isha: Uh hum. Religion does come into it and we haven't touched on that yet.

Joyce: Yes, and that's another story. In Jamaica there are only two formal training programmes for counselling, otherwise there is the church. There is a religious focus all the time. 'Have you been to see your pastor?' 'Did you pray about it?' The other alternative is Obeah, and the Western talking therapies that you and I have become accustomed to are gaining prominence. Although people turn to the pastor, they are in actual fact getting guidance rather than counselling.

Dr Pat: 'It's Like Healing the Soul'

This section offers a perspective on the integration of traditional African healing into the therapeutic process. Traditional healing informs services for clients at the Phoenix Women's Health Project, formerly based in south London. A common acknowledgement of people's pain assists the healing process and breaks isolation. Important factors in this approach are the inclusion of God, ancestors and the departed family. These practices have been handed down through the ages. It helps if the therapist and client have elements of the same background, such as being from an African or Caribbean background. The project focused on women because women are responsible for about 80 per cent of family health. Thinking about ways in which women can have longevity without too much stress is central to the services. Support groups and sister groups represent the family and community. Individuals are supported to reclaim their familiarity with other black people. Dr Patience Adin-Tetty suggests that the make-up of the staff group can influence the type of clients that the project attracts. In working with differences as well as similarity, even the region of the world is important. The following question signifies trainees' interest in this approach.

When people talk about an African-centred approach, what do they mean?

I explore this question through discussion with Dr Patience Adin-Tetty, referred to as Dr Pat, who explains her attempts to integrate an African-centred approach into her work with health care patients.

Isha: I remember the first time we met and you told me how your community in Ghana meet together and do basic things which are healing. We conversed about how healing is not necessarily sitting two people in chairs and talking, because that is not what you are bringing here in terms of the work that you are doing. Your experience of traditional healing informs the theory behind the work that you do here in England.

Dr Pat: Yes, in Ghana we always believe in the spirit and the soul and body. When things go wrong what the tribe usually does, they pick a day, Monday to Sunday. It is the day of birth, the day they were born, and then on this day they alert the rest of the family that they are going to have purification, because the theory underpinning this is that once the soul is hurt things will not go well. It's like washing the

soul. We have particular fruits and foodstuffs that are used for it. The morning will start with a special ceremony, they pray to the gods, with drink and with spirits like gin. This is then followed by water. They first call the name of God and then the name of the local spirit. Then all the ancestors are called to come and stand behind the person. So they do that in the early hours of the morning before the sun rises. Then they bathe, then there is another ceremony and they wear white. It is an acknowledgement by the whole tribe that the person is suffering. So they have breakfast made of moist yam. One has palm oil in it; the other, which is white, has no oil in it. The one for the spirit of the person has no seasoning in it, made of about a dozen eggs. They have this for themselves. Everybody comes and tastes of it, as if it's a rebirth, because they have been cleansed through the prayers and they are going to start a meal. People come and give advice and congratulations and bring gifts, for having gone through the difficult experience. They are going to restart life. Then in the afternoon, they may kill a chicken or a goat, depending on the type of trauma and the family resources. They cook and have light soup and then a thicker soup or fufu. I found out that different groups have different foods. There are a lot of children around and music and dancing to celebrate. Then in the evening they say goodbye and the person has a special bed, so that everything is clean and special for them to start again. It's amazing how this works, I've been trying to work out the theory of this, the people feel new and good about themselves and accepted again and can start again empowered and loved by your community.

> When the life of a group is threatened, ritual is used to psychologically and emotionally strengthen its members by creating a sense of order that will better enable them to deal with their problems in a constructive way. (Richards, 1992, p. 26)

Isha: So with the understanding and agreed sense of ritual and its part in your culture, you know what is available if you need help. Is that right?

Dr Pat: Things are changing now because of the foreign religions such as Christianity, Muslim and Western philosophy, it is different. In the cities, most people have forgotten. It's only when things get really bad that some families will do it. Most traditional people or people in the country would do this.

Isha: And you are saying that in most cases this approach works. Do you know of any situations where this did not work?

Dr Pat: Not really, I have been so impressed with it that I have thought that it is something that can be modified. It is the same with our bereavement, because there is so much acknowledgement of people's pain. You don't get a lot of the same syndromes you get here. It's as if we need each other to acknowledge and to help with our healing.

Isha: And there is a lot to be said for group attention on somebody. The more attention you get, the more likely you are to heal.

Dr Pat: Definitely.

Isha: Like group therapy and therapies where lots of people are supporting you because we get quite isolated. In group settings we have the experience where people may be of like mind or can appreciate what is happening and that is a way forward.

Dr Pat: Yes, because even back home where we have lots of people around, bad experience of sorrow or grief can isolate, so group attention can draw you back.

Isha: There is no mystery about what will happen because you know that this, this and this will happen.

Dr Pat: The mystery is in the inclusion of the departed family, your ancestors and God. This is where Western cultures make mistakes. It doesn't matter if Africans have got a god, they always acknowledge God. God with a big G comes first in every ceremony. They think that all these people are going to heal them and God's people are going to heal. On the other hand it's no mystery in that it is handed down, so the elders will explain this.

Isha: There is no Freud?

Dr Pat: Definitely not.

Isha: It's traditional and it's pure, it has been handed down through the ages?

Dr Pat: Yes.

Isha: Do you think that the fact of these traditions being carried out with your own people and by your own people makes a difference?

Dr Pat: Yes.

Isha: Do you apply your traditional theories in your work here at the project?

Dr Pat: Yes, my counselling is very unorthodox.

Isha: In what way is it unorthodox?

Dr Pat: I treat everyone as a sister. My tradition comes in, because back home where I grew up, you have a hundred thousand uncles. Any female figure over a certain age was an auntie and every male figure was an uncle and all the others down the road were sisters or brothers. In my head everyone who comes in through the door is a relation.

Isha: So that's part of the healing because they are accepted as part of your family. It goes a long way in helping people to reclaim their familiarity with other black people, so what are the particular issues that people bring because they are black and living in Britain? And what makes it work?

Dr Pat: We did a conference on relationships. The response showed that unfortunately, black women who have lived in this country with Western values, not in a negative way, find it difficult to cope with black men who are having it rough in this country, especially those who are having the same education as their white peers and have problems getting jobs. They internalise everything and bring it home and the black woman gets a raw deal, especially when sometimes, not far away, you can see a black man treating a white woman differently. Also the general feel of racism makes anyone living in a foreign country feel isolated. The weather here is not always conducive to going to visit your neighbour. There are all these problems. Sometimes at Phoenix we would have a little meal at lunchtime. People who were in the building would come and we would all sit and talk. I must say, I was naughty, I facilitated it without people being aware that I was facilitating these sessions, so that the people who came in for counselling would realise that they were not alone. People would share and quite often they are better motivated and held by their peers than a professional counsellor or whatever. It breaks the isolation.

Isha: What makes this black-on-black approach work? The organisation is staffed by black women. They work predominantly with other black women who need help. What makes the two work together and how do you know it works?

Dr Pat: People give you feedback. It is not every black person that wants black support. I can't put it into words but I relate to you far more easily than I would relate to a white person in your profession. It takes me far longer to establish that relationship with a white person. I don't know how to put it, but it's there. Like I might find it easier to relate to a Ghanaian than I may relate to you, but perhaps having lived abroad for so long, I have come to be part of the larger family so that

I relate to you as I relate to a fellow Ghanaian. Of course, familiarity breeds its own contempt, but generally because we are all foreigners and because of the racism around when we do get together it works better. Sometimes it is a barrier because we don't somehow internalise depression, we find it easier to come together and trust each other.

Isha: Is it a homogeneous group that come to you or do you have lots of different types of black women, for example African born, Caribbean born, British born, or a predominance of a particular type?

Dr Pat: It's been more Caribbean born until recently, but now it's more African born. Strangely enough it happens in waves. I suppose it depends on the staff too. There was a time when I had a lot of East Africans and then Muslims and then suddenly you are going through a cycle of Ghanaians. It varies and I think it depends on the people around and who are talking about it.

Isha: So if there is a predominance of staff from particular areas, they might attract clients from those areas. That is a kind of evidence that same group attracts same group in counselling. I think that is an interesting point because I think that we are not just one homogeneous mass and there is an assumption that we can all help each other. It's also about working with our differences as well and in some cases similarity, even the region of the world, because as black people that is important too.

Dr Pat: Yes.

> To attempt to apply Western psychological perspective straight into the African setting is to miss the understanding of different individuals. It may be taken to mean that African cultures cannot be understood in their own right and therefore need to be translated through interpretation of Western thought; a process that dismisses the whole process of communication. On the other hand, to attempt to understand the psychological make-up of an individual without any knowledge of their cultural make-up is to dismiss cultural heritage – a process that is currently prominent in counselling approaches to non-Western clients. (Ocheing, 2003, p. 40)

Reflections

Finding the right balance between appropriate services and therapeutic approach presents a challenge for therapists in the Western world. Ocheing, quoted above, considers the cultural bearings on

African-centred approaches in Western society. I asked Dr Pat to consider combining her traditional Ghanaian approach with her work with clients in Britain.

Isha: There is another question. Would you like to incorporate your traditional approach from Ghana into your work in Britain and do you think it would be viable?

Dr Pat: Yes, I would like to do it and I do think it would be viable, but not with the ritual, you can substitute that with food and especially with black people, we like acknowledging each other's challenges and suffering. Actually about four years ago I was thinking of applying this to bereavement because our bereavement process back home is so good. I took a course and when I discussed this on the course, I was told that this kind of thing used to happen before the Industrial Revolution. It was the Industrial Revolution that stopped it. So as much as we want to claim that it is a particular black thing, it seems as if it is something that has always been done, you know, and it worked and we are already doing it.

Conclusion

It is clear that African- and Caribbean-influenced approaches have much to offer therapists trained in the Eurocentric traditional therapies. All three therapists interviewed in this chapter highlight the importance of developing appropriate, culturally sensitive approaches to working with black issues. Their diverse experiences contribute to a vast field of therapeutic knowledge.

Beryl's combination of Eurocentric and black therapy training affords her knowledge and understanding of black issues in a spiritual context, at the same time using her awareness of ancestral baggage. She shares the challenges of her own personal development and growing confidence and uses her insights to engage with black issues in the therapeutic process. Her work highlights key areas of concern such as isolation, educational oppression, violence and internalised racism.

Joyce reveals the challenges of working across a cultural and geographic divide between Jamaica and her Eurocentric training in Britain. Joyce's work helps us to reflect on the impact of language and the context of the diaspora and recovering forgotten cultural elements.

She shares her understanding of HIV and homophobia in Jamaica and the shift to Western therapeutic approaches.

Dr Pat suggests that an African-centred approach using rituals and life ceremonies that militate against isolation can reinforce a sense of identity and community. Her primary intention is to recreate a sense of community to heal identity and self-love. This African-based approach seems to enable individual healing through community support: 'A community is a place of self-definition. Any group of people meeting with the intention of connecting to the power within is a community' (Somé, 1993, p. 67).

It is important to be aware of the unconscious or unaware processes operating behind certain behaviours or symptoms that can be detrimental to the self-esteem of a black person, whether they are client or therapist. All therapists need reassurance. Concerns about whether the issue of racism should be addressed are important and should not be ignored.

We can learn a lot from Beryl, who wanted to remember parts of her history that have been omitted from her present and use these experiences in her therapeutic work. She recalled with clarity the experiences of her ancestors and remembered cultural indicators that she could celebrate and enjoy. From this she has given herself a stronger framework within which to build her identity and self-esteem and from which she can support others.

This chapter has focused attention on the therapeutic transformation for both the black therapist and the black client. I have drawn on the wisdom of established practitioners and the experience they have gained from their developing practice. From these experiences it is clear that progress in understanding black issues requires emotional emergence from the impact of racism. This can be combined with knowledge of oppression and understanding of the constraints of Eurocentric dominance in training and theories of therapy and counselling.

Discussion with black counsellors demonstrates that multicultural approaches need to develop and integrate specific reference to black issues in the therapeutic relationship for both black and white therapists. Having a black client in front of us does not validate black issues therapeutic work unless therapists are equipped to acknowledge and explore the black issues that go with this situation. A multidimensional approach that revises traditional theories and integrates awareness about black issues and racism is necessary. Paying attention to the racist components of psychology assists clients to heal from and undo the damaging effects of internalised racism and other oppressions.

Understanding black issues means paying attention to language and social codes that may influence power relationships and black clients' responses. These social codes also influence power relationships between black counsellors and between white counsellors and their responses to their different cultural groups.

It is important to be aware of the extent to which therapists shut down on the wider context of identity oppression. An example of this happened when I was challenged about whether I address difference with my white clients. I had to admit that I am less likely to address this difference, and as a black woman I am more likely to address the context of similarity with black clients, yet I encourage white trainees to explore their difficulties when addressing difference with black clients. Perhaps this acknowledgement is a fitting example of how ingrained the oppression of racism and Eurocentric approaches has become.

Pointers for therapists (including trainees and trainers)

- Provide group therapy or one-to-one experience where common acknowledgement of people's pain can assist the healing process and break isolation. This may require black people to work together on their issues.
- Draw on group attention to break the isolation of sorrow and grief; this can encourage individuals to reconnect with their communities.
- Develop an awareness of how colonialism and Eurocentric traditions have permeated the developing countries.
- Be aware that negative issues that threaten the emotional well-being of individuals may threaten the life of their relevant cultural groups.
- African-centred approaches may be integrated into therapeutic support and inform the theory behind work carried out in Britain.
- Draw on the client's knowledge or experience of ancestors and his or her spirituality.
- Don't make assumptions that a British-born and -raised African will identify with approaches used by Africans born and raised in their country of origin.
- Acknowledge clients as part of your community; this assists the healing process and helps individuals to reclaim their familiarity with others.
- Work with differences and similarities, including those found in language, belief systems and regions of the world.
- White therapists should draw on these suggestions to develop work in cross-racial settings or within white groups, especially where background and cultural heritage have been denied.

- Keep dialogue on black issues open in personal development forums so that practice develops appropriately.
- Be aware of internalised oppression at whatever level seems appropriate to each individual, whether displayed consciously or not.
- Although most black people will have been impacted by racism, do not take this for granted. Some individuals have been raised in family and community systems that elevate them above distresses of this type.
- Read, travel and experience dialogue about black issues.

10
Going All the Way

Chapter 9 explored different training approaches to black issues used by three black therapists. This chapter outlines some key aspects of learning and practice for counsellors and therapists working with black issues. Drawing on the transformative process of black issues workshop exercises with trainee counsellors, I present the narrative of trainers and trainees recounting their workshop experiences. For me, 'going all the way' means addressing a training process that can support some of the ideas, concepts and experiences that this book has highlighted. To be true to this, I begin the process of providing a framework for integrating black issues into training courses.

Approaches to therapeutic support may differ, but for practitioners keen to work transculturally, an active involvement in the process of black issues can be integrated into most models of counselling, psychotherapy and psychology. The style and model of an integrated approach depend on therapists' flexibility and willingness to dialogue about black issues with their clients, their supervisors and in their own personal development. As an anti-oppressive practice, such an approach may be experienced differently by black therapists than by white therapists. The potential for racism to be reinforced may be greater when the therapist is white and the client black, whereas a black therapist may be inclined to identify with the black client. Both black and white therapists must therefore be aware of their potential to ignore internalised racism in black clients. It is important to pay attention to any difficulties in relationship dynamics and dialogue about black issues.

An important learning from the study was that a space should be allowed for trainees to find their voice and explore their concerns about working with black issues. This is an important parallel to client work. The three questions presented below are further examples of trainees' concerns about their practice, the theories that support their work and their personal process when working with black issues.

What do we do when we know a client is holding back on race issues?

The answer to this question is really no different than when the challenge is one of clients holding back on other issues, such as gender and sexuality. However, concerns about addressing black issues appear greater because of the levels of fear attached to racism. I have found that both trainees and experienced professionals become afraid to go in there, afraid to go all the way and afraid to make mistakes and get messy. Although this fear rings true of client work in general, where there may be conflict owing to the hurtful experience of oppressions, it is usually greater between white therapist and black client. However, we must continue to challenge ourselves on these fears and thus develop a greater potential to engage with the effects of racism on the psyche and soul.

First and foremost, therapists need to break down their own prejudice and fear about the process a black person goes through when he or she is hurt by racism. Therapists need to approach black issues with the same openness, regard and respect that they would use when processing other issues. It is important not to further deny the experience of racism by ignoring race issues because the client may be holding back. It is also important not to allow feelings about racism to prevent exploration of other black issues, or indeed other oppressions. Stuckness in addressing these issues implies that therapists need to get support for their own feelings about racism so that they can prepare themselves for the client's responses, just as they would be expected to do with any other issue. This means that senior practitioners and supervisors must develop ways to model and open dialogue about these concerns and not perpetuate the oppressions by responding with a 'colour-blind' approach.

Is it true that racism causes depression?

Lack of confidence and low self-esteem can result from having to cope with racism in addition to everyday pressures of life. Frequent media coverage of racist dynamics suggests that racism is almost an everyday occurrence. Many black people live with the threat of the physical and emotional hurt of racism. For some, hopelessness and despair can set in. This can result from constant emotional pressure owing to low status and lack of opportunity, a sudden racist incident or perhaps a developing awareness of the part that racism has played in their lives. This type of depression can be associated with recognition trauma.

Support to manage the effects of racism has been limited by lack of understanding and by institutional racism. This is the nature of the beast. Activities such as art, recreation, talking and music can be used to explore the process of racism in everyday life. These activities can also be introduced in therapeutic relationships, as they support the development of cultural identity. The therapist should be innovative and creative in providing appropriate support to facilitate strategies to cope with the specific ways in which racism can contribute to depression.

How do we support and listen well to the anger that black people experience when they become aware of their oppression?

Addressing racism can be an uncomfortable process. Clients may openly express their rage or exhibit defences that appear impenetrable. They may present as wearing 'no entry' signs, showing the harsh, uncompromising face of battle. The armour can be a tough reminder that no more pain must enter; yet the defences are fragile and have to be reinforced every day. Sometimes it can appear that there is no escape from the daily reminder that skin colour difference is another class barrier for the black person. Behind the armour lie the anger of injustice and the hurt of generations that have barely been understood. This is an aspect of recognition trauma. Therapists run the risk of becoming institutionalised to ignore recognition trauma if their training does not attend to these issues. Feelings about racism are sometimes viewed as abnormal, theorised away as ordinary pain or avoided, but the impact of racism continues even when hidden. Accumulation of past racism can affect how present, everyday racism is managed. During my study, colleagues and trainees helped to identify supportive ways to work with these responses.

A mixture of enthusiasm, concern and fear was expressed by both trainees and trainers during the process of examining ways of understanding black issues in the therapeutic process. My study showed that active facilitation and opportunities to address these experiences and emotions are key to finding a voice and creating the dialogue essential for working through recognition trauma and understanding black issues. The interactive process of dialogue and stimulating workshop exercises, combined with a supportive confidential space to evaluate, created a bridge for the transformation process of individuals involved in the training. In the following list, I present some training points based on what trainees said could be usefully included in their training:

- discussions about how similarities, differences, power and oppression can affect the therapeutic relationship

- the open discussion by black and white people of black issues and the sense that comments made about black issues are accepted
- an acknowledgement that white group members can feel oppressed
- open discussions where people can speak freely without fear of being judged or labelled
- experiential learning that includes exercises to examine feelings about black issues
- the identification and availability of reading and resource material that addresses black issues
- black support groups to reinforce black trainees' confidence during training
- examples of live counselling sessions or case studies where black issues are addressed
- information about the meaning of black issues for different generations
- drama, role-play
- the establishment of a good group contract at the beginning of training that empowers members to respect and accept other group members and cultures

The following pointers may be helpful when integrating the theme of black issues into a training programme:

- Include 'black issues' as criteria for assessment within equalities competencies.
- Expect placement, personal development and external supervision to support trainees with black issues and include this in their report requirements.
- Complement reading lists with texts that explicitly address racism and black issues.
- Provide definitions and examples of 'intercultural' and 'transcultural' approaches to counselling.
- Make links between black issues and the issues of other ethnic groups.
- Allow discussion time for the exploration of black issues, oppressions, internalised oppression, white racism and white oppression.
- Be willing to contribute knowledge and engage in discussions about the developmental process and cultural heritage and belief systems of black people.
- Be willing to engage in the process of white people's cultural heritage and historical and social role in the context of black issues.

- Role-model attempts to dialogue about black issues even when it gets difficult.
- Expect support to discuss black issues in supervision, line management and personal development forums. Put it on the agenda at team meetings.
- Address parallels between cultural issues and minority oppressions.
- Provide opportunities to explore mythology, folklore and stereotyping.
- Take risks, make mistakes and learn from the process.

Your training team should be one in which risks can be taken, mistakes can be made and trainers can learn from the process of addressing black issues. As an example of this type of dialogue, I present the following transcript of a team meeting recorded after some black issues workshops had taken place during the training. Except for the researcher (me), all ten staff were white. Core tutors, external supervisors, personal development facilitators and external moderators were present. (Phrases in *italics* were spoken by me.)

What the tutors said

How do we know what impact the black issues workshops have had on staff and students and the development of practice on the counsellor training programme?

The impact has had a domino effect. We are changing; therefore students change, and therefore practice has an impact on clients.

A difficult beginning. A difficult thing to admit that I am not as aware as I thought I was.

Work with university clients has shifted due to being given permission and encouragement to address these issues of diversity.

Proud to be part of a training that is dealing with this. As I read assessments, journals, case notes, professional logs, philosophies and how students are finding their way to write about this. The assessment section that says how does difference, similarity, equality issues, oppression affect your role as counsellor etcetera. I have noticed that sometimes people are bolting it on, and on the other hand I am also observing that prompted by this input, there is another way it is becoming embedded in the course due to how we are locating it on the course and integrating it in different ways to previously.

People are saying positive things. Are we brave enough to say what we are uncomfortable about?

About staff relationships and being the lone black tutor, my white staff peers saying we are all doing it. Yet I was still, as the black tutor, holding the fort. I was unable to sit back and let you take some of the flack.

Important to role-model how everybody is challengeable, and we all have this material in us. Out of the pain comes our best modelling and our best teaching.

What the supervisor said

I have been challenged by my supervisees about what is going on in the group. I left a black student who was in the minority and felt silenced. I excused her silence as the effect of a new situation. I let her go because of my racism. There was discomfort. Eventually the student was able to talk about being in the minority and the group engaged with this, which eased things. Thinking about this in terms of client–counsellor relationships. A black student brought the issue of meeting a white client for the first time and I have begun to think about this. I have also noticed more about other differences, like being Jewish, Irish or asylum seeker.

In my supervision group I noticed students getting very defensive when they first started to do the black issues work. I think they were afraid to be called racist. So they wanted to say we don't need any work on this. I believe that this has changed and now it has become easier. The work has now opened up and a whole gamut of issues which link in. I want to engage with this more deeply and get down to talking about black counsellor, white client and gay counsellor and straight client, for example.

My experience of myself as a white man, working with a group of black women supervisees, working with both black and white clients. It seems that they were able to settle into some security and solidarity as the year progressed and they were able to discuss the differences and assumptions they made about each other. I have been in touch with an important learning curve where I have learned more about the experience of black counsellor and white client.

It is very challenging to do this listening without getting into stereotyping. I haven't quite got to grips with this aspect of it.

Tutors' comments about practice sessions

In my recent experience of practice assessments students were not picking up black issues, but they were evidencing the capacity to reflect on why they had not picked it up in the sessions and some of their fears. They were evidencing the capacity to go away and think about it and say what stops them doing something, saying something, but they were not evidencing it at the moment a client may need to have something validated. Something still is not happening relationally at the moment when something crucial may need to happen. Although what is happening is that some of them have much more awareness now.

Also some of them are ticking the box of having to jump the criteria of addressing black issues. They are naming something like I am white and they are black and then not taking it any further and as you were saying bolting it on the end. I am constantly challenging this, for some of them this might be a development because they may not have taken the time to recognise this before, so I am not clear what the evidence is.

There was a time when students and colleagues thought that you address the difference between black and white as soon as you open the session. 'I am black and you are white or I am white and you are black and how do you feel about this?' I think our students are realising there is more than that, because there is a lot more information about how it feels to be in this position. In a recent practice session level-two students were doing this. They were not addressing it. When I came into the room to support them, they were a bit scared. As though they should be doing something because I was there. I would stop them and ask them about the difficulty of addressing the difference or similarity and they would say they were scared. Then I would ask them to have a go and get it wrong. They found it helpful to have a go and then they could take a risk and process what their fear was about. It was not about formalising their counselling, it was about just taking a risk to address black issues.

When we worked with a split group, I led the white group and one person could not speak, she was so full of feeling. I tried to let them know that I get lost and stuck with this too and don't know where I am going with this either. In writing about lesbian issues and therapy, I realise that it feels very different when I am in it. So we cannot underestimate the emotional impact. I am assuming this has a similar impact on students, based on the response afterwards, i.e.

emails and contact from students asking for more support. It is such cutting-edge work that it might be written about, but I am not sure how many trainings really go for it and really engage with it.

The opening up of being white is one of the key issues. At first students thought black issues was about racism. Racism is only one thread of black issues. Being white is a huge one. As part of my process I have had to take some more therapy myself and learn what it is like to listen to white people and what it is like to be white. In the skills course, I owned that to the students and in doing so got the black students to listen to white students. This can also act as a way of interrupting a pattern of black expert which can deny black students their listening and learning time. The amount of feelings about being on the receiving end of racism can stop that listening in the other direction. Listening to themselves and each other, black on black, reaching out for each other, white on white and then across the board. It has been a huge learning for me too.

What the personal development facilitator said

The whole session was about being white. People were talking about guilt, fear, shame and difficulties about staying with being white, making choices, because of the assumptions about being racist. Somehow they had to carry that. It was powerful.

Ragina, an Asian tutor from another training course, offers a useful example of modelling her experience of working creatively with Asian cultures; she proposes that clients need a place to live out the contradictions of their cultural experiences:

In the role of a helper-expert I am given a status because I know something about the counselling process that clients don't. So not looking could mean they have respect for me. I would not automatically infer they are not interested or avoiding. My Asian clients have feelings and concerns to share as a white person does, but they disclose differently. They might shake their head and mean yes or they might want to make me a cup of tea. That is out of respect. There are stigmas around mental health and whereas I understand the place of boundaries, I might sometimes break out of the boundaries to give them confidence about it. I wouldn't necessarily interpret an offer to make tea. We work from emotion; for example, someone considers that the counsellor is a kind of guru, therefore they would experience you through that emotion. Some clients address me as 'Didi', this means sister, or as 'Beta', which means daughter. I have addressed some clients as 'Aunt Ji' or 'Mata Ji'. An expectation that you live up to that title sometimes gets in the way if you are trying to work in a Eurocentric way. So you adapt to this as a cultural issue not a transference issue, then it doesn't get in the way.

As a trainer I first get students to identify an awareness of who they are and what their own value systems consist of. What do they believe in and what makes cultural sense for them? It has to begin from their own perspectives. Diversity work means accepting that a black or Asian person may have been raised in a culturally specific way and worked with certain ethics. Therapists need to understand why they do what they do.

We all work from a theoretical perspective. Trainees need to work out, Does the theory fit? For example, in the person-centred way, to believe that you are good no matter what you do, that is in every culture, but to assume you will be good may be naïve. It is important to be able to acknowledge one's vulnerabilities, deficiencies. It is important that these are given space to be acknowledged within one's culture. So in our culture we acknowledge Kali, that there is both good and evil in us. Ravana stole Rama's wife. He was not evil, he done an evil thing, so God could kill him and achieve the cycle of life and death. There was reasoning behind this. He wanted to achieve Mukti.

I refer a lot to my own culture when teaching. Trainees see me as not just someone spouting Western culture, so then they understand the process of making sense of it. For training it is very important that one's culture is recognised. If you cannot understand why something is important to you, it is difficult to understand why it is important to someone else. We are born with an ascribed identity and we also have an achieved identity. I am who I am at the moment because I have chosen things. For example, the way I live, my education. It is important to understand the importance of Asian people having space to be themselves. I have achieved this identity as a counsellor. Growing up, I quite often felt not heard. There was a sense of injustice. When people don't hear you, they don't see what your needs are. I hope that my students will recognise their own prejudices, their stereotypes and pre-transference. That even within a given culture they will not make assumptions. They will develop cultural awareness, so that they can allow clients to be heard.

Reflections

The importance of making choices is emphasized in Ragina's modelling. She has come through a Eurocentric training, and although she teaches the value of this, she includes her cultural belief system rather than compromising it. In her client work she understands the value of working with the client's cultural reference points. Listening to Ragina talk about her work gave me insights into ways to be more humble in the therapeutic partnership. I am not always aware of the power dynamics involved in my client work. A white client once said to me, 'You are not allowed to tell me what you really think of me.' I was challenged by her awareness of the power dynamics of my role as a black therapist with a white client. Clients may not always be aware of these dynamics; however, I am sure that developing greater awareness and an ability to address power dynamics will reinforce relational contact and further support the context of black issues and other oppressions. As therapists we must be aware of the dangers of transferring oppressions and the role of oppressive therapist.

A tutor discusses further need

For the skills group and in terms of further need, it seemed to mean demonstrating that I am not a racist person, or if I am racist, then trying to keep it hidden. Something has to happen for change to be created. So what do I need to facilitate these students in this? There is a big unknown; it is more than about just demonstrating racism or absence of it. About what gets co-created between people, about history, sedimented learning that I still haven't got to yet in my own thinking about black issues/black people. I am somewhere along that road. As though I am looking at a plant somewhere above the ground and I am not sure what the roots are. And I don't know how I can help students to get there when I am still in the process of developing this for myself.

We need more supervision using supervisors with a commitment to being on the ball addressing and carrying forward black issues. Not having to explain and struggle about issues because we are not being carried forward. Our own supervision and therapy should reflect this.

What trainees said

White female trainee: There was just one thing, it's not massive, but sometimes I have felt that perhaps sometimes what we are asked to do, it is almost not simple enough. It's not that I want to be treated like a child. It is difficult because I am talking about everyone, and me, but I want to own it at the same time. Part of the lack of response is not feeling safe, which we have discussed already. Also sometimes for me it is so complicated what is going on, to be able to simplify and say it's okay. This is a hard one because I would not want it to be taken away from me and I need to go through the process. Also I really don't know exactly what I am saying, but like the guy who is the artist, it took me a while to understand what you wanted us to look at. You know in terms of how our assumptions would be if we had a black client. I also felt, Oh, I am not sure if I want to say because of who is in the group, the size of the group, safety and everything. I also felt it could have also been missed by some people, missed by me. Sometimes it's like a bit of confusion, what are we being asked to think about here? It's like you have to think about the client relationship, but for me it was like I have to think about what I am thinking about this guy while I am listening to him. He is my client, he is on this tape recorder, he is a young black man, and he is a young black male artist. You know get in there and really think about it and you're safe and no one here is gonna think you are shit. But you have got to feel safe to say it. I feel sometimes this opportunity was missed. But maybe we/I got to that point later.

Isha: It sounds to me like you are saying that this needed to be held more and acknowledged, that I was aware that people were afraid and that there was different levels of understanding and learning and that if the tutors had been further along in our process to do that, it would have re-assured you.

White female trainee: Yes, you have articulated it much better than me; that's exactly what I mean.

Black African female trainee: For me, in the creativity session when we were asked to make a mask, I did not think I could make anything, but somehow I made a mask. This had a strong impact on me emotionally. The colours reminded me of my history, the vibrancy of orange burning tigree (vegetation against the landscape). I was put in touch with my African-ness. The very last workshop discussion when you, Isha, presented your slide and the interview with the black artist summed it up. He touched on everything. To sum it up, I would say he was talking about; he was the sum of his history. 'This is the I that I am' I think was the phrase that he used. To me it related to the sun god, the water, the history of slavery, everything made this person, from his ancestry and history to experiencing life in the present made him the person that he is. It sounded as if he wouldn't change that person for anything. I found that quite useful.

Turkish Asian female trainee: The second workshop was very useful. It was interesting to see how people fitted into the two groups that were set. If you identified white, go into that group; if you identify as black, go into that group. It was interesting to see the number of what we wouldn't really consider as 'black' in quotes in the same group that I belong. If I were to explain that I would say that all the people that came into my group saw themselves as members of the oppressed non-white group.

Summary of Research Outcomes

Table 2 summarises the main points that came out of my study based on black issues workshops (McKenzie-Mavinga, 2005). I have also listed some recommendations for psychotherapy and counselling training courses.

Table 2   Summary of Research Outcomes

1. Interviews with experienced practitioners	Black issues a missing element
2. Participants shared concerns	How to understand and work with black issues
3. Emerging themes	History, guilt, trust, racism
4. Emerging concepts	Shared concerns, finding a voice, recognition trauma
5. Other inferences	Impact of workshops and black trainer on training programme
6. Colleagues	Similar level of understanding to trainees
7. Impact on areas of training	Less support in placement than in other areas
8. Narrative discussions	Produced more comprehensive data
9. Most poignant theme	Concerns about racism
10. Lack of opportunity	To discuss other black issues
11. General impact	Challenges the silence of institutional racism; supports equality and race issues by making them explicit; creates space for dialogue on black issues

1. Psychotherapy and counsellor training should make black issues explicit within their 'Diversity and Equalities' module early in the curriculum and alongside the issues of other minority groups so that they are not ignored or glossed over.
2. Creative methods for learning, such as art, music and movement, storytelling, poetry and folklore, can be used to develop exploration. Space should be created for trainees to explore concerns.
3. A 'Black Issues' module that includes an exploration of historical context, guilt, trust and issues of racism should be included in training.
4. Opportunities to explore internalised racism and whiteness should be provided in the context of the black–black dyad and the white–white dyad.
5. Acknowledgement of recognition trauma must be made using multicultural and transcultural theory (e.g. Helms, 1990; Tuckwell, 2002; Dalal, 2002).
6. Acknowledgement that black issues are not just about racism or race issues should be made to provide opportunity for the wider context of black issues to be explored.
7. Addressing black issues must be included and supported as a competency throughout training.
8. Training organisations should provide more opportunities for people of colour to become trainers and facilitators and include their skills and experiences.

In the next section, I present ideas for setting up a space to contemplate black issues within training. The early stages of black issues work should be about creating a space for sharing experiences and opening a dialogue about concerns. The theme of black issues can be integrated into transcultural workshops or given its own time and space within the curriculum. It is important to allow space for the concerns of other ethnic and cultural groups to be explored. Links should be made between racism and other oppressions. Examination of the parallels with group and individual process and the therapeutic process may also be helpful. Trainee feedback suggests that trainers should be clear about their expectations of trainees and acknowledge that the theme of black issues may evoke powerful feelings that can be supported.

Preparation and Workshop Plans

Explore and compare different theoretical approaches and their usefulness with respect to black issues. Discuss texts on multicultural, transcultural and intercultural psychotherapy and counselling. Remember that whatever happens is process, so discover what you know and what you need to know more about. Learning about black issues needs to be linked to listening skills and counsellor competencies. Trainers can ask themselves and the trainees the following questions. What helps you learn in this area? What helps you voice your achievements and concerns? How can you challenge your belief systems, prejudice and experience of oppression? How can Eurocentric theory contribute, rather than dominate, when addressing black issues?

The workshop plans that follow are presented in three stages to support varying levels of postgraduate counsellor trainee development. These exercises can be incorporated into the curriculum over the duration of the training.

Stage 1: shared concerns

Stage 1a

Preparation: Give trainees reading on definitions of multicultural, intercultural and transcultural therapy.
Aim: To open a dialogue about working transculturally with black issues and encourage trainees to share their experiences and concerns.

a. Present definitions of intercultural and transcultural therapy and counselling. Present a definition of black issues (see the 'What Are Black Issues?' section of the Introduction). Use theory where appropriate. Acknowledge and permit powerful feelings that may arise. Examine ways of containing these feelings and be aware of the trainees' different levels of awareness and their support needs.
b. Create an exercise where trainees can share their different or similar cultural backgrounds. Include artefacts, objects and the context of language.
c. Create ways to encourage trainees to share and celebrate their experiences, knowledge and concerns about black issues. Use creative writing, poetry, art, storytelling, drama and play. In small groups, give trainees the task of selecting one or two of their experiences or concerns and discuss the content and cultural context of these.
d. Ask each group to reflect on how they felt in the small-group work and what they thought was going on among group members (e.g. defensiveness, not knowing, who appeared to be leading, silent, talking the most). Do group members think that the topic of black issues impacted their group process?
e. Ask trainees to draw on their experience of the exercise and decide what they would include in a counselling model on black issues.
f. Share in the large group.

Texts: d'Ardenne and Mahtani (1989); Pederson (2000); Lago and Thompson (1996); Feltham and Horton (2000).

Stage 1 offers an introduction to the transcultural aspects of therapeutic work. The theme of black issues can be introduced as an integral part of transcultural work. Be mindful that trainees' responses to these exercises will be influenced by their cultural experiences and their personal levels of awareness and experience of racism or other oppressions.

Stage 1b

Preparation: Give trainees papers or suggested reading as in Stage 1a.
Aim: To make explicit sameness and difference and understand oppression, racism and internalised racism in therapeutic relationships and the context of black issues.

a. Contradictory statements exercise: unlearning the colour-blind approach. In small groups, discuss one of the following statements in relation to black issues:
   - I treat all my clients the same; otherwise, I would be accused of favouritism or discrimination.
   - For people to be treated equally, they cannot all be treated the same.
   - Each person should be treated according to his or her need.
   - It's all in the unconscious, so what's the problem about difference?
   - We are all the same inside.

b. Visible and invisible difference. In pairs or small groups, ask trainees to identify positives and negatives in response to the following questions:
   - Identify a time when you listened well to someone different from or similar to you. What went well? What can you improve on?
   - How might your counselling skills be affected by difference and similarity in skin colour, hair texture, gender, sexuality, ability, language, dress and so on?

c. Offer or create a definition of oppression and internalised oppression. Find out:
   - what trainees understand by racism and internalised racism
   - how their understanding of these concepts might affect their counselling skills
   - what they need to learn and develop to become effective counsellors in this area

d. In pairs, discuss any thoughts, feelings and defences that the exercises have raised for trainees. Attempt to be non-judgemental and give good attention. Make a note of the positive responses and difficulties. Don't expect difficult feelings and stuckness to be resolved immediately. Share in the main group.

Texts: Kareem and Littlewood (1992); Lago and Thompson (1996).

Stage 2: finding a voice

My study showed that powerful feelings in response to the theme of black issues created silence, emotional blocks and eventually ways of expressing how trainees felt about the experience. Stage 2 proposes exercises to encourage trainees to articulate thoughts, feelings and learning needs about black issues. Responses to black issues can be linked to theory about defences and transference/counter-transference.

Stage 2a

Preparation: Give trainees reading on the process of black awareness/white awareness, plus case material on counter-transference and race.
Aim: To encourage awareness of black issues and to help trainees consider personal identity and experiences of black issues.

 a. Discuss issues presented in the reading texts.
 b. Ask trainees to split into groups of people whom they think appear the same. Discuss what this exercise was like.
 c. Ask the trainees to split into two groups, with black and white trainees in separate groups. This exercise may evoke powerful feelings about attachment and separation. Sometimes confusion about which group to identify with becomes apparent, particularly for individuals of mixed black/white or of Mediterranean heritage. It is important to allow and support those individuals to make their own choices. Facilitators should join the relevant groups. Instruct each group to discuss what it is like being in that group. Individuals should share what they want their group to know about them and what they want the other group to know about them as black/white trainees. They can then be asked to share in the main group what they want the other group to know about them as individuals from the context of their group and personal identity.
 d. Creative personal development session. Make historical links to black issues using creativity. Trainees can create an object, image or piece of writing that represents their historical links with black issues from childhood to adulthood. Encourage trainees who feel they have had no links to black issues to reflect on what this means for them and their counselling skills. Present the results to the main group.
 e. Discuss how the issues raised can be linked to counselling and therapy.

Texts: Dalal (2002); Tuckwell (2002); Fanon (1986).

Stage 2b

Preparation: Give trainees reading on racism in psychology or therapy or offer case studies of black clients exploring racism.

Aim: To encourage dialogue about black issues and experiences of racism and develop a black empathic approach (see Chapter 3). Allow time for discussion of feelings about racism, but do not allow the whole session to focus on racism. Time must be given to other black issues (e.g. the black family, belief systems, being black in Britain, our rich black heritage).

    a. A discussion about taboo subjects may be useful to assist understanding of silences and hidden experiences both within cultural groups and within the therapeutic process.
Present some art or creative writing produced by a black person.

    b. In small groups, discuss each piece of art or writing in the context of black issues and counselling/therapy approaches. What is the artist/author presenting? What do the metaphors/images express? How do trainees experience the information? How would trainees respond to experiences of racism in a counselling/therapy setting? What do trainees need to learn more about?

    c. Can trainees identify any oppression, internalised oppression or experience of racism in the art/writing? How would you respond to these experiences in a counselling/therapy setting? Discuss. Present to the main group.

    d. In small groups, discuss case study material involving black clients with both black and white counsellors/therapists from the literature or trainees' practice. Discuss case study material involving white clients where black issues or racism is apparent.

Texts: Eleftheriadou (1994); Kareem and Littlewood (1992); Howitt and Owusu-Bempah (1994); Marshall (2004); Dupont-Joshua (2003).

Stage 3: the processing of recognition trauma

By stage 3, trainees are usually ready for more in-depth exploration of their personal development and their responses to black issues. Black trainees may need support to explore the impact of their history and experiences of racism. This may involve challenges about internalised racism, especially when black trainees perform the role of the expert, which may compromise time and space for their own learning and development. White trainees may need support to explore their inherited role as members of the oppressor group and feelings of guilt and fear attached to this role. All trainees should be supported to explore their feelings about racism. Time should also be given to celebrating students' rich cultural experiences.

Stage 3a

Preparation: Give students reading on trauma, together with information that explains the impact of racism and oppression in African/Asian history and the history of trauma within or among other groups (e.g. holocaust, war, ethnic cleansing). Ask trainees to read Part II, 'Recognition Trauma'.
Aim: To understand and support the process of recognition trauma.

  a. Discuss reading texts in the context of the therapeutic process.
  b. Identify and explore experience of trauma, recurrent trauma and recognition trauma.
  c. Discuss Part II of this book.
  d. Create a safety exercise where trainees' responses to the concept of recognition trauma can be aired and shared. Remind trainees that they can use their counselling skills to listen to and support each other with these issues. Support trainees to develop congruence when faced with powerful feelings about the impact of racism.
  e. In pairs, discuss ways of supporting powerful feelings related to black issues.

Texts: Helms (1990); Vanoy Adams (1996); Fletchman Smith (2000).

Stage 3b

Preparation: Give trainees reading on identity, intersecting identities, archetypes, stereotyping, the shadow, the gaze and mirroring (see also Chapter 5).
Aim: To support the reflective process, explore transpersonal aspects and promote engagement with black issues.

  a. Discuss issues that arise from the reading and make links to black issues and racism.
  b. Present and discuss newspaper or magazine cuttings that portray both positive and negative images and experiences of black people.
  c. In groups, discuss case study material that involves black clients or counsellors. What went well? What could have been done differently? Consider the role of collusion and challenge in counselling practice.
  d. Discuss relationships between black people and their use of supervision and personal development forums to support practice. What do trainees need to support their black issues work?
  e. Discuss relationships between white people and their use of supervision and personal development forums to support practice. What do trainees need to support their black issues work?
  f. Triads. Encourage trainees to practise being explicit about black issues, then discuss approaches to engaging with or supporting black issues when they are not made explicit by clients. Role-play supervision where black issues are raised. Assist trainees to develop assertiveness about their support needs when addressing black issues.
  g. Evaluate the impact and learning from these workshops.

Texts: Laungani (2004); Lago (2006).

Other useful exercises

- Get trainees to describe a cultural experience to a partner and then have the partner explore through role-play what it might be like to have this cultural experience. Re-enact situations or case studies using a drama therapy approach.
- Make puppets and masks that represent cultural heritage or experiences.
- Tell stories using mythology and folklore to understand black issues.
- Explore the meaning of music and rhythm in different cultures and groups.
- Share and discuss early memories of being black and being white.
- Get trainees to line up in order of their skin colour, with the darkest at one end of the line and the lightest at the other. Discuss thoughts and feelings about this exercise. Discuss experiences of difference based on skin tone, hair colour and hair texture.

Conclusion

Going all the way means journeying through whatever it takes to get there. The journey to understanding black issues is not a straight road. It can be a road that leads deep into the risky territory of cultural exclusion and oppression. In addition, traditional psychotherapy and counselling have been tentative about acknowledging the need to work with the impact of racism. This has made the journey an intensive one that involves the process of internalised racism.

Internalised racism can play havoc with the unconscious; therefore, the black individual needs a place to be black and a place to explore differences and similarities among black people. Only the individual seeking therapeutic support can determine what is useful about the matching or non-matching of therapist and client. Black people are prone to accusations from white people that they are being racist when they choose to work with someone 'like them' or raise issues about their experiences of white racism. We are told that we are making things worse by naming racism and identifying the oppressor. Often the expression of our pain is mistaken for attack by white people, or we are placed in the victim role by being told that we have a chip on our shoulder. This rejection and lack of empathy can cause black people to express anger towards white people and accuse their black peers of racism. Given these dynamics, it is important to remember that the insidious effects of racism on different groups affect all of us. We may feel that we want to blame and punish, or we may feel guilt and remorse. Blame assigned to any one group hinders the personal recovery of both victim and oppressor. It is therefore important to stay focused on history, healing and whatever therapeutic assistance may be useful for recovery and transformation from the pain of this experience.

Fanon's work on the transformation process involved in the context and consequences of white racism demonstrates that an emphasis on this aspect of therapeutic work has been in the pipeline for the past four decades. It is clear that the personal development processes of black people in Britain have been adversely affected by collective and generally accepted negative images of black people, as described in the concept of the black Western archetype. Fanon (1986) became involved in finding a more positive black gaze to identify with: 'As I begin to realise that the Negro is the symbol of sin, I catch myself hating the Negro. But then I recognise that I am a Negro. ... I have only one solution; to rise above this absurd drama' (p. 197).

During case management, supervision and transcultural workshops, trainees continue to ask many questions about the risks involved when therapists address issues pertaining to race. It strikes me that therapists work hard to facilitate issues of race and culture, but often without adequate supervision and guidance to truly integrate this process into their work. Defences against experiences of racism need to be examined for this work to progress.

My study brought to light the need for a safe space to discuss racism as a component of black issues. In this chapter the voices of both trainers and trainees have been presented, expressing the need for all areas of training to support the process of working with black issues. The dominance of black issues by racism has been highlighted. The concepts and experiences that emerged during the study have been used to outline exercises and training strategies. It is important that external training elements such as supervision and placement take on board their responsibility to support trainees through this aspect of their learning journey.

Afterword

My study (McKenzie-Mavinga, 2005) only scratched the surface of training concerns about black issues in the therapeutic process. Sharing the journey with trainees and trainers has made my research less isolating. I am eternally grateful to all the individuals and groups that contributed to the knowledge and wisdom gained during this process. Their contributions have made it possible to hear the voices of trainees, artists and, most of all, black individuals.

Through this experience I have gained a greater awareness of my own difficulties in understanding. The difficulties of silenced, vulnerable and defensive people remind me of my own not-knowing, vulnerable, silenced and defensive self. I have wondered how the experience of racism can be addressed within counsellor training or whether it can be taught at all, given the emotional responses that this theme evokes. But then that is the business of counselling and therapy. I have pondered the concept of safety raised by the topic of black issues and what this means in the context of racism and its relationship to the personal experiences of trainees and clients. I remain concerned about the historical transference of racism within the dynamic of discussions about black issues. Many questions remain unanswered: What portion of training time should courses devote to discussions about black issues and racism, which evoke such powerful feelings? What portion of time should be allocated to listening to the developmental experiences of black people, both in training and in the therapeutic setting? How can the silences caused by Eurocentric approaches, fear and mistrust be broken? Will this book be just another transcultural reference, or can it be a contribution to the transformation of practice?

References

Ackbar, N. (1996). *Breaking the Chains of Psychological Slavery*. Jersey City, NJ: Mind Productions.

Alleyne, A. (2005). Invisible Injuries and Silent Witness: The Shadow of Racial Oppression in Workplace Contexts. *Psychodynamic Practice* 11(3), 283–99.

Angelou, M. (1998). *Even the Stars Look Lonesome*. London: Virago.

Besson, G. (2001). *Folklore and Legends of Trinidad and Tobago*. Trinidad: Paria.

Bethel, M. (1995). Bringing Myself into Fiction. In C. Boyce Davies and M. Ogundipe-Leslie (eds.), *International Dimensions of Black Women's Writing*. London: Pluto.

Blyden, E. (1994). *African Life and Customs*. Baltimore, MD: Black Classic Press.

Boyce Davies, C. and Ogundipe-Leslie, M. (eds.) (1995). *International Dimensions of Black Women's Writing*. London: Pluto.

Clarke, L. (1981). *Douens*. Trinidad: KaRaEle.

CRE (Commission for Racial Equality) (2002). *A Guide for Further and Higher Education Institutions*. London: CRE.

d'Ardenne, P. and Mahtani, A. (1989). *Transcultural Counselling in Action*. London: Sage.

Dalal, F. (2002). *Race, Colour and the Process of Racialization*. Hove, UK, and New York: Brunner Routledge.

Davey, J. and Cross, M. (2004). *Barriers, Defences and Resistance*. Milton Keynes, UK: Open University Press.

Davies, D. and Bhugra, D. (2004). *Models of Psychopathology*. Milton Keynes, UK: Open University Press.

Denzin, N. (1989). *Interpretive Interactionism*. Applied Social Research Methods Series, vol. 16. London: Sage.

Dupont-Joshua, A. (ed.) (2003). *Counselling in Intercultural Settings*. Hove, UK, and New York: Brunner Routledge.

Eleftheriadou, Z. (1994). *Transcultural Counselling*. London: Central Book Publishing.

Ellenberger, H. (1994). *The Discovery of the Unconscious*. London: Fontana.

Fanon, F. (1986). *Black Skin, White Masks*. London: Pluto.

Feltham, C. and Horton, I. (eds.) (2000). *Handbook of Counselling and Psychotherapy*. Thousand Oaks, CA: Sage.

Fernando, S. (1998). *Race and Culture in Psychiatry*. London: Tavistock/ Routledge.

Fernando, S. (2006). Foreword. In R. Moodley and S. Palmer (eds.), *Race, Culture and Psychotheropy*. Hove, UK: Routledge.

Feurtes, J. N. and Gretchen, D. (2001). Emerging Theories of Multicultural Counseling. In J. Ponterotto, J. M. Casas, L. A. Suzuki and C. M. Alexander (eds.), *Handbook of Multicultural Counselling*. London: Sage.

Field Belenky, M., Clinchy, B., Goldberger, N. and Tarule, J. (1986). *Women's Ways of Knowing*. New York: Basic Books.

Fletchman Smith, B. (2000). *Mental Slavery*. London: Rebus.

Foundation News (November 2003). South London African Women's Organisation. SLAWO.

Freud, C. (1909). *Analysis of a Phobia in a Five Year Old Boy*. (Standard edition 10(3); PFL 8.165 (27, 43, 46)). In J. Strachey (ed.) (1977). *Freud, S. 8 Case Histories 1. Dora and Little Hans*. New York: Penguin.

Hartill, G. (1998). *The Web of Words*. In C. Hunt and F. Sampson (eds), *The Self on the Page*. London: Jessica Kingsley.

Helms, J. (1990). *Black and White Racial Identity Theory, Research and Practice*. Westport, CT: Greenwood.

Helms, J. (1995). *An Update of Helms 'White and People of Color Racial Identity Models'*. In J. Ponterotto, J. M. Casas, L. A. Suzuki and C. M. Alexander (eds.), *Handbook of Multicultural Counselling*. London: Sage.

hooks, b. (1984). *Feminist Theory, from Margins to Centre*. New York: South End.

hooks, b. (1991). *Yearning*. London: Turnaround.

hooks, b. (1992). *Black Looks*. Boston, MA: South End.

hooks, b. (1996). Feminism as a Persistent Critique of History. In A. Read (ed.), *The Fact of Blackness*. London and Seattle, WA: Bay Press, Institute of Contemporary Arts.

Howitt, D. and Owusu-Bempah, J. (1994). *The Racism of Psychology*. Hemel Hempstead, UK: Harvester Wheatsheaf.

Jacobs, M. (1995). *D. W. Winnicot*. London: Sage.

Jung, C. (1930/1950). *Psychology and Literature: The Spirit in Man, Art and Literature*. In A. B. Samuels, B. Shorter and F. Plant (eds.), *A Critical Dictionary of Jungian Analysis, Collected Works*, vol. 15. London: Routledge.

Jung, C. (1970). The Archetypes and the Collective Unconscious. In Sir Herbert Read et al. (eds.), *The Collected Works of C.G. Jung, vol. 9*. London: Routledge and Kegan Paul.

Kareem, J. and Littlewood, R. (1992). *Intercultural Therapy*. Oxford: Blackwell.

Klein, M. (1946). *Envy and Gratitude and Other Works 1946–1963*. London: Virago.

Klein, M. (1986). *The Psychoanalysis of Children*. In J. Mitchell (ed.), *The Selected Melanie Klein*. London: Penguin.

Krause, I. (1998). *Therapy across Culture*. London: Sage.

Lacan, J. (1977). *Écrits: A Selection*, trans. A. Sheridan. London: Tavistock.

Lago, C. (2006). *Race, Culture and Counselling*. Milton Keynes, UK: Open University Press.

Lago, C. and Thompson, J. (1996). *Race, Culture and Counselling*. Milton Keynes, UK: Open University Press.

Laungani, P. (2004). *Asian Perspectives in Counselling and Psychotheropy*. Hove, UK, and New York. Brunner Routledge.

Lawrence, D. (2003). Racial and Cultural Issues in Counselling Training. In A. Dupont-Joshua (ed.), *Counselling in Intercultural Settings*. Hove, UK, and New York: Brunner Routledge.

Lorde, A. (1984). *Sister Outsider*. New York: Crossing.

Marshall, S. (2004). *Difference and Discrimination in Psychotherapy and Counselling*. London: Sage.

McKenzie-Mavinga, I. (1991). Black and White Psychotherapy. Paper, Freud Museum, London.

McKenzie-Mavinga, I. (2005). A Study of Black Issues in Counsellor Training. Doctoral thesis, Metanoia Institute and Middlesex University, London.

McKenzie-Mavinga, I. and Perkins, T. (1991). *In Search of Mr McKenzie*. London: Women's Press.

Mearns, D. (1994). *Developing Person Centred Counselling*. London: Sage.

Mearns, D. and Thorne, B. (1988). *Person Centred Counselling in Action*. London: Sage.

Mitchell, J. (ed.) (1986). *The Selected Melanie Klein*. London: Penguin.

Moodley, R. and Palmer, S. (eds.) (2006). *Race, Culture and Psychotherapy*. Hove, UK: Routledge.

Morrow, L., Rakhsha, G. and Castaneda, C. (2001). Qualitative Research Methods for Multicultural Counselling. In J. Ponterotto, J. M. Casas, L. A. Suzuki and C. M. Alexander (eds.), *Handbook of Multicultural Counselling*. London: Sage.

Moustakas, C. (1990). *Heuristic Research*. London: Sage.

O'Brien, M. and Houston, G. (2007). *Integrative Therapy: A Practitioners Guide*, 2nd edn. London: Sage.

Ocheing, S. (2003). Working with an African Perspective in Counselling Practice. In A. Dupont-Joshua (ed.), *Counselling in Intercultural Settings*. Hove, UK, and New York: Brunner Routledge.

Ottley, C. (1979). *Folk Beliefs; Folk Customs and Folk Characters Found in Trinidad & Tobago*. Trinidad & Tobago: Crusoe.

Pederson, P. (1987). Ten Frequent Assumptions of Cultural Bias in Counselling. *Journal of Multicultural Counselling and Development* January, 16–24.

Pederson, P. (2000). *Hidden Messages in Culture Centered Counselling*. Thousand Oaks, CA: Sage.

Ponterotto, J., Casas, J. M., Suzuki, L. A. and Alexander, C. M. (eds.) (2001). *Handbook of Multicultural Counselling*. London: Sage.

Read, A. (1996). *The Fact of Blackness*. London and Seattle, WA: Bay Press, Institute of Contemporary Arts.

Richards, D. (1992). *Let the Circle Be Unbroken*. Lawrenceville, NJ: Red Sea.

Rogers, C. (1990). *Client Centered Therapy*. London: Constable.

Rycroft, C. (1968). *A Critical Dictionary of Psychoanalysis*. Harmondsworth, UK: Penguin.

Samuels, A., Shorter, B. and Plant, F. (1986). *A Critical Dictionary of Jungian Analysis*. London and New York: Routledge.

Schaverien, J. (1995). *Desire and the Female Therapist*. Harmondsworth, UK: Penguin.

Scheurich, J. J and Young, M. D (1997). Colouring Epistemologies: Are Our Research Epistemologies Racially Biased. *Educational Researcher* 26(4), 4–16.

Somé, M. (1993). *Ritual, Power, Healing and Community*. Portland, OR: Swan Raven & Company.

Somé, M. (1999). *The Healing Wisdom of Africa*. New York: Tarcher Putnam.

Straker, G., Watson, D. and Robinson, T. (2002). Trauma and Disconnection. *International Journal of Psychotherapy* 7, 145–58.

Sue, D. and Sue, D. (1998). *Counselling the Culturally Different*. New York: Wiley.

Tuckwell, G. (2002). *Racial Identity, White Counsellors and Therapists*. Milton Keynes, UK, and Philadelphia, PA: Open University Press.

Vanoy Adams, M. (1996). *The Multicultural Imagination*. London and New York: Routledge.

Watson, V. (2004). The Training Experiences of Black Counsellors. PhD thesis, University of Nottingham, UK.

Wilson, A. (1987). *The Psychological Development of the Black Child*. New York: Africana Research Publications.

Wilson, A. (1990). *Black-on-Black Violence*. New York: Afrikan World Info Systems.

Wilson, A. (1993). *The Falsification of Afrikan Consciousness*. New York: Afrikan World Info Systems.

Wilson, S. (1992). *The Drummer's Path*. Rochester, VT: Destiny.

Suggested Reading

Ackbar, N. (1991). *Visions for Black Men*. Tallahassee, FL: Mind Productions.

Angelou, M. (1986). *And Still I Rise*. London: Virago.

Barker, C., Pistrang, N. and Elliott, R. (1994). *Research Methods in Clinical and Counselling Psychology*. New York and Chichester, UK: Wiley.

Barrott, J. (2004). Understanding Black Issues – A Response. Association for University and College Counselling, British Association for Counselling and Psychotherapy.

Bhugra, D. and Bhui, K. (1998). Psychotherapy for Ethnic Minorities: Issues, Context and Practice. *British Journal of Psychotherapy* 14(3).

Bolton, G. (1999). *The Therapeutic Potential of Creative Writing*. London: Jessica Kingsley.

British Association for Counselling and Psychotherapy (1 April 2002). *Code of Ethics*. London: BACP.

Burgess, R. (ed.) (1985). *Issues in Educational Research: Qualitative Methods*. London: Falmer.

Burke, A. (1984). Racism and Psychological Disturbance among West Indians in Britain. *International Journal of Social Psychiatry* 30, 50–68.

Coffey, A. and Atkinson, P. (1996). *Making Sense of Qualitative Data: Complementary Research Strategies*. Thousand Oaks, CA: Sage.

Creswell, J. (1998). *Qualitative Inquiry and Research Design: Choosing among Five Traditions*. Thousand Oaks, CA: Sage.

Denzin, N. and Lincoln, Y. (eds.) (1998). *Strategies of Qualitative Enquiry*. Thousand Oaks, CA: Sage.

Dey, I. (1998). *Qualitative Data Analysis: A User-Friendly Guide for Social Scientists*. London: Routledge.

Dhillon-Stevens, H. (2005). Personal and Professional Integration of Anti-oppressive Practice and the Multiple Oppression Model in Psychotherapeutic Education. *British Journal of Psychotherapy Integration* 1(2), 47–62.

Dillard, J. (1998). *Multicultural Counselling: Toward Ethnic and Cultural Relevance in Human Encounters*. Chicago, IL: Nelson-Hall.

Ely, M., Vinz, R., Downing, M. and Anzul, M. (1997). *On Writing Qualitative Research: Living by Words*. London: Falmer.

Etherington, K. (2000). *Narrative Approaches to Working with Adult Male Survivors of Child Sexual Abuse*. London: Jessica Kingsley.

Etherington, K. (2001). Writing Qualitative Research: A Gathering of Selves. *Counselling and Psychotherapy Research* 1(2), 119–25.

Fernando, S. (1988). *Race and Culture in Psychiatry*. London: Tavistock/Routledge.

Fernando, S. (ed.) (1995). *Mental Health in a Multi-Ethnic Society*. London: Routledge.

Finch, J. (1986). *Research and Policy: The Uses of Qualitative Methods in Social and Educational Research*. Lewes, UK: Falmer.

Holder, J. (1999). *Soul Purpose*. London: Piatkus.

hooks, b. (1994). *Teaching to Transgress*. New York: Routledge.

hooks, b. (1999). *Wounds of Passion*. New York: Holt.

Hunt, C. and Sampson, F. (eds.) (1998). *The Self on the Page*. London: Jessica Kingsley.

Jacobi, J. (ed.) (1996). *Psychological Reflections*. London: Routledge & Kegan Paul.

Jacobs, M. (2001). Psychodynamic Psychotherapy. In E. Spinelli and S. Marshall (eds.), *Embodied Theories*. London: Continuum.

Jobanputra, S. (2005). *Racism and Psychology: Learning from Black Students*. PhD thesis, University of Westminster, London.

Kirk, J. and Miller, M. (1986). *Reliability and Validity in Qualitative Research*. Beverly Hills, CA, and London: Sage.

Lee, W. (1999). *Introduction to Multicultural Counselling*. Philadelphia, PA: Accelerated Development.

Littlewood, R. and Lipsedge, M. (1982). *Aliens and Alienists*. London: Penguin.

Lorde, A. (1982). *Zami. A New Spelling of My Name*. London: Sheba.

Mama, A. (1995). *Beyond the Masks*. London: Routledge.

Mason, J. (2002). *Qualitative Researching*. London: Sage.

May, T. (1997). *Social Research: Issues, Methods and Process*. Milton Keynes, UK, and Philadelphia, PA: Open University Press.

May, T. (2002). *Qualitative Research in Action*. London: Sage.

McKenzie-Mavinga, I. (2003). Creative Writing as Healing in Black Women's Groups. In A. Dupont-Joshua (ed.), *Counselling in Intercultural Settings*. Hove, UK, and New York: Brunner Routledge.

McKenzie-Mavinga, I. (2003). Linking Social History and the Therapeutic Process. *Research and Practice on Black Issues, Counselling & Psychotherapy Research* 3(2), 103–6.

McKenzie-Mavinga, I. (May 2004). Finding a Voice – Understanding Black Issues in the Therapeutic Process. Association for University and College Counselling, British Association for Counselling and Psychotherapy.

McKenzie-Mavinga, I. (2005). A Space to Contemplate: Understanding Black Issues in Counsellor Training and the Therapeutic Process. Trainers booklet, London Metropolitan University.

McKenzie-Mavinga, I. (2005). Understanding Black Issues in Postgraduate Counsellor Training. *Counselling & Psychotherapy Research* 5(4), 295–300.

McKenzie-Mavinga, I. (2006). Is Counselling Colour Blind? *Healthcare Counselling and Psychotherapy* 6(3), 11–14.

McLeod, J. (1999). *Practitioner Research in Counselling*. London: Sage.

McLeod, J. (2001). *Qualitative Research in Counselling and Psychotherapy*. London: Sage.

Miller, G. and Dingwall, R. (eds.) (1997). *Context and Method in Qualitative Research*. London: Sage.

Mishane, J. (2002). *Multiculturalism and the Therapeutic Process*. New York: Guilford Press.

Moodley, R. (2003). Matrices in Black and White: Implications of Cultural Multiplicity for Research in Counselling and Psychotherapy. *Counselling and Psychotherapy Research* 3(2), 115–21.

Moodley, R. and Palmer, S. (2006). *Race, Culture and Psychotherapy*. London: Routledge.

Moodley, R., Lago, C., and Talahite, A. (eds.) (2004). *Carl Rogers Counsels a Black Client*. Ross-on-Wye, UK: PCCS Books.

Morrison, T. (1988). *Beloved*. London: Pan.

Moustakas, C. (1990). *Heuristic Research*. London: Sage.

Moustakas, C. (1994). *Phenomenological Research Methods*. London: Sage.

Patel, N., Bennett, E., Dennis, M., Dosanjh, N., Miller, A., Mahtani, A. et al. (eds.) (2000). *Clinical Psychology, Race and Culture*. London: British Psychological Society.

Pederson, P., Draguns, J., Lonner, W. and Trimble, J. (2002). *Counselling across Cultures*. Thousand Oaks, CA: Sage.

Pope Davis, D. and Coleman, H. (eds.) (2001). The Intersection of Race, Class and Gender in Multicultural Counseling. *Journal of Multicultural Counseling and Development* 28, 98–112.

Punch, K. (2001). *Developing Effective Proposals*. London: Sage.

Rack, P. (1982). *Race, Culture and Mental Disorder*. London and New York: Tavistock.

Rastogi, M. and Weiling, E. (eds.) (2005). *Voices of Color*. Thousand Oaks, CA: Sage.

Reason, P. (ed.) (1988). *Human Enquiry in Action*. London: Sage.

Reason, P. (ed.) (1988). *Participation in Human Enquiry*. London: Sage.

Reason, P. and Bradbury, H. (2001). *Handbook of Action Research*. London: Sage.

Ridley, C. (1995). *Overcoming Unintentional Racism in Counselling and Therapy*. London: Sage.

Robson, C. (2002). *Real World Research*. Oxford: Blackwell.

Roland, A. (1978). *Psychoanalysis, Creativity & Literature*. New York: Columbia University Press.

Scott Mio, J. and Awakuni, G. (2000). *Resistance to Multiculturalism*. London and Philadelphia, PA: Bruner/Mazel.

Valle, R. and King, M. (eds.) (1978). *Existential-Phenomenological Alternatives for Psychology*. New York: Oxford University Press.

Index